History and Becoming

Plateaus – New Directions in Deleuze Studies

'It's not a matter of bringing all sorts of things together under a single concept but rather of relating each concept to variables that explain its mutations.'
Gilles Deleuze, *Negotiations*

Series Editors

Ian Buchanan, Cardiff University
Claire Colebrook, Penn State University

Editorial Advisory Board

Keith Ansell Pearson
Ronald Bogue
Constantin V. Boundas
Rosi Braidotti
Eugene Holland
Gregg Lambert
Dorothea Olkowski
Paul Patton
Daniel Smith
James Williams

Titles available in the series

Visit the Plateaus website at www.euppublishing.com/series/plat

HISTORY AND BECOMING
Deleuze's Philosophy of Creativity

Craig Lundy

EDINBURGH
University Press

To my parents, Robert and Susan

Edinburgh University Press Ltd
22 George Square, Edinburgh

www.euppublishing.com

Typeset in Sabon
by Servis Filmsetting Ltd, Stockport, Cheshire, and
printed and bound in Great Britain by
CPI Group (UK) Ltd, Croydon CR0 4YY

A CIP record for this book is available from the British Library

ISBN 978 0 7486 4530 5 (hardback)
ISBN 978 0 7486 4531 2 (webready PDF)
ISBN 978 0 7486 5437 6 (epub)
ISBN 978 0 7486 5436 9 (Amazon ebook)

Contents

Acknowledgements

The creation of this book has been, without doubt, an absolute joy. For that I have several people to thank. Foremost of those is Paul Patton, whose wisdom and support I have had the pleasure and good fortune to call upon since the earliest stages of this project. Other friends and colleagues who I would particularly like to thank for their helpful feedback, engaging conversation and inspiration are: Robin Durie, Daniel W. Smith, Eugene Holland, Simon Tormey, Timothy Rayner, Nathan Widder, Michael Hale and Daniela Voss. I am grateful to James Williams for inviting me to present a formative version of Chapter 5 at his excellent symposium 'Deleuze in Context', held at the University of Dundee. Thanks are also due to Carol MacDonald and the team at Edinburgh University Press for their hard work in producing this book. My family – Robert, Susan, Derek and Dawn – are deserving of special mention for helping me achieve my goals. This project would have not begun let alone ended without their ongoing encouragement and support. Finally, I would like to thank Stevie Voogt for her always well-measured advice, unwavering devotion and, above all, her friendship.

This book draws on material that has previously been published. I am thankful to the publishers for permission to utilise extracts from the following articles:

'Emerging From the Depths: On the Intensive Creativity of Historical Events', *Journal of French and Francophone Philosophy – Revue de la philosophie française et de langue française*, 18 (1), 2010, 67–85.

'Deleuze and Guattari's Historiophilosophy: Philosophical Thought and its Historical Milieu', *Critical Horizons*, 12 (2), 2011, 115–35.

Abbreviations

Deleuze

B *Bergsonism*, trans. Hugh Tomlinson and Barbara Habberjam. New York: Zone Books, 1991 [1966].

BCD 'Bergson's Conception of Difference', in John Mullarkey (ed.), *The New Bergson*, trans. Melissa McMahon. Manchester and New York: Manchester University Press, 1999 [1956].

DI *Desert Islands and Other Texts: 1953–1974*, ed. David Lapoujade, trans. Michael Taormina. New York and Los Angeles: Semiotext(e), 2004 [2002].

DR *Difference and Repetition*, trans. Paul Patton. London: Athlone Press, 1994 [1968].

F *Foucault*, trans. Sean Hand. London and New York: Continuum, 1999 [1986].

LS *The Logic of Sense*, ed. Constantin V. Boundas, trans. Mark Lester with Charles Stivale. London: Continuum, 1990 [1969].

N *Negotiations: 1972–1990*, trans. Martin Joughin. New York: Columbia University Press, 1995 [1990].

NP *Nietzsche and Philosophy*, trans. Hugh Tomlinson. London and New York: Continuum, 1983 [1962].

TRM *Two Regimes of Madness: Texts and Interviews 1975–1995*, ed. David Lapoujade, trans. Ames Hodges and Mike Taormina. New York and Los Angeles: Semiotext(e), 2006 [2003].

Deleuze and Guattari

AO *Anti-Oedipus*, trans. Robert Hurley, Mark Seem and Helen R. Lane. London and New York: Continuum, 1984 [1972].

ATP *A Thousand Plateaus*, trans. Brian Massumi. Minneapolis: University of Minnesota, 1989 [1980].

WP *What Is Philosophy?*, trans. Graham Burchell and Hugh

Tomlinson. New York: Columbia University Press, 1994 [1991].

Deleuze and Parnet

D   *Dialogues II*, trans. Barbara Habberjam and Hugh Tomlinson. London and New York: Continuum, 2002 [1977].

Introduction

Gilles Deleuze is widely and rightly regarded as a philosopher of creativity, one of the greatest of the last century, if not several before. Throughout his work – whether it be on the history of philosophy, politics, literature or any other of his multifarious interests – can be found a whole host of concepts that help us to analyse the process of creation, express its salient features and inspire our various practices of it. As evidenced by the rapid appropriation of Deleuzian philosophy by an extraordinarily diverse range of fields, there is no doubt that Deleuze's 'call to arms' for creative production of and experimentation with thought is being heeded and duly acted upon. But in this rush for novelty, for a new formation that breaks from the past and gives rise to foreign experiences and ways of living, it is also often the case that much of importance is erroneously left behind. More specifically, it is often forgotten that history has a critical role to play in the act of transformation and the process by which something new emerges. It is the intention of this book to articulate this role, and in so doing demonstrate the vital importance of Deleuze's philosophy of history to his wider creative agenda.

Of all the concepts that Deleuze employs throughout his writings on the process of creativity, it is arguably 'becoming' that is of most significance. Becoming, of course, has a long and distinguished history in philosophy, stretching back to at least Heraclitus. More often than not, however, philosophies of becoming have found themselves in the shadow of philosophies of being – those philosophies, from Plato to Heidegger, that privilege presence over absence, identity over difference and 'what is' over the process of alteration. Deleuze's writings, from the choice of his subjects to the thrust of his conclusions, are all contoured by an attempt to step out from the shadow of this dominant history of philosophy, whether by an act of subversion or one of escape. As he says in a well-read passage:

> The history of philosophy has always been the agent of power in philosophy, and even in thought. It has played the represser's role: how can

1

you think without having read Plato, Descartes, Kant and Heidegger, and so-and-so's book about them? A formidable school of intimidation which manufactures specialists in thought – but which also makes those who stay outside conform all the more to this specialism which they despise. An image of thought called philosophy has been formed historically and it effectively stops people from thinking. (D 13)

But as we can intimate from this passage, it is not just the dominant history of philosophy that Deleuze is taking to task. If the history of philosophy has played the represser's role, it is because history itself is by nature a despotic force that tames thought through the process of historicisation: 'Nothing positive is done, nothing at all, in the domains of either criticism or history, when we are content to brandish ready-made old concepts like skeletons intended to intimidate any creation' (WP 83). Such remarks on the nature of history are peppered throughout Deleuze's work and proffered in all variety of contexts. But what exactly does Deleuze mean by history, and how are we to understand its relation to becoming within the parameters of a philosophy of creativity? In what follows I will embark upon a series of explorations into the relation of history and becoming in key sections of Deleuze's corpus. What will guide these various studies is the intuition that Deleuze's philosophy provides us with a novel and important notion of creativity as *historical creativity* – that is, a way of thinking about, on the one hand, history as an ontological force of creativity, and on the other, creativity as part of an historical process.

To adjoin history and creativity in this manner may at first appear to be a terrible mistake, for as we have just seen, Deleuze patently considers history to be a repressive force. Although Deleuze also admits that history is in a certain respect necessary for creation, there is no denying his ambivalence towards it. As he remarks in an interview with Antonio Negri:

What history grasps in an event is the way it's actualized in particular circumstances; the event's becoming is beyond the scope of history. History isn't experimental, it's just the set of more or less negative preconditions that make it possible to experiment with something beyond history. Without history the experimentation would remain indeterminate, lacking any initial conditions, but experimentation isn't historical. [. . .] Becoming isn't part of history; history amounts only [*sic*] the set of preconditions, however recent, that one leaves behind in order to 'become', that is, to create something new. (N 170–1)

In this book, I will in no way attempt to dismiss such statements or argue with Deleuze over their validity. Instead, I will endeavour to show that there is more to the matter of Deleuze and history than these statements initially portray.

Given that nearly all of Deleuze's explicit remarks on history occur within the context of an explanation of becoming, how one understands and approaches Deleuze's thoughts on history will depend upon which of several possible renditions of becoming one employs. On my reading, there are roughly three kinds or treatments of becoming in Deleuze's work. The first of these is the becoming of the abyss or the becoming of the depths. This is the infamous river of Heraclitus, what Deleuze and Guattari will later refer to as the pure phylum of becoming. It is also the absolute becoming of schizophrenia, that which brings about both the complete rupture and the line of destruction. In contrast to this abyssal becoming, Deleuze develops another kind of becoming that is most clearly presented in *The Logic of Sense*. This is the becoming of what Deleuze calls the pure incorporeal Event. It is also unlimited, but this time in an infinitive sense – the infinitive 'verb' as opposed to the 'adjective'. As this becoming, in Deleuze's imagery, hovers over and strafes an entire depth beneath it, I will also refer to it as surface becoming. There is, however, a third becoming in between these two. This becoming is not of the depths or the surface, but is rather the *movement between* the two. It is therefore developmental and successive rather than envelopmental and simultaneous; it is the *unravelling* of a form and/ or thing rather than the form of the infinitive or abyss of 'all things'. Most significantly, this ongoing movement is also what describes the relation between history and becoming:

> [B]ecoming is distinct from history. There are all sorts of correlations and *movements back and forth between them.* (TRM 377, translation modified, emphasis added)[1]

The critical question therefore is: what is the ontological status of this movement back and forth, and how does it differ from the becoming and history on either side?[2]

Aside from specifying the nature of becoming at various points in Deleuze's philosophy of creativity, equal attention must of course be given to ascertaining what Deleuze means by history. An immediate and relatively uncontroversial response presents itself: when Deleuze refers to history vis-à-vis becoming, by history he invariably means historicism – that is, a form of history which (1) proceeds in a linear-chronological fashion, (2) obeys a standard ontology of cause-effect, (3) concerns itself with the task of representing the world (or its essence) and (4) is teleological. In giving this list, it should be noted that Deleuze's attack of history varies from place to place, sometimes taking issue with its representational character and on other occasions with the cause-effect mechanism adopted by many forms of chronological history. As a result, the above list of attributes should be thought of as forming a broad and disjunctive conception of history-as-historicism rather than a set of conditions that must all be met. What is more or less consistent through all the various critiques of history-as-historicism, however, is the construal of history and becoming whereby the latter corresponds to a productive force for change (*puissance*), while the former is associated with the power of domination or control (*pouvoir*). Thus while becomings are said to create, history is said to capture and represent that which is created: 'history is one with the triumph of States' (ATP 394). This image of history is furthermore aligned by Deleuze with the ontological category of the 'actual', as opposed to the 'virtual' nature of becoming. History, as such, is a string of actualities that represent (capture) a virtual and productive force of becoming (creation). However, while this presentation of history is fairly straightforward, the studies in this book will each show how this is not the final word on Deleuze and history but only the first. For if Deleuze is to have anything worthwhile to offer our understanding of history and its role in the process of creativity, there must be more to the story than mere history-as-historicism, State history and/or history-as-actuality.

Holding such a belief is a precondition for anyone who believes in the possibility of a Deleuzian philosophy of history. Amongst the Deleuzian community there have been two standout attempts to explore this possibility in a sustained manner. The first of these is Manuel DeLanda's highly impressive *A Thousand Years of Nonlinear History*. There is much to like about this work. Its relevance to the project I am here undertaking, however, is somewhat limited. This is because *A Thousand Years* is much closer to being a work *of* Deleuzian history than a work about it. In other words, DeLanda addresses Deleuze's philosophy of history not by analysing it but rather by attempting to implement it (without directly specifying its nature) in a series of historical studies. Admittedly, even this description is somewhat inaccurate. For instance, the influence of Fernand Braudel is much more apparent than Deleuze (there are more than twice as many references to Braudel than Deleuze), and what use of Deleuze there is in DeLanda's book, much of which occurs in the 'Conclusion and Speculations', is almost exclusively limited to *A Thousand Plateaus*. This observation is not necessarily a criticism, for DeLanda's stated purpose is to use (selective parts of) Deleuze and Guattari's philosophy (among others) for his own tangential project (of a renewed materialist history). Nevertheless, this fact does restrict the usefulness of DeLanda's book to a project that has set itself the task of elucidating the relation between history and becoming within a Deleuzian philosophy of historical creativity.

As Eugene Holland has noted, if a general criticism could be made of DeLanda's overall interpretation and use of Deleuze and history, it would be that DeLanda gives an insufficient amount of attention to politics and in particular the influence of Marx on Deleuze and Guattari's historical theory (Holland 2006: 182). This lack of respect for Marx is no inadvertent oversight on DeLanda's part. To the contrary, DeLanda makes no secret about his desire to divorce Deleuze and Guattari from 'the bankrupt political economy of Marx', despite their unquestionable admiration for and use of Marx (see DeLanda 2009: 235 and DeLanda 1997: 331n). However, while I fully endorse the sentiment behind DeLanda's appropriation of Deleuze and Guattari – that 'this would be a better way of honouring Deleuze and Guattari's memory and work than any dogmatic attachment to what they actually said' – a dismissal of Marx's political economy will arguably require at least a little more justification than what DeLanda provides, even if DeLanda claims to hold the high ground of 'historical evidence' (DeLanda 2009: 236).[3] But while his reading of the so-called 'evidence' can most certainly be contested, it will not be an aim of this book to do so. This is not because I am an idealist or insensitive to the physical evidence DeLanda rests his work on. Rather, it is because I do not believe, as will become clear throughout this book, that such a revisionary programme based on fitting parts of Deleuzian philosophy to the 'best available historical evidence' is capable of doing justice to that 'actual' evidence or Deleuze's philosophy, let alone his philosophy of history.

The other major work in the field is Jay Lampert's *Deleuze and Guattari's Philosophy of History*. In this more explicit exposition of Deleuze's thoughts on history, Lampert provides many interesting insights into the subject, analysing with extraordinary acumen some of the more important themes. His detailed exegesis of the three syntheses of time (which takes up a third of his book) is a particularly valuable contribution to the area of Deleuze and history. Somewhat fortuitously, my interests lie in different directions. While the philosophy of time, as we will see, is of critical important to the investigations contained in this book, Deleuze's philosophy of space will be given equal if not greater consideration. This is partly due the fact that history is much more than just 'the past', and a philosophy of history cannot be ontologically reduced to a philosophy of time. But it is also due to the simple observation that the majority of Deleuze's key remarks on the nature of history and its relation to becoming invariably take place within the context of a topological discussion. I am specifically thinking here of Deleuze and Guattari's nomadology and geophilosophy, but there are other notable examples that I will analyse in detail. Thus while Lampert's work is largely guided by Deleuze's syntheses of time – a quite reasonable and understandable eventuality, given the traditional affinities between philosophies of history and time – my project will instead gain its impetus from Deleuze's syntheses of space, his philosophy of depth/surface and the topological concerns that feature in his later work with Guattari.

A second way in which my work differs from Lampert's is in its appreciation and use of Nietzsche and Bergson. Although Lampert certainly discusses Nietzsche and Bergson, for example in their relevance to the syntheses of time, he does not explore Nietzsche's or Bergson's *own* philosophies of history to see how they might inform Deleuze's. By contrast, I will demonstrate how Deleuze's philosophy of history can be seen as a continuation of an alternative tradition of historical thought that favours ontological creativity over representation. Towards this end, more attention will be given to Nietzsche's explicit writings on history (in particular his essay 'On the Utility and Liability of History for Life') as well as Bergson's influence on Deleuze beyond his role in the second synthesis of time.

Bergson in particular is largely responsible for a major distinction between my project and Lampert's. Put in brief, Lampert's account of Deleuze's philosophy of history favours simultaneity over succession. This is because despite the intricacy of Lampert's reading, he does not go beyond the binary of history (-as-historicism) and pure becoming, instead constructing a multi-levelled structure to explain how the two coexist in varying ways at the same time. For Lampert there are two kinds of history: one that corresponds to State history, and another that he calls revolutionary history. While the former is 'centrist', 'reactive' and 'paranoiac', the latter is 'an equivalent term to "becoming"', by which he means a wide range of things including the nomadic, the 'schizoanalytic phenomena of libidinal production, the overflow of codes and alliances, contingencies, ruptures, collectivities, retrospections, bifurcations, and lines of flight, differences without origin, neo-archaism and ex-futurism, rhythms and refrains' (Lampert 2006: 7). Although it is difficult to draw a generalisation from this list, it would seem that the becoming Lampert has in mind is what was referred to above as pure incorporeal becoming – that surface becoming which moves at an infinite speed, making possible the occurrence of *simultaneous* becomings. It is thus not surprising that this revolutionary or 'good' form of history essentially concerns the nature of simultaneity.

To verify this, one need read no further than Lampert's opening paragraph:

> Deleuze and Guattari's philosophy of becoming seems at times opposed to the very idea of historical succession. But suppose that we want to do without the concept of history, or to rebuild a concept of history without succession. [. . .] How might we conceptualize [. . .] phenomena free from the constraints of succession? If events are not related in terms of progression, then they will have to be related in terms of co-existence or simultaneity. (Lampert 2006: 1)[4]

There is no question that Lampert is interested in historical succession. But for him, the primary objective is to explain (away) this succession of historical actualities via a theory of virtual simultaneity: 'History therefore consists of diachrony within synchrony; or, to put it in reverse, succession is delayed simultaneity' (Lampert 2009: 72). Or again:

> The succession of befores and afters is a triple by-product of there being three simultaneous simultaneities. What takes the place of the classical concept of history is nothing other than these multiple forms of co-existence with their multiple subordinate forms of serial distribution. (Lampert 2006: 9)[5]

There is indeed a decent amount of evidence for this position. For example, when explaining the nature of Bergson's 'great synthesis of Memory', Deleuze clearly promotes the profoundness of virtual coexistence over succession. And looking ahead, this preference manifests itself in Deleuze and Guattari's later assertion that: 'All history does is to translate a coexistence of becomings into a succession' (ATP 430). But while there is no denying Deleuze's heavy reliance upon Bergson for his theory of virtual coexistence, this point must not be overplayed: on the one hand, Bergsonian ontology cannot be summed up by the theory of memory as virtual coexistence, and on the other hand, Deleuze's use of Bergson goes beyond his role in the second synthesis of time. One must therefore be careful

when equating Deleuze and Bergson with a theory that gives preference to a coexistence of virtual becomings over a succession of actual
history, for it is not at all certain that the ontology of virtual/actual
and simultaneity/succession can be so neatly apportioned between
becoming and history to begin with.[6] Once these designations are
questioned, both sides of the dualism of history and becoming are
affected. As soon as cracks appear in the presumption that history is
synonymous with the historicist succession of actuality, these cracks
immediately spread to its underside. This means that if there is to be
another kind of history in Deleuze's work, it must be distinct from
both historicism *and* its inverse. Put otherwise, if there are to be two
kinds of history in Deleuze's work that are genuinely distinct, they
must be more than just two sides of the same coin: history cannot
be saved by rushing into its negative. For this reason, the reduction
of succession to simultaneity, whereby succession is nothing other
than a 'by-product' or 'artifact' of simultaneity, arguably takes us
no further in eliciting a history that is genuinely different in nature
to 'bad' history, regardless of how complex a latticework of simultaneity one constructs. Thus while Lampert attempts 'to rebuild a
concept of history without succession', what my work is in search of
is a form of history that is capable of going beyond the caricatured
forms of succession (as historicist-progression) and simultaneity (as
virtual becoming).

DeLanda, for that matter, tosses the same coin. Like Lampert,
DeLanda also tries to reassert the significance of historical reality.
One of the main targets for criticism in his work are those
approaches that he calls 'top-down'. Such philosophies prioritise the
ideal and proceed 'downwards' to actual historical reality. In order
to redress the ascendency of these philosophies, DeLanda adopts
the contrary approach: 'My account is bottom-up in that I make an
effort not to postulate systematicity when I cannot show that a particular system-generating process has actually occurred' (DeLanda
1997: 18, 270). This methodology obliges one to begin with actual
materiality before proceeding 'upwards'. As such, DeLanda hopes to
bring about a philosophy in which 'geological, organic, and linguistic
materials will all be allowed to "have their say"' (DeLanda 1997:
22). To a certain extent, my project is similar to DeLanda's. For
example, in the studies that follow I will consistently argue against
those accounts that reduce historical reality to philosophical theory.
I will also emphasise the dynamic process whereby abstract machines
and virtual events are created rather than insist upon the ontologi-

cal priority of incorporeal events. But despite these synergies, it will be impossible for this book to adopt the method and ontology of DeLanda's work, given that it is little more than the negative of what it opposes. Because of this, it will not be the objective of this book to reassert historical actuality or to forward a theory that 'take[s] real history as its starting point' before moving on to 'philosophical conjecture' (DeLanda 1997: 12). Instead, I will show how the two were never *really* separated to begin with; I will show how historical reality is always *already* more than the actual and in productive relation with the virtual and incorporeal. As such, I will argue that if a Deleuzian philosophy of history is to be properly non-linear and contingent (as opposed to a linear historicism), then it will not merely consist in a bifurcation or 'virtuous circle' between actual history and virtual philosophy. On the contrary, history must *itself* be acknowledged as in part virtual and philosophical becoming as in part actual, as the two depart their initial placeholders and transmute their very nature.

This book therefore seeks a form of history in Deleuze's work that is not historicism yet equally not its inverse – a form of history, in short, that is irreducible to both historicism *and* pure becoming. As with the third kind of becoming identified above, this history will not be confined to one side of the dualism that history forms with becoming, but will rather be in between them. In this respect, it will be legitimate to describe this history as a kind of becoming and vice versa. In my terminology, the two will merge in the middle to compose a productive composite or differential 'history/becoming'. Thus while Lampert attempts to show 'the revolutionary potential of co-existential history' (Lampert 2006: 140), I will instead advocate the revolutionary potential of compositional history, or more exactly, the creative composite of 'history/becoming'. If this composite differs from a coexistential simultaneity, it is because a genuine composite of history and becoming or succession and simultaneity will be no more of one than the other. And if it differs from a straight 'bottom-up' progression from actual history to virtual philosophy, it is because it refrains from preferencing either direction by showing how creation always already requires a compositional and differential relation.[7]

Explaining what I mean by this composite more precisely will occupy the bulk of this book. It will be described in five ways: as an intensive-depth, dynamic, nomadic, universal-contingent, and as an historiophilosophy. In the final chapter of *Difference and Repetition*,

Deleuze engages in a discussion of creativity that revolves around the relation of depth and surface and the movement between them. As he argues, all extensive reality is the product of an intensive process that comes from the depths and emerges at the surface. While the creative movement from depth to surface is referred to as a 'becoming', 'history' concerns the retrospective identification and representation of this productive process. Or does it? By drawing on the philosophies of depth as found in several thinkers that Deleuze himself relies upon – Bergson, Braudel, Péguy and Nietzsche – Chapter 1 of this book, 'The Depths of History', will posit the existence of a form of history that can be legitimately characterised as an intensive-depth. This history will not be against becoming but rather in productive relation with it. It will not be against pure becoming or history-as-actuality, but it will show how any purity on its own is not enough when it comes to genuine experimentation. As a consequence, this chapter will show that if an intensive force is to move from depth to the surface, then the historical processes of production will need to be enlisted, not overcome.

Chapter 2, 'The Surfaces of History', will again focus on this movement from depth to surface. On this occasion, however, an alternative approach to the problem will be adopted, respective to the shift in emphasis between *Difference and Repetition* and *The Logic of Sense*. Whereas the former work exhibits a preoccupation with depth and its intensive uprising, the latter is explicitly written from the perspective of the surface (TRM 65). As a result of this modification, *The Logic of Sense* rearticulates Deleuze's philosophy of becoming, advancing a form that I refer to as 'surface becoming'. Although the majority of its pages are dedicated to detailing the logic and nature of sense and surfaces, in the final few series of *The Logic of Sense* Deleuze also admits that this logic requires a complementary *history* – a history that is *dynamic* as opposed to *static*. In Chapter 2 I will therefore explore how Deleuze's alternative form of history might be thought of as dynamic, in contrast to the static nature of pure incorporeal surface becoming (and historicism, for that matter). More specifically, I will illustrate how pure incorporeal surfaces are not more primary than the dynamic historical processes that produce them, for the two are always already in mutually productive union. In showing how neither depth nor surface has a priority over the other, however, the emphasis of this analysis will ultimately be placed elsewhere: on that which lies *between*. I will therefore conclude Chapter 2 by suggesting how Deleuze foregrounds a notion of 'the between' in *The Logic of Sense* that will guide much of his later work with Guattari.

Chapter 3, 'Nomadic History', will devote itself to unravelling this theme of 'the between' in greater detail. Returning to our original problematic, the question will be put again: what is it that differentiates history and becoming? What is it that lies between them, passing back and forth from one to the other? The answer is the 'and' itself – that which separates and conjoins history 'and' becoming. Substantialising the 'and' in this manner is by no means intended to be facetious. The reason for focusing on the 'and' is to indicate how the relation between history and becoming is outside of the terms it bisects and irreducible to either side alone. Deleuze and Guattari's project of 'nomadology' is perhaps the most mature and sustained examination of this relation to and *of* the outside. The nomadology can also, I will argue, be conceived of as a philosophy of history, or better yet, a philosophy of historical creativity. Such a claim might raise immediate objections, given that Deleuze and Guattari quite clearly regard their nomadology as the opposite of history (ATP 23). This opposition, however, only holds for the particular conception of history-as-historicism. Furthermore, there is every reason to believe, based on my analyses of Chapters 1 and 2, that beyond (or in-between) the opposition of history and becoming lies a composite form that renders the two together within the process of creativity. This belief is confirmed by the Nomadology plateau. As the plateau unfolds, the sharp and strict dualisms that are deployed in its early phases, such as history and becoming, are complexified, broken and ultimately transformed in accordance with 'the magical formula we all seek – PLURALISM = MONISM – via all the dualisms that are the enemy, an entirely necessary enemy, the furniture we are forever rearranging' (ATP 20). The apparent opposition of history and becoming is thus shown by the nomadology – through words and deeds – to be but a moment that gestures to a further compositional form, one that is capable of surpassing historicism and pure becoming by inhabiting the space between them.

Chapter 4, 'From Prehistory to Universal History', will locate in Deleuze and Guattari's joint writings another means by which this productive relation between history and becoming could be described: as universal-contingent. Taking the State rather than the nomad as its starting point, this chapter will investigate how it is that history is said 'to begin'. What is the relation between the history of an event and its prehistory? Does one successively follow the other, or do they not both always exist simultaneously since time immemorial? Through an analysis of the birth of the State, this chapter will examine Deleuze and Guattari's conceptions of succession and simultaneity, and question their straight assignations to history and becoming. As with previous studies, this chapter will also demonstrate why their relation must not be construed as an antagonistic opposition but rather as a differential composition. This will be achieved by drawing upon the history of social machines that Deleuze and Guattari develop throughout *Capitalism and Schizophrenia* – a universal history specifically marked by its contingent and creative character.

Now armed with an understanding of Deleuze's philosophy of historical creativity, Chapter 5, 'What is History in *What Is Philosophy?*', will put it to the test. Using Deleuze and Guattari's final monograph as a case study, this chapter will interrogate the role that history and becoming play in their definition of philosophy. As this analysis will demonstrate, although history does not appear to feature in *What Is Philosophy?* other than as a foil for Deleuze and Guattari's 'geophilosophy', historical creativity in fact and in principle is laced throughout their examination of the nature of philosophy. As a result, *What Is Philosophy?* will be reopened to history – a form of history that is far from repressive, since it is an active part of the creative process from the start and forever more – in turn giving rise to what could be called an historiophilosophy.

From these five analyses, this book will show how Deleuze has the potential to transform the way history is both conceived and used contra becoming and the process of creation. Ideally, it would be able to live up to Eugene Holland's call for a 'minor' history – by which he means a philosophy of history that doesn't just diagnose history but changes it (Holland 2008b).[8] Such a philosophy of history would indeed be creative and worthy of Deleuze's legacy. But short of this, it is hoped that this book will go some way towards providing thought-provoking possibilities for a philosophy of historical creativity that can be of use to theorists and practitioners of history, becoming and creativity.

1

The Depths of History

In his collection of essays *On History*, Fernand Braudel offers us a moving image for the nature of events. Commenting in reference to a display of fireflies he says, 'their pale lights glowed, went out, shone again, all without piercing the night with any true illumination. So it is with events; beyond their glow, darkness prevails' (Braudel 1980: 10–11). Although it is the glow of an event that catches our eye and fascinates us, Braudel argues that such superficialities belie greater complexities, for events emerge from an impenetrable milieu – a darkness or contingency – and this black night must be taken seriously. This means that even the brightest of stars must be related to the indeterminate realm that they light up. Two methods for achieving this offer themselves. On the one hand, we could carve out the event from its field of indeterminacy by graphing its flight from above; we could, in other words, come to know the life of the event by externally tracking its movement. But on the other hand, we could follow the firefly as it weaves through the night by placing ourselves *within* its line of flight; we could, according to this other method, come to know the life of an event by living with it.

   When developing their theory of the event, Deleuze and Guattari seize upon a similar conceptual distinction. As they state:

> [T]here are two ways of considering the event. One consists in going over the course of the event, in recording its effectuation in history, its conditioning and deterioration in history. But the other consists in reassembling the event, installing oneself in it as in a becoming, becoming young again and aging in it, both at the same time, going through all its components or singularities. (WP 111)

Much like Braudel, this passage describes how Deleuze and Guattari seek to get inside the environs of an event in order to gain an understanding of it that goes deeper than firefly watching. This theory of the event, however, can be directly traced to Deleuze's reading of Charles Péguy's work *Clio* (Péguy 1931: 266–9).[1] In the two versions that he wrote of this essay, Péguy illustrates a theme that is common to all of his historical commentaries: factual details, on their own, are insufficient for understanding an historical event; what is also needed is an appreciation of the *spirit* of an age, people and/ or movement – its *mystique*.[2] But as Deleuze and Guattari echo the insights of Péguy and Braudel, a curious transformation takes place. Whereas for Péguy and Braudel the reassembling of (and placing oneself within) the event was a way of practising and understanding history, for Deleuze and Guattari this alternative method is directly positioned *against* history and renamed 'becoming'. How then has this occurred?

In this chapter, as with the studies that will follow, I will show how there are two different forms of history at work in Deleuzian ontology: one which could be characterised as opposed to becoming, and another which is in productive union with it. Drawing from the intimations of Braudel and Péguy above, the location of my first foray into this other history will be 'beyond the superficial glow' and 'within the event': it will occur *in the depths*. In its colloquial context, depth is often used to indicate the past and history. For example, to understand a present situation 'in depth' is in many respects (though not all) to have experience, familiarity or knowledge of its past. However, as we will see, it is equally plausible to consider Deleuze's notion of intensive-depth, set out in the final chapter of *Difference and Repetition*, as compatible with a kind of history.

The purpose of Deleuze's analysis of intensive-depth is to get behind the process of creativity and explain how it is that new formations emerge. As he argues, underneath every identifiable extensity is a prior productive process whereby intensive forces erupt from the depths into an explicated surface. These intensive forces, in Deleuze's terminology here, are becomings, while history accounts for the extensive recording of intensities. However, if we return to some of Deleuze's sources for this reading – Braudel, Péguy and two of his most significant ontological touchstones, Bergson and Nietzsche – what we will find is an alternative theory of intensive production that is (in part) historical. History, as such, will be found in the depths of Deleuze's philosophy of creativity – a form of history that is not static and fixating but rather a productive force for change. But if this relocation is to be successful and meaningful, three questions must be adequately addressed. Firstly, can history be intensive? If so, is the placing of ourselves into the depths, so that we may *move with* an intensity as it becomes, a viable ontology and methodol-

14

ogy of history? And finally, what is it that this other history allows for and why is it important? In responding to these questions, this chapter will go far in not only reconciling history with becoming in the work of Deleuze, but also in indicating how Deleuze can provide a significant contribution to the lineage of thinkers who believe in a truly creative historical ontology.

Historical intensities

Deleuze's concept of intensity, it might initially seem, would not be a prudent place to look for an alternative conception of history. This is because history, as we will shortly see, is often associated by Deleuze with those things that are decidedly unintensive and uncreative. The most obvious place for history would therefore appear to be on the side of extensity rather than intensity. To a certain extent this state of affairs is undeniable. Nevertheless, it must also be acknowledged that this is not all that history can be or become. Aside from the figure of extensive history, there is another form of history in Deleuze's work that can be legitimately described as intensive. But before we can posit this other historical creativity beyond the borders of extensive history, it will be necessary to first establish what Deleuze means by intensity. In the process, possibilities for an intensive concept of history (and vice versa) will begin to emerge.

Taking up Kant's brief discussion of intensive magnitudes in the 'Anticipations of Perception' (Kant 2008: 110–14), Deleuze distinguishes between two forms of quantity: intensive and extensive. Although intensive quantities can be measured and ordered, they differ from extensive quantities in that they do not adhere to a whole–part metric that would allow them to be manipulated by procedures such as addition. For example, if one body of water measuring 10°C is added to another body of water measuring 20°C, the two do not add up to 30°C. Likewise, the sensation of my body moving at 20 kph is not reducible to a summation of the sensations my body experiences moving at 15 kph and 5 kph. We of course need not limit ourselves to examples of temperature or speed – psychological experiences such as love and anger are equally suitable. For example, one cannot add up lesser values of love in order to produce a higher order of love (God's love is of a different *order* to ours). In each case, the quantities at issue are intensive and as such are incapable of being divided *without effectuating a change in its nature* (DR 237, 254).

The inability of intensive quantities to be divided without changing in kind means that each intensity exists as what Bergson, drawing from Riemann, referred to as a continuous multiplicity. Deleuze makes this debt clear when he modifies Bergson's two multiplicities of continuous and discrete (or heterogeneous and homogeneous) into implicit and explicit: 'We must henceforth distinguish between two types of multiplicities [. . .]: implicit as opposed to explicit multiplicities; those whose metric varies with division and those which carry the invariable principle of their metric' (DR 238).[3] As this passage shows us, an intensive magnitude is a heterogeneous or implicit multiplicity that cannot be divided without effectuating a change in nature. This means that every heterogeneous multiplicity is a *singular-composite*: singular insofar as it is indivisible (without changing what it is into something else), yet a composite of differentiated elements. Another way of putting this would be to say that each heterogeneous multiplicity is an ordered whole of difference. But as Bergson's ontology continues, each of these ordered wholes can themselves be related to other orders that differ precisely in the degree of their difference – the different ways in which each order makes a singularity of difference. Intensive quantities obey the same ontology. On the one hand, every intensity is ordered as a continuous heterogeneity (as opposed to discrete homogeneities that give themselves to be added and divided without prejudice). But on the other hand, each of these intensities is itself within an order or continuum of difference, hierarchised according to ascending and descending degrees.[4] Thus every intensity is an ordered whole within an order, and their demarcation from one another determines at once both their internal heterogeneity (endo-consistency) as well as the external relations of that continuous heterogeneity to another (exoconsistency). Difference can then be said to occur both *at* every level and *between* every level *in precisely that way in which they differ.*[5]

As the above presentation of intensity suggests, an intensity is defined by the singular nature of its difference. The identity of an intensity is thus produced by difference. This theme of *constitutive difference* is of course a central concern throughout *Difference and Repetition*. It is, however, Deleuze's final treatment of difference that is arguably of most significance to an examination of the nature of history. In this concluding chapter, Deleuze's primary concern is not so much with the difference between the past, present and future (the topic of Chapter 2) but rather 'differences of level, temperature, pressure, tensions, potential, *difference of intensity*' (DR 222). It is these differences that are the stuff of history; if history is concerned with the relations between past, present and future, it is because these relations are a necessary part of the intensive differences by which reality is produced. This means that while a philosophy of history is no doubt dependent upon a philosophy of time (as we will see throughout this book), an investigation of the latter cannot stand for the former, since history is not reducible to time.[6] Looking ahead to the direction Deleuze will take his philosophy of history with Guattari, it is not difficult to see that theories of space will be equally as important as time: nomadology, for example, will be opposed to traditional history first and foremost on spatial and topological grounds; geophilosophy, to continue, will draw its inspiration from a history that is decidedly geographical (Braudel's geohistory). These future projects, however, are dependent upon Deleuze's conception of intensity-as-difference – a conception that complements the earlier philosophy of time in *Difference and Repetition* by specifically addressing the issue of space.

Crucial to this differential philosophy of space is the argument that the world cannot be finished or exact, for if it was then it would either be dead or cease to exist (DR 222). The world is therefore *in extrapolation*: a process of continual emergence that is constantly undergoing adjustment and readjustment – negotiation – of various differences in intensity. These differences in intensity must in turn be conditioned and correlated if we are to make sense of the newly emerged. However, in the act of 'making sense of' difference, difference becomes reified and stratified; difference becomes fixed, and as such emptied of its difference. This means that while an intensive difference is productive of extensive reality, in so doing it abolishes itself as a difference. More precisely, intensity-as-difference covers over, cancels out and/ or extends itself into an extensity or quality that in one and the same stroke identifies the existence of the intensive difference while effacing it: intensity, in other words, is suicidal. As Deleuze says:

> Intensity is difference, but this difference tends to deny or to cancel itself out in extensity and underneath quality. It is true that qualities are signs which flash across the interval of a difference. In so doing, however, they measure the time of an equalization – in other words, the time taken by the difference to cancel itself out in the extensity in which it is distributed. (DR 223)

Or further:

> Intensity is developed and explicated by means of an extension [*extensio*] which relates it to the extensity [*extensum*] in which it appears outside

17

itself and hidden beneath quality. Difference of intensity is cancelled or tends to be cancelled in this system, but it creates this system by explicating itself. (DR 228; see also DI 96)

The paradoxical nature of intensity is thus as follows: on the one hand, the intensive is that which resists being sensed 'independently of the qualities which cover it and the extensity in which it is distributed'; but on the other hand, intensity is the *only* thing which can be sensed, 'since it is what gives to be sensed, and defines the proper limits of sensibility' (DR 230; see also 236–7). This means that although intensity destroys itself, it only does so as a result of its own productive and metamorphic power. Put otherwise, the explication of an intensive force is not so much a dissipation as it is a creative explosion.

Deleuze emphasises this distinction between a dissipation of force and an affirmative explication of it in his discussion of thermodynamics. As he notes, despite its affinity with process and change, classical thermodynamics was overly concerned with the eventual equalisation of that change (DR 223). In so doing, classical thermodynamics turned away from an appreciation of the intensive processes that produce the states of equalisation. Today's 'far-from-equilibrium' thermodynamics seeks to correct this oversight. As Manuel DeLanda explains it: '[W]hile equilibrium thermodynamics focuses on what happens once the intensive differences have been cancelled, far-from-equilibrium thermodynamics studies systems that are continuously traversed by a strong flow of energy or matter, a flow which does not allow the differences in intensity to be cancelled, that is, a flow that maintains these differences and keeps them from cancelling themselves out' (DeLanda 2005: 82). Far-from-equilibrium thermodynamics thus does not efface intensities by dissipating/equalising their force but rather pushes them towards future productivities by keeping them open. Employing alternative Deleuzian terms, one could say that far-from-equilibrium thermodynamics does not allow processes of becoming to coalesce into fully static and explicated beings.

By invoking the ontological dualism of becoming and being, the question of history's place in this schema is brought into relief. Throughout his career Deleuze will repeatedly contrast becoming to history. For example, in an interview looking back at his work, Deleuze reflects: 'The thing is, I became more and more aware of the possibility of distinguishing between becoming and history'

(N 170). In *Difference and Repetition*, this notion of history is specifically attacked as *historicism* and contrasted with the virtual structure of the Idea (DR 186).[7] History understood in this manner is thus opposed to the unknown and the creation of the new, for it is designated the task of capturing and representing what is created in an order of causal-linear succession (chronology and/or teleology).

But while this reading of history in Deleuze is more or less undeniable, it does not by itself stand for a Deleuzian philosophy of history. According to the above topology, histories are extensive series that spiral away on the surface from those intensive breaks that cause a change in kind. For instance, the historical series of 'before the war', 'after the revolution', 'postcolonial history' or 'prehistoric times' are all extensive series that proceed from an intensive moment/movement of becoming: after the intensive creations of May '68 are captured, to take one of Deleuze's favoured case studies, we are presented with various extensive histories that spiral from and towards that point, making sense of it in various ways (or perhaps even ignoring the event itself). Two questions, however, immediately assert themselves: (1) must this scenario always occur in a one-two step process, creation occurring first and capture second? and (2) could not history already be a part of the productive process that leads to extensive historical series? Both of these questions can be answered by showing how history is itself constitutive.

This can be achieved by returning to our discussion of thermodynamics. The issue of thermodynamics is crucial, for it is the science that is arguably most concerned with asymmetrical movements – the kind of movements that are most often associated with the onwards march of history. More specifically, according to Deleuze, thermodynamics is concerned with the asymmetric movement from the intensive to the extensive. Thermodynamics thus addresses the serial movement *from depth to surface*, as opposed to those sciences that are only concerned with analysing surface series of extensity. The problem for classical thermodynamics, to recap, is that in pursuing the equalisation of intensive processes, it promotes an ontology in which a final future state acts as an inescapable attractor – what Bergson would call radical finalism (Bergson 1998: 39 and 91). With equalisation as its modus operandi, classical thermodynamics is only capable of proving its own presuppositions. This in turn discredits the effectivity of the process in realising the final state – the road travelled rendered inconsequential. In contrast to this, far-from-equilibrium thermodynamics attempts to avert this equalisation and thus evade a radical finalism. As a result, the productivity of intensity remains open and active, undecided and contingent. This means that the line drawn from depth to surface is not an ineffectual shadow of the final state, but is truly productive of what it is that comes about. But what are these various paths to equilibria if not differentiated histories by which a thermodynamic force moves towards explication? As DeLanda puts it when distinguishing classical from far-from-equilibrium thermodynamics:

> [I]nstead of the single global equilibrium of the classical theory we now have multiple equilibria, which means that *history matters*. While with a single possible outcome the different paths followed by systems on their way there can be ignored, with multiple possible outcomes *the details of the history followed matter*. (DeLanda 2005: 83)

When the result is known in advance, who cares for history? Such a history is a mere formality – an extensive series that always leads to and issues from the already known. But in far-from-equilibrium thermodynamics history can no longer be taken for granted; history becomes constitutive at precisely that point where the future becomes open. When the future is genuinely unknown, it matters a great deal whether we turn left of right at the next junction, for these details will contour the field of possibility, creating and closing alternatives. While it is not my intention here to suggest a vulgar tree diagram of history, it must nevertheless be acknowledged that in any particular instance certain outcomes are more likely (physically attractive) than others. This empirical fact cannot be denied. But as much modern science testifies, attractors need not be radically mechanistic or deterministic: while there may be 'basins of attraction', this does not preclude their emergent alteration. The critical point is, however, the following: the contingencies of historical encounters are in part responsible for the movements from one phase-space or basin of attraction to another. Thus to allow for the contingency of the event is to affirm the historical processes of production, not to deny them. Unlike the historical series of extensive surfaces, the historical processes of production are utterly different in kind, for they are indeed productive of historical extensities.

It must be admitted, however, that this analysis of productive intensity has yet to establish a clear link with what I am referring to as the historical processes of production. To properly achieve this we must look more closely at what Deleuze means by *depth*.

Historical depth

As noted above, extensive quantities can be divided and added together due to their adherence to whole–part relations. This aspect is, however, more than just a simple capability: extensive quantities are themselves only given insofar as they express a whole–part relation. For example, what is high is determined by its relation to what is low, what is right is determined by its relation to what is left, and so on. But as Deleuze points out, surely 'right' must be more than just 'to the right', it must be more than just an inverted 'left', for if it was not then the two would fail to genuinely differ in kind. Therefore, if 'right' is to maintain a difference in kind to 'left', then the extensity of 'right' within an external relation must be predicated upon the intensive determination of 'right' within itself. This is to say that the measure of an intensive quantity is always given according to its *own* metric. Intensities submit to no standard, for they are what produce standards – standards are made of them.

Insofar as the measure of an intensity always comes from within, what is being measured is none other than the *depth* of that intensity. It is therefore in depth and through depth that the productive processes of intensities take place. As Deleuze says, while an extensive quantity measures distance, length or size, these determinations themselves 'flow from a "deeper" instance – depth itself, which is not an extension but a pure *implex*' (DR 229). And again:

> Extensity does not develop or appear without presenting a left and a right, a high and a low, an above and a below, which are like the dissymmetrical marks of its own origin. The relativity of these determinations, moreover, is further testimony to the absolute from which they come. Extensity as a whole comes from the depths. Depth as the (ultimate and original) heterogeneous dimension is the matrix of all extensity [. . .] (DR 229)

Deleuze is here developing his earlier reading of Nietzsche, in which '*high* and *low*, *noble* and *base*, are not values but represent the differential element from which the value of values themselves derives' (NP 2). This 'differential element', we can now see, is intensive-depth – the 'absolute' from which extensive relations and values are derived. Depth is, however, a *heterogeneous* absolute, a matrix that 'makes whole' of a multiplicity: 'The original depth [. . .] is indeed space as a whole, but space as an intensive quantity: the pure *spatium*' (DR 230). But if it is in depth that a measure of worth is given, then in order to gauge it we must delve into it; extensive assessment will not suffice, we must place ourselves within depth in order to feel its own internal pulse or rhythm.

When so put, Deleuze's intensive-depth can be seen to have much in common with the notion of productive-depth used by his conceptual forebears. Take Bergson to begin with. I have already shown how Deleuze's understanding of intensity draws from Bergson's heterogeneous multiplicity. It is, however, Bergson's heterogeneous multiplicity of *duration* in particular that is most instructive for Deleuzian depth. In solving Zeno's paradox of the footrace between Achilles and the tortoise, Bergson demonstrates how Achilles will never pass the tortoise so long as time and motion are reduced to a homogeneous plane of space. As with the trajectory of an arrow, each stride of both Achilles and the tortoise is an indivisible movement, meaning it cannot be divided without changing it in kind. Each stride, as it were, comes from the depths of their respective durations. While these different durations can in turn be mapped onto an extensive space – the ground they are racing on – this does not mean that their intensive durations can be *reduced* to this shared homogeneous space:

> But the truth is that each of Achilles' steps is a simple indivisible act, and that, after a given number of these acts, Achilles will have passed the tortoise. The mistake of the Eleatics arises from their identification of this series of acts, each of which is *of a definite kind* and *indivisible*, with the homogeneous space which underlies them. (Bergson 2001: 113)

When the duration of Achilles is defined by the homogeneous space he shares with the tortoise, Zeno's paradox arises: every time Achilles attempts to bridge the final gap he must first cover half that distance. Thus as long as Achilles' stride can be extensively divided without changing it in kind (that is, without the realisation that it is no longer Achilles who is racing) he will be unable to reach the tortoise. But if the stride of Achilles is taken as a continuous motion of duration, an indivisible intensity that is greater in magnitude than the intensive quantity of the tortoise, then Achilles will be able to take that final step to victory. Zeno knows as well as anyone that Achilles must win. He knows that while his paradox appears to hold 'on paper', 'in the flesh' Achilles will clearly streak by the tortoise. Bergson's insight is to take this distinction between the static representation of motion in homogeneous space and the vital movement of heterogeneous time in duration seriously: 'Why resort to a metaphysical hypothesis, however ingenious, about the nature of space, time and motion, when immediate intuition shows us motion within duration, and duration outside space' (Bergson 2001: 114)? This means that to consider the race in real duration, one must draw a continuous line of heterogeneity from the depths of the past to the present moment that is emerging. It is only by doing so that we can gauge the confluence of multiple durations (e.g. Achilles', the tortoise's and ours) and thus experience the passing of time. For this reason, if time is to be vital and ongoing, it must be connected not as a discrete plane of homogeneity but as a continuous multiplicity of heterogeneity. The present moment must not be severed from the depths of the past, *but made thick with it*:

> Let us [. . .] grasp ourselves afresh as we are, in a present which is thick, and furthermore, elastic, which we can stretch indefinitely backward by pushing the screen which masks us from ourselves farther and farther away; let us grasp afresh the external world as it really is, not superficially, in the present, *but in depth*, with the immediate past crowding upon it and imprinting upon it its impetus; let us in a word become accustomed to see all things *sub specie durationis*: immediately in our galvanized perception what is taut becomes relaxed, what is dormant awakens, what is dead comes to life again. (Bergson 2007: 106, emphasis added)

Although it is not mentioned in the above passage, what Bergson is specifically describing here is his notion of philosophical intuition. Unlike the intellect, which concerns itself with analysing static extensive matter, intuition for Bergson is the form of knowledge through which one follows an intensive movement. Beginning with his analysis of intuition in *Bergsonism*, Deleuze will rely upon this form of knowledge throughout his career (see ATP 409 and WP 40). This form of knowledge, however, will also call on *depth* to delineate its nature: intuition is precisely that which has depth, as opposed to (1) the instinct which is flattened intuition (Bergson 1998: 182), and (2) the intellect which is cut out from intuition (Bergson 1998: 268); Bergsonian intuition is that which *moves* from the depths of duration, as opposed to the intellect which serves to solidify the movements of intuition for static investigation (Bergson 2007: 18–19, 103–4); and finally, intuition is a selection mechanism capable of ensuring appropriateness to and for each organism by gauging the thickness or richness – in other words, depth – of an organisms' 'zone of indetermination' (Bergson 2007: 19). In each case, while it is always an extensive surface that offers itself up for analysis, this analysis is itself dependent upon an appropriate intuition that always occurs within (or more accurately comes forth from) the depths:

Let us then go down into our inner selves: the deeper the point we touch, the stronger will be the thrust which sends us back to the surface. Philosophical intuition is this contact, philosophy is this impetus. Brought back to the surface by an impulsion from the depth, we shall regain contact with science as our thought opens out and disperses. (Bergson 2007: 103)[8]

Furthermore, insofar as this impetus from the depths to the surface concerns a proper duration rather than an extensive image of static time, it concerns a movement from the past to the present – the 'thickening' of a present moment as it is stretched backwards. Thus the placing of ourselves into the intensive-depths is the placing of ourselves within the past as it moves towards the present, making a continuity or composite of the two (a whole duration). What defines this continuity is that it cannot be dissected into isolated parts without changing it in kind, for as soon as this is done, we are in the realm of surface extensities. This means that an historical trajectory from the past itself to the present, as opposed to those historical series which fully reside on the surface, cannot be cut and rearranged without changing its nature. If one is to appropriately understand the past as it moves to the present, one must therefore consider an entire duration in its depths, for as this depth changes so too will what is an appropriate understanding of it: 'But the truth is that we shall never reach the past unless we frankly place ourselves within it' (Bergson 2004: 173).

The resonance of this last quote with the remarks of Braudel and Péguy reported at the start of this chapter is evident. Let us then explore in more detail what these two thinkers make of history and what they hope to achieve with it. As mentioned, Braudel's ambition is to promote 'a genuinely new form [of history]' (Braudel 1980: 18). According to Braudel, the dominant practice and theory of history ignores and/or stifles life. In light of this: 'It is precisely our task [as historians] to get beyond this first stage of history', in order that we can reach this other history capable of tackling social realities 'in themselves and for themselves' (Braudel 1980: 11). Because it is this other form of history that is best suited to investigating life, Braudel proclaims: 'As I have said before, it is life which is our school' (Braudel 1980: 17). Braudel even goes so far as to make the two synonymous: 'Just like life itself, history seems to us to be a fleeting spectacle, always in movement, made up of a web of problems meshed inextricably together, and able to assume a hundred different and contradictory aspects in turn' (Braudel 1980: 10). By now it is obvious that for Braudel history need not be opposed to life, move-ment, contingency or becoming. Indeed, the question that confronts the historian is: 'How should one tackle such a complex, living entity' (Braudel 1980: 10)? Just as Bergson insists that the two forms of knowledge (intellect and intuition) demand their own respective methods of inquiry, so too Braudel notes that 'each form of history demands an appropriate erudition' (Braudel 1980: 12). Furthermore, when prosecuting a Braudelian history, one must not reduce all and sundry to the one extensive time, but must rather be attuned to the various different durations involved. When one fails to do so:

> This necessarily entails enormous errors of perspective and of reasoning, for what they are thus attempting to reconcile, to fit into the same frame-work, are in fact movements which have neither the same duration, nor the same direction, some belonging to the time of men, of our own brief, transient lives, others partaking of the time of societies, for whom a day, a year hold hardly any meaning, for whom, sometimes, a whole century lasts but a moment. Though we must of course be clear that social time does not flow at one even rate, but goes at a thousand different paces, swift or slow, which bear almost no relation to the day-to-day rhythm of a chronicle or of traditional history. (Braudel 1980: 12)

Braudel's insistence on the multiple nature of duration similarly holds for the complexity of history's schematisation:

> There is no unilateral history. No one thing is exclusively dominant: neither the conflict between races, whose collisions or reconciliation sup-posedly shaped the whole of man's past; nor powerful economic rhythms, creators of progress or ruin; nor constant social tensions; nor that diffused spiritualism that those like Ranke see as the sublimation of the individual and of the whole vast body of history; nor the reign of technology; nor the demographic expansion, that vegetable expansion with all its eventual consequences for the life of communities. Man's complexity is yet other. (Braudel 1980: 10)

As to how this complexity can be appropriately approached, Braudel's answer is Bergson's: these different durations and complex histories are found 'in the depths and most often in silence, whose domain, immense and uncertain as it is, we must now approach' (Braudel 1980: 10).

As a follower of Bergson, it is not surprising that Péguy will also share much with this approach.[9] We have already seen how Péguy distinguishes between two ways of considering the event, one which consists in recording its effectuation in history and another which involves reassembling the event and installing oneself in it. Deleuze will rely on these heavily in order to contrast history and becoming. However, if we look beyond this oft-quoted passage to the rest of Péguy's historical essays, we can see that what Péguy has in mind is an alternative historical method that does not merely trade in histori-cal extensities on the surface but rather investigates historical events *in depth*. As Péguy writes, musing on what he would wish for instead of the litany of (republican) documents he consistently receives to be published in his journal *Les Cahiers de la Quinzaine*:

> History will always tell us about the big chiefs, the leaders of history, more or less well, less rather than more, that's its *métier*; and if history does not, then historians will, and if historians do not then the professors (of history) will. What we want to know, and what we cannot invent, what we want to know more about, are not the principal roles, the leading stars, the grand drama, the stage, the spectacle; what we want to know is what went on behind, below, beneath the surface, what the people of France were like; in fact, what we want to know is the *tissue* of the people in that heroic age, the texture of the republican party. What we want to know is the texture, the very tissue of the bourgeoisie, of the Republic, of the people, when the bourgeoisie was great, when the people was great, when the republicans were heroic, and the Republic had clean hands. And to leave nothing unsaid, when Republicans were republicans, and the Republic was the republic. What we want is not a Sunday version of history, but the history of every day of the week, a people in the ordi-nary texture of its daily life; working and earning, working for its daily bread, *panem quotidianum*; a race in its reality, displayed in all its depth. (Péguy 2001: 4)

Péguy's concern is thus not with the facts of history per se, but with the *cultures* that produce those facts. This may put him at odds with those forms of history that consist in the analysis of histori-cal extensities. But insofar as it does, it suggests to us another kind of historical technique and understanding – one that demands we become acquainted with a culture 'displayed in all its depth' if we are to appropriately intimate its historical processes of production.

As it happens, exemplifying this alternative historical ontology and methodology was Péguy's original purpose for writing the essay that the above passage is taken from. In 1907, Péguy was approached by the well-known Dreyfusard, Joseph Reinach, to write a history of the Dreyfus Affair. Declining to do so himself, Péguy in turn asked his friend Daniel Halévy to produce an historical account for his *Cahiers*. However, after publishing Halévy's piece, titled 'Apology for Our Past', Péguy responded less than a year later with his own rival version, titled 'Memories of Youth' ('Notre Jeunesse'). This was necessitated, Péguy believed, by the inability of Halévy's history to convey the appropriate spirit (*mystique*) of the Dreyfusard movement. Halévy most certainly had the majority of factual details correct, but what he failed to express was the life of the event – the vital and evolving forces that shaped the historical event and continued to be felt in the present.[10] 'Memories of Youth' was thus an attempt by Péguy to show how an alternative form of history is possible, one that is not disinterested and aloof but alive and continually creative. Moreover, in order to remain faithful to the historical event – to become worthy of the event, as Deleuze puts it[11] – Péguy sought to place himself back within its depths in order to feel its vibrancy and live its contingency. Péguy's history, as such, was not written from the privileged perspective of hindsight, replacing possibility with a retrospective historicism. Rather, it was expressed from within the depths of an historical movement that continues to speak to us today.

It should be noted that these thinkers of depth have not been called upon randomly. On the contrary, Braudel and Péguy are both specifically cited as inspirational sources for Deleuze and Guattari's alternative to traditional history (WP 95–7 and 110–13). And to the extent that this alternative revolves around a theory of becoming that is predicated upon Bergson's notions of the virtual, multiplicity and duration, it is equally clear that Bergson's philosophy of historical depth is of great pertinence to Deleuze's.[12] However, in recognising the affinity between Deleuze's understanding of depth – the pure spatium from which intensive production emerges – and the conceptions of depth in Bergson, Braudel and Péguy, the place and purpose of history in these accounts is called into question. Whereas depth for Bergson, Braudel and Péguy is in many respects an historical depth that is intensively productive in relation to the present and future, for Deleuze depth is a realm of becoming that is in turn overlaid by historical extensities. How then are we to explain this discrepancy?

It could be suggested that Deleuze repositions Bergson, Braudel and Péguy against history in order to emphasise the futural focus of his own philosophy. But while there is some truth to this, the case must not be overstated. Indeed, if the above historical thinkers can be said to have a common thread, it is precisely the great concern they all show for the future and the new. Given this, even if the bringing forth of the new is Deleuze's ultimate concern, the critical question remains: what role does history play in this process, what is the relation between the depths of the past and that which is yet to come?

In responding to this problematic, Deleuze invokes an earlier analysis in *Difference and Repetition*, noting how the philosophy of space he is setting out reprises his philosophy of time:

> We should not be surprised that the pure spatial syntheses here repeat the temporal syntheses previously specified: the explication of extensity rests upon the first synthesis, that of habit or the present; but the implication of depth rests upon the second synthesis, that of Memory and the past. Furthermore, in depth the proximity and simmering of the third synthesis make themselves felt, announcing the universal 'ungrounding'. Depth is like the famous geological line from NE to SW, the line which comes diagonally from the heart of things and distributes volcanoes: it unites a bubbling sensibility and a thought which 'rumbles in its crater'. Schelling said that depth is not added from without to length and breadth, but remains buried, like the sublime principle of the *differend* which creates them. (DR 230)

What is of most interest in this passage for our current study is the centrality afforded depth: it is *in depth* that the third synthesis of the future makes itself felt, and it is *depth* that is the 'sublime principle' of creation. Deleuze's focus here is thus not with that which is beyond depth, but the beyond that *depth points towards*. This is why Deleuze rounds off his discussion of intensive-depth by stating: 'The fact that they [intensities] cannot be added in any order whatsoever, or that they have an essential relation to an order of succession, refers us back to the synthesis of time *which acts in depth*' (DR 231, emphasis added). From this we can see that although depth is associated with the second synthesis of the past, both are not contrary to creation but are active participants in the process. Accordingly, if the explanation of intensive-depth as an alternative form of history is significant, it is because it has the potential to address exactly how history can provide an opening towards the future, rather than a closing down.

Opening towards the future

Some initial thoughts on how history can be an opening towards the future have already been suggested in our brief discussion of far-from-equilibrium thermodynamics. There we saw how 'history matters' when there are multiple possible outcomes in a process, since the realm of possibility is progressively determined. This in turn led me to claim that to allow for the contingency of the event is to affirm the historical processes of production, and more fundamentally, that history can itself be vital and creative. But on this point we must be clear: my claim is not just that the empirical facts of history have an impact on what comes next but rather that the intensive features of history are productive of the empirical extensive facts of history (hence two kinds of history).

This claim can be extemporised by asking the following question: what is the nature of potentiality in far-from-equilibrium thermodynamics? Is the future said to remain open due to 'epistemological unforeseeability' (meaning it only *appears* open due to our ignorance), or does modern thermodynamics go so far as to advocate 'ontological lawlessness' (meaning an ontological reality where anything and everything is possible)? For Deleuze the answer is neither. Although the future must remain unknown, this does not mean that 'anything goes'. What goes is rather intensive-depth. While laws of nature correspond to extended empirical domains, each domain is itself created by a difference of intensity. This means that intensive-depths concern a transcendental and not empirical principle (DR 240–1). If the intensive-depths are 'lawless', it is therefore not just because of their chaotic nature, but also because they are that which produces laws – intensive-depths produce identities through their difference. As such, the potentiality in far-from-equilibrium thermodynamics is more than mere epistemological unforeseeability yet cannot be described as simple lawlessness. What it instead calls for is a different conception of energy itself, a conception that does not define energy through extensity or a constant empirical principle but rather as a pure intensity with a generative difference buried within its depths that forms a transcendental principle (DR 240–1, 25).

But if even laws of nature are dependent upon their intensive-depth, what is it that is capable of grounding or determining the nature and direction of intensive movements? Deleuze's associations of the spatial to the temporal syntheses gives us our firmest indication of how his analysis of intensive-depth will be completed: insofar as the second synthesis gestures to a third, Bergson's synthesis of 'Memory and the past' gestures to Nietzsche's synthesis of the future. Nietzsche will thus be the critical figure in Deleuze's work for showing how it is that the past opens onto the future. Let us then explore some of the ways in which Deleuze uses Nietzschean ethics and ontology to complete his analysis of intensive-depth and direct it towards the opening of the future. Through this analysis, we will see how even that concept presumed to be most opposed to history – the untimely – is in fact a demonstrative tool for showing how history must and should be used for the bringing forth of the new.

As Deleuze stipulates at the start of Chapter 5 of *Difference and Repetition*, intensity *is* difference:

> The expression 'difference in intensity' is a tautology. Intensity is the form of difference in so far as this is the reason of the sensible. Every intensity is differential, by itself a difference. [. . .] The reason of the sensible, the condition of that which appears, is not space and time but the Unequal in itself, *disparateness* as it is determined and comprised in difference of intensity, in intensity as difference. (DR 222–3)

This means that intensity does not merely appropriate difference, but has difference in its heart – difference is what pulses through it. Insofar as difference is that which is unequal, as opposed to the equalisations of identity, intensive difference *includes* the unequal in itself. However, if intensity is to make of difference its *raison d'être*, it must do more than just include difference: intensity must *affirm* difference or make difference an object of affirmation (DR 234). Deleuze's understanding of affirmation and negation is most fully developed in his work on Nietzsche (though it can also be sourced to his earlier work on Bergson – see BCD 49 and 53). Put in brief, Deleuze focuses on the distinction in Nietzsche between those who produce their own value from within (masters) and those who determine their value by opposing another's (slaves). While the former can be said to affirm their existence, the latter negate that which they are not. As this summary already illustrates, the distinction that is being made between the two is akin to the distinction between intensive-depth and extensive surface: the distinction between those who produce from their own depths, and those who gain their value through an external relation of negation: 'To affirm is [. . .] *to create* new values which are those of life, which make life light and active' (NP 185). This chapter has already made several other allusions to this creative aspect of affirmative difference. For example, I pointed out how intensity *creates* its cancellation and as such does not negate itself in explication but rather affirms itself. Building on this, I argued that, unlike extensities, intensities cannot be measured according to some external standard but must be determined from within according to their own metric; intensities, in other words, must be judged according to the standards which they produce, for this is what ensures that intensities can indeed differ in kind. In this manner, intensity involves an affirmation of difference that can be contrasted by Deleuze's Nietzsche with the negation of that which differs.

We of course must be careful here, since Nietzsche quite famously praises the ancient Greeks for their profound superficiality (Nietzsche 1976: 683). This surface-art, however, is not at odds with the intensive-depth I am attempting to unravel, for the Greek superficiality Nietzsche is alluding to more specifically refers to the lack of any hidden *ressentiment*. Put otherwise, in each case a Greek is what he is; there is no building up of *ressentiment* for a future moment of revenge but rather an immediate show of strength that allows surfaces to faithfully convey the difference in kind of their depth. Deleuze emphasises this point by using another of Nietzsche's exemplary masters, the 'bird of prey':

> Everything is like the flight of an eagle: overflight, suspension and descent. Everything goes from high to low, and by that movement affirms the lowest: asymmetrical synthesis. High and low, moreover, are only a manner of speaking. It is a question of depth, and of the lower depth which essentially belongs to it. There is no depth which is not a 'seeker' of a lower depth: it is there that distance develops, but distance understood as the affirmation of that which it distances, or difference as the sublimation of the lower. (DR 234–5; see also LS 347n)

As with the eagle, it is depth and descent that preoccupies Nietzsche's studies. Despite his discoveries at and of the surface, Nietzsche, according to Deleuze, does not remain there, 'for the surface struck him as that which had to be assessed from the renewed perspective of an eye peering out from the depths' (LS 129). Thus once again, it is from within the perspective of depth that the future is sighted. Nietzsche may be Deleuze's pre-eminent philosopher of the future and the leading source for his third synthesis of time, but he is also the philosopher of depth and the creator of a 'new concept of genealogy' – a conception that plunges into the depths of an historical movement in order to make possible 'a determination of the values of the future' (NP 2–3).

This link between Nietzschean depth and the future is formalised in the final chapter of *Difference and Repetition* by Deleuze's alignment of the pure spatium of intensive-depth with the will to power. After describing how the spatium of intensive quantity is 'the theatre of all metamorphosis or difference in itself which envelops all its degrees in the production of each' (DR 240), Deleuze makes the following assertion: 'The will to power is the flashing world of metamorphoses, of communicating intensities, differences of differences, of *breaths*, insinuations and exhalations: a world of intensive intentionalities, a world of simulacra or "mysteries"' (DR 243). If this association of the pure spatium of depth with Nietzsche's will to power is significant, it is because Deleuze will in turn use it to forward a generative principle of selection: the eternal return. While the will to power is for Deleuze's Nietzsche the pure spatium of difference and becoming – difference unmitigated and uninhibited, free to become what it will (what it wills) – the eternal return is *that* which 'ceaselessly rumbles in this other dimension of the transcendental or the volcanic *spatium*' (DR 241); while the will to power is the play of difference, the eternal return is the being of that difference – it is *that* which is said of difference. In Deleuze's words: 'eternal return is the being of this world, the only Same which is said of this world and excludes any prior identity therein' (DR 243). By showing how the will to power and the eternal return relate to one another in this way, Deleuze effectively uses Nietzsche to show how the pure spatium of depth – that which was also aligned with the past and Bergson's great cone of memory – is inextricably linked with and partly responsible for the production of the new: 'one does not hold without the other' (DR 243).

Deleuze further elaborates this dual aspect or partnership of the will to power and the eternal return in his treatment of Nietzschean affirmation. As he explains in *Nietzsche and Philosophy*, affirmation is a quality of the will to power. Specifically, this quality is 'the enjoyment and play of its own difference' (NP 188). This affirmation, however, itself becomes an object of affirmation: 'a second affirmation takes the first as its object' (NP 189). In doing so, affirmation is redoubled: 'as object of the second affirmation it is affirmation itself affirmed, redoubled affirmation, difference raised to its highest power' (NP 189; see also DR 243). When taken as an object of affirmation, becoming is given a being and difference is given a repetition, leading to a double affirmation of the will to power and the eternal return – becoming and the being of becoming.

The consecration of this double affirmation is personified by the marriage of Dionysus and Ariadne:

> The first affirmation is Dionysus, becoming. The second affirmation is Ariadne, the mirror, the fiancée, reflection. But the second power of the first affirmation is the eternal return or the being of becoming. The will to power as the differential element that produces and develops difference in affirmation, that reflects difference in the affirmation of affirmation and makes it return in the affirmation which is itself affirmed. Dionysus

developed, reflected, raised to the highest power: these are the aspects of Dionysian willing which serve as principles for the eternal return. (NP 189)

In their marriage, Ariadne grounds Dionysus – the earthing of the God of becoming. As with an electrical charge, this grounding or earthing is what completes a circuitry, what allows a flowing current of power to be energised *into* something, allowing something in turn to be done (the light goes on). It is in this respect that the eternal return is correctly called a selection mechanism – a mechanism which activates the will to power flowing through it and accordingly determines 'what is to be done' by employing a centrifugal force that dispels lesser or weaker alternatives: will only that which you would will again for all eternity. But most importantly, this circuitry of the eternal return must not be conceived of as a simple cycle – a cycle in which the same things return. In such a cycle, the identity of that which returns is presupposed, demanding in turn that what returns already possess quality and extensity. Such a cycle is 'not so much an eternal return as a system of partial cycles and cycles of resemblance' (DR 242) – generalities, in short, that already obey an extensive law of nature. But for Deleuze's Nietzsche, on the other hand, if the eternal return is a cycle, if it folds back on itself, then what it folds back on is difference – the return of difference as the only same of the eternal return. Ariadne, as the eternal return, is therefore the grounding of the ungrounding, she is what guarantees difference returns. Thus if intensity is said to include the unequal in itself (the first characteristic of intensity) and furthermore to affirm this difference (the second characteristic of intensity), we can then say that this affirmation occurs as a double affirmation: enveloping and enveloped, implicating and implicated (the third characteristic of intensity).

The philosophy of history of Deleuze's day – and arguably still ours – fails to adequately respect this ontology of the double affirmation and more particularly the eternal return. It makes a simple cycle of the eternal return (cyclical history) and contrasts it with a linear conception of time and history (standard cause/effect). However, as Deleuze criticises, 'it is a meagre achievement on the part of our philosophy of history to oppose what is taken to be our historical time with the cyclical time supposed to be that of the Ancients' (DR 241), for both are ultimately incapable of allowing for any genuine difference to remain; both close off the possibility of an undetermined future in which novelty emerges. This is why Nietzsche's eternal return is said to be a belief of the future (DR 90, 241 and 242), but a future *founded in depth*:

> Depth, distance, caves, the lower depths, the tortuous, and the unequal in itself form the only landscape of the eternal return. Zarathustra reminds the buffoon as well as the eagle and the serpent that it is not an astro-nomical 'refrain', nor a physical circle . . . It is not a law of nature. The eternal return is elaborated within a ground, or within a groundlessness in which original Nature resides in its chaos, beyond the jurisdictions and laws which constitute only second nature. Nietzsche opposes 'his' hypothesis to the cyclical hypothesis, 'his' depth to the absence of depth in the sphere of the immutable. The eternal return is neither qualitative nor extensive but intensive, purely intensive. In other words, it is said of difference. (DR 242–3)

Although Bergson could also be credited with establishing a circuit of depth-surface that is productive and not vicious (Bergson 2004: 127–9), Deleuze insists that this creative return is Nietzsche's invention (DR 242). This is most likely due to Deleuze's general char-acterisation and deployment of Bergson in *Difference and Repetition* as the philosopher of the second synthesis, as well as his concomitant positioning of Nietzsche vis-à-vis the third synthesis. As Deleuze would well know, both Bergson and Nietzsche have much more to offer the matter than such a deployment would suggest. But if we momentarily humour Deleuze on this allotment, we can see what his structured argument is driving at: while the pure past of the second synthesis grounds successive presents as they transpire, this ground-ing is 'necessarily expressed in terms of a present, as an ancient *myth-ical* present' (DR 88). As a result, the ground of the second synthesis remains unacceptably encased in the mode of representation.

The problem of the pure past as ground is therefore as follows: how is it that the ground can detach itself from what it grounds, can refrain from taking on the characteristics of what it grounds and find its meaning independent of what it grounds? We have already seen one answer: the will to power and the eternal return, Dionysus and Ariadne, the great ungrounding and that which gives it meaning, the Same that is said of difference. In offering another response within the context of the three syntheses, Deleuze again delves into mythol-ogy. As Deleuze recounts, Mnemosyne, the figure of the pure past, is only completed in her conjunction with Eros: 'It is always Eros, the noumenon, who allows us to penetrate this pure past in itself, this virginal repetition which is Mnemosyne. He is the companion,

the fiancé, of Mnemosyne' (DR 85). We thus have two ceremo-
nies: while Ariadne takes to the sky with Dionysus,[13] Mnemosyne
holds her hand out to Eros, 'the erotic effect of memory itself' (DR
88). Dionysus and Eros, who together are known by the epithet
Eleutherios ('the liberator'), are therefore that which is capable of
escaping the relational confines of representation by providing the
ungrounding upon which the ground depends: 'Just as the ground is
in a sense "bent" and must lead us towards a beyond, so the second
synthesis of time points beyond itself in the direction of a third which
denounces the illusion of the in-itself as still a correlate of representation' (DR 88).

Although the above analysis has drawn heavily on the will to
power and the eternal return in order to illustrate how a Nietzschean
philosophy of depth and, by extension, historical depth might open
towards the future, these concepts are arguably not necessary to
prove the point. Long before Nietzsche's thought of the eternal return
struck, when he was still a young philologist under the influence of
Jakob Burckhardt and Johann Bachofen at the University of Basel,
Nietzsche was already grappling with the relation between history
and creativity, most directly in his essay 'On the Utility and Liability
of History for Life'. Deleuze is of course aware of this, evidenced by
his persistent affinity with Nietzsche's recommendation that we act
'counter to our time [. . .] for the benefit of a time to come' (Nietzsche
1983: 60). Nevertheless, Deleuze misappropriates this phrase, sever-
ing it from its original historical context in order to place it in the
service of a philosophy that positions the future against the past
and becoming against history. In order to achieve this contortion,
Deleuze omits the first half of the sentence every time he refers to
it (NP 107; DR xxi; LS 265; TRM 346), quite simply ignoring the
fact that Nietzsche is concerned with the impact that *philology* and
history must have on life – as the title of the essay stipulates – not
philosophy. The full sentence reads as follows:

> But I have to concede this much to myself as someone who by occupa-
> tion is a classical philologist, for I have no idea what the significance of
> classical philology would be in our age, if not to have an unfashionable
> effect – that is, to work against the time and thereby have an effect upon
> it, hopefully for the benefit of a future time. (Nietzsche 1995: 86–7)

The significance of drawing attention to the first half of this quote
is to show how Nietzsche need not be thought of as against history
en masse, but merely a *particular kind of history*, namely, those

histories that are *against life*. For Nietzsche, if becoming is to be distinguished from history, it is only in order that they become integrated in a *history for life*; if 'history isn't experimental', as Deleuze claims (N 170), then Nietzsche's point is that it must be made so, and if the untimely is the leaving behind of history 'in order to "become"' (N 171), then what it must become is a *history for the future*.[14]

As proto-considerations for the eternal return, Nietzsche's essay on a history for life can be seen as an early attempt to explain how history can be used for the production of the future.[15] Nietzsche was aware that the form of history which came to ascendency in the nineteenth century was a force that stifled life. Yet in critiquing this form of history Nietzsche was careful to acknowledge that life is still in need of history: 'That life requires the service of history must be comprehended, however, just as clearly as the proposition that will subsequently be proved – that an excess of history is harmful to life' (Nietzsche 1995: 96). By this, Nietzsche did not merely mean that history is a negative necessity. Rather, history can and must be used as a vital force if a healthy life is to be achieved. History, as such, when used appropriately, is not an impediment to life but an enabler of it. History is not something to be denied, one should rather engage with it as an oracle: 'The voice of the past is always the voice of an oracle; only if you are architects of the future and are familiar with the present will you understand the oracular voice of the past' (Nietzsche 1995: 130). The particular oracle Nietzsche has in mind here is the Delphic oracle that voices the refrain: 'Know thyself'. Come to know (intuit) your inner duration; hear the rumble of the eternal return in the depths of its crater. In every case, form a relation with the past but do not attempt to simply mimic or negate it. Instead, use it as an inspirational force in order to create something new, just as Nietzsche did with the Greeks and Deleuze with Nietzsche. Henk de Jong has perhaps said it best:

> But we should never forget that when Nietzsche so vehemently attacked historicism he did so *in the name of history*. When advocating the unhistorical and the transhistorical, when condemning historicism from this double perspective, it was *history* that made him do so. [. . .] [Nietzsche] wanted to imprint on his readers that the past was of the greatest importance to us, precisely because it helped us see how in the past individuals succeeded in transcending their own past. To put it in a paradoxical tautology, the past could liberate us from the past because only the past showed us how to liberate ourselves from it. In this strange way Nietzsche can be said to have been even more of a historical thinker, to have been

36

even more an advocate of the ultimate significance of history, than most of his historicist opponents. His later *Zur Genealogie der Moral* is perhaps the best proof of all this. (de Jong 1997: 273)

Despite Deleuze's modification of Nietzsche, the project of a Deleuzian philosophy of history that reattaches history to the production of the new is by no means a contradiction. All we need do is reattach Deleuze's concept of intensive-depth to a form of history contrary to historicism. More precisely, all we need do is show how Deleuze's concept of intensive-depth is entirely consistent with the form of history that Deleuze's own conceptual antecedents developed. We can then join with Deleuze in his critique of representational and revisionary history (DR 90) while simultaneously positing another kind of history in Deleuze that is not opposed to the future, difference and/or becoming, but is instead an active ingredient in its emergence.

∗   ∗   ∗

In the course of this chapter I have examined the concepts of intensity and depth, as found in *Difference and Repetition*, and compared them with those as found in Bergson, Braudel, Péguy and Nietzsche, in order to intimate how history and becoming relate to one another within a Deleuzian philosophy of creativity. This project has been predicated upon the observation that Deleuze's hostility towards history is highly superficial. While it is true that Deleuze criticises history for its association with representation, explication, being and the actual, this is by no means the final word on history in Deleuze, but only the first. Aside from this image of history-as-historicism, there is another history in the work of Deleuze, a history that draws its inspiration from the lineage of historical thinkers who themselves attempted to escape the dominant tradition.[16] While it might be thought that Deleuze employs these thinkers to attack history *in toto*, I have shown how this negative construal can be replaced by a more positive project: namely, the affirmation of a creative conception of history – an historical creativity.

History, in this respect, can be said to operate along two different axes. On the one hand, there are extensive histories: histories which order a series of extensive positions. These histories more or less resemble eulogies – a retrospective chronicle of a life. But on the other hand, for each of these overlapping and encompassing historical series there is a correlate process of production. Each extensive series is the explication of a productive intensity; each one, as it were, has its own requisite depth or zone of intensity – that internal and novel story of genesis that is responsible for its identifiable distinction and differentiation from others. Insofar as 'history matters' in the production and selection of each zone of intensity, history, as such, has a second axis, and this is found in the depths of intensity. This axis of history calls for a different kind of erudition, a method of intuition that allows us to follow an intensive movement along its progression from the depths to the surface.

By allowing for this distinction, history need no longer be opposed to becoming or the production of the new. Rather history, as an intensive-depth, might be precisely that which enables an opening towards the future. Far from being a force of capture or domination (*pouvoir*), history might rather be an integral and active constituent in the process of creation (*puissance*), thus transforming the supposed opposition of history and becoming into a productive or differential composite. If this productive form of history is not immediately obvious in Deleuze, it is because it lies beneath the surface, in the depths of Deleuze's thought. It is therefore imperative that we place ourselves within this historical thought, where it is actively working and producing. For any investigation of Deleuze's philosophy of history and becoming that limits itself to easily accessible historical extensities must content itself with chasing fireflies, superfluous to the milieu that produces them and that they in turn produce.

2

The Surfaces of History

Of Deleuze's two seminal solo works, *Difference and Repetition* and *The Logic of Sense*, it is the former that is commonly considered to be his magnum opus. *Difference and Repetition* certainly reads more like a great tome, a work of gravitas, while *The Logic of Sense* proceeds in a contrastingly skittish fashion. It is precisely this distinction, however, that indicates the manner in which the two works form a conceptual dualism: while the former is a work of depth, the latter is an inquiry into multifarious surfaces. Deleuze puts it as follows:

> For my part, when I was no longer content with the history of philosophy, my book *Difference and Repetition* still aspired nonetheless toward a sort of classical height and even toward an archaic depth. The theory of intensity which I was drafting was marked by depth, false or true; intensity was presented as stemming from the depths [. . .] In *Logic of Sense*, the novelty for me lay in the act of learning something about surfaces. The concepts remained the same: 'multiplicities,' 'singularities,' 'intensities,' 'events,' 'infinities,' 'problems,' 'paradoxes' and 'propositions' – but reorganized according to this dimension. The concepts changed then, and so did the method, a type of serial method, pertaining to surfaces; and the language changed, a language which I would have wanted to be ever more *intensive* and one which would move along a path of very small spurts. (TRM 65)

The Logic of Sense can therefore be seen as a reorganisation or reorientation of *Difference and Repetition* along the lines of the surface. In light of this shift, it will be necessary to replay the analyses of history and becoming carried out in Chapter 1, but this time from the perspective of the surface rather than depth.

At first, it might appear that this reorganisation involves little more than an inversion of the locations in which we find various concepts. For example, whereas in *Difference and Repetition* intensive becomings emerge from the depths into explicated actualities on the surface, in *The Logic of Sense* the surface is defined by its processes of virtual becoming in contrast to the depths of actuality. Similarly, whereas depth in *Difference and Repetition* is otherwise known as 'the transcendental or the volcanic *spatium*' (DR 241), in *The Logic of Sense* it is the surface that is described as the 'transcendental field' (LS 102 and 125). The situation is, however, more complicated than that, for as Deleuze indicates above, while it might be the same concepts that are under examination, they will differ due to the contrasting dimension they are being appraised in and deployed.

As a result, although *The Logic of Sense* continues Deleuze's development of a theory of intensity and fleshes out further his understanding of becoming, this becoming is in some respects distinct from what we have seen thus far. In my terminology, the driving conception of becoming in *The Logic of Sense* can be referred to as 'surface becoming'. Describing the nature of this surface becoming will be the first task of this chapter. As we will see, surface becomings are incorporeal and virtual forces that stretch over a sea of corporeal bodies and actual states of affairs. By virtue of their logic, they extract sense from the chaos they fly over and engender states of equilibrium through a process known as 'static genesis'.

In this initial analysis of surface becoming and static genesis I will address a principle concern of *The Logic of Sense*: the provision of a logic that explains how incorporeal surfaces are independent from yet impact upon the depths of corporeality. But in so doing, the limits of this logic will also be revealed. While a logic of sense and surfaces can stipulate the relation between an incorporeal surface and the various corporeal bodies that it corrals, it cannot account for the process that produces incorporeal surfaces themselves. Unlike the logic of surface becoming and static genesis, this other process of creation, according to Deleuze, is *dynamic*. It therefore proceeds in an entirely different manner to surface becoming: it is incremental as opposed to instantaneous, unravelling as opposed to enclosing, unfinished as opposed to pre-accomplished, and developmental instead of envelopmental. And most importantly for us, this dynamic process is also described by Deleuze as *historical* (LS 186).

What is this history? Clearly, it must be distinct from surface becoming, due to its successive rather than simultaneous nature. But it is equally true that this history cannot be the form of causal-linear historicism that Deleuze criticises, due to its dynamically productive nature. The historical process that Deleuze describes and employs in the latter series of *The Logic of Sense* will thus lie somewhere *between* these two extremities of 'pure' becoming and historicism. It will also lie between the depths of corporeal bodies and the incorpo-

40

real surface, insofar as it is what generates the movement from the former to the latter through a process of historical creativity.

Locating a conception of historical creativity between the surface and depth in *The Logic of Sense*, however, is a contentious manoeuvre. This is because the surface is itself described in this text as 'the between': the surface, for example, is *that* which lies between and relates a series of things and a series of propositions (LS 186); surface becoming, to continue, is defined by its always being 'spread between' its various instantiations in states of affairs. We therefore have a problem: if surface becoming is itself 'the between', then how are we to ontologically understand the movement between depth and surface (irrespective of which one is designated the 'transcendental field')? Answering this question is of paramount importance if we are to in turn understand the nature of the movements back and forth between history and becoming. I will therefore conclude this chapter by showing how there is another form of 'the between' forwarded in *The Logic of Sense* – a Herculean form that evades its dualism with depth and offers a novel conception of creation. Following this, we will be well positioned to pursue Deleuze's philosophy of history and becoming in his later work with Guattari.

The logic of surface becoming

In the first series of *The Logic of Sense*, Deleuze offers us a Platonic dualism. This dualism is not that of Model and copy, Idea and matter/body or intelligible and sensible. It is rather the distinction between copies and simulacra. If 'being' is the matter of copies, those limited and measured expressions of an Idea, then 'pure becoming' is the matter of the simulacrum, that which 'eludes the action of the Idea' and 'contests *both* model *and* copy at once' (LS 2). What both model and copy share are their susceptibility to measurement – it is in part by measuring the resemblance between them that the latter is determined to be a more or less good copy of the former. A pure becoming, however, evades such measurement by referring to an ongoing movement that is irreducible to specific qualities/quantities: '"[H]otter" never stops where it is but is always going a point further, and the same applies to "colder", whereas definite quality is something that has stopped going on and is fixed' (Plato 1961: 24d). That becoming refuses to answer to an ontology of being is unsurprising. But what is of interest is that such becomings, according to Deleuze, flee their fixation in opposite directions at the same time.

Deleuze draws inspiration for this theory from the literary work of Lewis Carroll, and in particular the story of *Alice in Wonderland*. As Deleuze notes in the case of Alice, she becomes larger and smaller at the same time, becoming larger than she was and smaller than she will be:

> This is the simultaneity of a becoming whose characteristic is to elude the present. Insofar as it eludes the present, becoming does not tolerate the separation or the distinction of before and after, or of past and future. It pertains to the essence of becoming to move and to pull in both directions at once: Alice does not grow without shrinking, and vice versa. (LS 1)

We thus arrive at the following philosophy of time. On the one hand there is the living present. This living present 'is the temporal extension which accompanies the act, expresses and measures the action of the agent and the passion of the patient' (LS 4). This present, in other words, pertains to corporeal bodies and their states of affairs. Insofar as such bodies can be collected into a unity, there is in turn a cosmic present, called Chronos, which 'embraces the entire universe' (LS 4). For Chronos, 'only bodies exist in space, and only the present exists in time' (LS 4, 162). But simultaneous with this reading of time is another – Aion – which corresponds to the incorporeal nature of events rather than the substantive corporeality of bodies: the infinitive verb rather than the adjective. As such, this alternative time always eludes the present, constantly splitting it into the already past and eternally yet to come.

At first, this dualism, whereby a 'veritable becoming-mad' (LS 1) continues to evade its capture in present bodies, may already appear familiar to us. As we saw in Chapter 1, intensive becomings are always distinct from the extensive quantities and qualities that come to represent them. However, whereas our previous analysis located the play of becoming *in the depths*, the becoming of Aion occurs *on the surface*.[1] Now it is no longer a case of *de jure* depths and *de facto* surfaces, but mixtures in the depths of bodies and pure incorporeal events which hover or strafe over that depth.

This shift is in fact motivated by the same philosophical opponent as *Difference and Repetition*: Platonic representation. In Plato, all that evades the action of the Idea must be banished to the depths of darkness. But as we saw in Chapter 1, Deleuze seeks to take this darkness of contingent becoming seriously. Whereas the strategy to achieve this in *Difference and Repetition* involved placing oneself into the depths, Deleuze's response in *The Logic of Sense* will consist in bringing these becomings, as becomings, to the surface itself:

> In Plato, an obscure debate was raging in the depths of things, in the depth of the earth, between that which undergoes the action of the Idea and that which eludes this action (copies and simulacra). [. . .] In Plato, however, this something is never sufficiently hidden, driven back, pushed deeply into the depth of the body, or drowned in the ocean. *Everything now returns to the surface.* This is the result of the Stoic operation: the unlimited returns. Becoming-mad, becoming unlimited is no longer a ground which rumbles. It climbs to the surface of things and becomes impassive. [. . .] What was eluding the Idea climbed up to the surface, that is, the incorporeal limit, and represents now all possible *ideality*, the latter being stripped of its causal and spiritual efficacy. (LS 7)

The rumbling of becoming in the depths is thus itself brought to the surface. Such rising to the surface, as it happens, is a recurring theme in Carroll's writings. As one example, Alice's adventures underground describes how her initial struggle to make sense of bodies-in-depth gives way to figures that are without thickness. Depth is flattened into width, and as everything becomes visible, Alice is able to climb to the surface and disavow false depth (LS 9). What Carroll plays with in his stories are the various incorporeal senses that can be given to a corporeal body; incorporeal senses are able to skirt along the surface like skipping stones, continually changing their assignations of and to the depth of bodies. Put otherwise, for any mixture of bodies, various incorporeal surfaces encompass or envelop that mixture instantaneously. Incorporeal surfaces are thus expressions of unlimited becoming that move at an infinite speed.[2]

We must, however, be careful here when speaking of unlimited becoming, for what Deleuze has in mind is in fact something quite distinct from the becoming that we looked at in Chapter 1. When elaborating on the nature of incorporeal events, Deleuze describes their surface as 'a chessboard on which [things or bodies] are organized according to plan' (LS 10).[3] As we can see here, what an incorporeal surface or sense does is provide an organisation to a set of words and things. It gives out, in other words, a logic. This logic, moreover, is not given incrementally, but all at once. We can thus say that there are two distinctive characteristics of surface becoming: (1) this becoming is eminently organisational – it is a *power of arranging*; and (2) it is a becoming which *already* stretches itself to its infinitive limits.

These characteristics by no means suggest that surface becomings are permanent or uncreative. Indeed, if Deleuze is fond of Carroll it is because Carroll continuously creates new surface arrangements, constantly pushing sense beyond its limits so that nonsense and new senses emerge: 'Carroll has a gift for renewing himself according to spatial dimensions, topological axes. He is an explorer, an experimenter' (TRM 63). Nevertheless, surface becomings, according to Deleuze, are sterile, fixed and immobilized (LS 31). Unlike the becoming of the abyss and the movement from this pure spatium to the surface, becomings on the surface are neither primary nor unfinished. They may be open to change, but at any particular moment they are completely determined. They may also be unlimited, but for precisely this reason they are always fully as opposed to partially completed. For example, on the Aionic line of Alice's becoming older and younger, she *already occupies* all of the possible places at once; the infinitive event of growing, in a certain respect, is entirely indifferent to the actual integers that Alice may happen to occupy at any one present time, for according to the infinitive she was always already there and yet to arrive. For this reason, Alice's becoming is *motionless*.[4] In Deleuze's words, these unlimited becomings are *neutral*:

> Neutrality, the impassibility of the event, its indifference to the determinations of the inside and the outside, to the individual and the collective, the particular and the general – all these form a constant without which the event would not have eternal truth and could not be distinguished from its temporal actualizations. (LS 100)

In order to explain how an unlimited becoming can be constant, neutral and sterile, we will need to consider what Deleuze refers to as static genesis.

Deleuze's investigation into static genesis is an attempt to explain how states of equilibrium come about. As James Williams puts it is his introduction to *The Logic of Sense*: 'Static genesis is about the emergence of static states, in the sense of an identifiable equilibrium – and hence a basis for judgement and comparison, but also a necessary expression' (Williams 2008: 196). From this description, it is immediately clear that this investigation into genesis will concern *already expelled* forces – that is, forces which have already reached equilibrium, and as such can be analysed by the intellect. Much like our analysis in Chapter 1 of the explicative results of an intensive process, Deleuze's study of static genesis is intended to explain how the 'definition of sense, Ideas and infinitives can lead to an account of the genesis of identified actual things' (Williams 2008: 124). The purpose of Deleuze's static genesis is thus to demonstrate how infinitive or incorporeal surface becomings extract sense and in so doing create identifiable states.

This gives us the following peculiar situation: on the one hand, infinitives of surface becoming play a critical role in determining the genesis of actual things; but on the other hand, these becomings are by nature sterile, neutral and constant. These two facets, however, need not be contradictory. For example, a cookie-cutter does not produce a mass of dough, but when applied to it, it does extract a formation respective to its particular shape (the edge that the infinitive delineates). As Alice knows, 'the more the events traverse the entire, depthless extension, the more they affect bodies which they cut and bruise' (LS 10). We can then say that this is the effect of the surface's neutrality: not that it physically creates things but rather that it provides the constant infinitive sense or organisational structure by which individuation occurs. It is for this reason that static genesis is said to proceed by processes such as 'prolongation', 'convergence', 'envelopment', 'stabilisation' and 'limitation' (LS 109–10).

The suggestion that creation occurs with an act of limitation is not entirely novel. Bergsonian ontology begins, for instance, with the intuition that perception is born through the act of extracting via disassociation a singular image from the universal aggregate of images (that aggregate in which 'images act and react upon one another in all their elementary parts' (Bergson 2004: 1)). And in Nietzsche, creation requires one to delimit one's view (by both 'forgetting' and turning away from the abyss of becoming) so that a directed course of action can be achieved (Nietzsche 1995: 89). Even Braudel makes the same point: 'For to construct something must always mean to limit oneself, must it not' (Braudel 1980: 20)? In each case, an image or vision only emerges when guided by a directed act of limitation. The same can be said for Deleuze's static genesis: it is concerned with the role that incorporeal limits (infinitives) play in the creation of actual things.

This was illustrated in our previous discussion of Aion and Chronos. Although the two could be said to differ fundamentally, there is at least one aspect they share: both are *readings* of time, that is, static organisations of *all* of time; they are both *spectral*, offering various 'fields' or 'complexes' of time (LS 116). The various readings of unlimited becoming, moreover, are themselves highly confining. This can be demonstrated by noting how the paradoxical nature of Aionic lines are only really paradoxical when the parameters of becoming are predetermined. For example, the infinitive line of 'shrinking-growing' is completely distinct from the infinitive of 'reddening-greening' (becoming more red and more green). Alice may indeed do both when she travels underground, but if the infinitive nature of Alice's shrinking is paradoxical, it is only by virtue of its structural relation with growing, not reddening. This is why there is no one Aionic realm but rather a simultaneous multiplicity of Aionic *readings*, each of which exudes its own particular form of consistency.

Given this description, it could be said that surface becomings have a kind of being. This being is stipulated by the particular form of each becoming's infinitive – by the way it corrals a 'series of ordinary points [. . .] selected according to a rule of convergence' (LS 110). Although this being may be distinguishable from the actual points it envelops, it is also markedly distinct from both the Heraclitean becoming of the volcanic spatium and the movement by which this lava erupts into a cooled-surface, neither of which could be said to share the impassive and neutral nature of surface becoming. For this reason, while surface becoming may be unlimited and transmutable, what sets it apart is its fundamentally static nature – the way that it sets parts on a 'chessboard' 'according to plan' (LS 10).

We can now see that the significance of static genesis not only lies in its stated object (the bringing about of equilibrium states), but more profoundly in the static nature of the genesis itself. But this in turn indicates the limitations of the static genesis: it lacks a genuine dynamism. By definition, static genesis and surface becomings cannot show us how surfaces are themselves dynamically generated. For this reason Deleuze recognises that the logic of sense and surfaces will only take us so far – the static genesis will require a dynamic genesis as its necessary complement. The explanation of this genesis, moreover, will correspondingly demand an alternative method: aside from the logic of surfaces, a history of surfaces will also be needed.

The history of developmental becoming

The 'Twenty-Seventh Series of Orality' marks a turning point in *The Logic of Sense*.[5] Up to this point Deleuze's analysis has been primarily concerned with an investigation into the logic and nature of incorporeal surfaces and sense, asserting in particular their independence from bodies on the one hand and their role in singularising bodies 'as such' on the other. However, after showing how it is that the surface 'renders possible', how it is that 'the expressed makes possible the expression' (LS 186), Deleuze admits that this analysis is limited and in need of a complementary examination:

> [W]e find ourselves confronted with a final task: to retrace the history which liberates sounds and makes them independent of bodies. It is no longer a question of a static genesis which would lead from the presupposed event to its actualization in states of affairs and to its expression in propositions. It is a question of a dynamic genesis which leads directly from states of affairs to events, from mixtures to pure lines, *from depth to the production of surfaces*, which must not implicate at all the other genesis. (LS 186)

As we can see here, the static genesis posits a surface becoming or incorporeal event, and as a consequence favours the movement from the pure event to bodies and states of affairs: 'But it is an entirely different question how speaking is effectively disengaged from eating, how the surface itself is produced, or how the incorporeal event results from bodily states' (LS 186–7). Another genesis is therefore required: a dynamic genesis.

Deleuze's dynamic genesis differs from the static in both object and direction, the static going from an incorporeal surface to a corporeal actuality and the dynamic from the depths of bodies to the production of a surface. It would, however, be misleading to suggest that the two geneses are symmetrical, for the dynamic is not merely the reversal or inverse of the static. The two therefore differ not only in object and direction, but more profoundly in the nature of their movement and method: while the former is static and logical, the latter is dynamic and historical.

This association of a dynamic development with history may seem contentious. However, as I pointed out in Chapter 1, this impression only persists as long as we insist on reading history as historicism. It is therefore important to remember that the dynamic historical development that Deleuze addresses from the 27th series onwards is by no means a standard or traditional notion of history. Most crucially, it is not foregone: the purpose of the dynamic genesis is not to illustrate a historicist or teleological progression towards an incorporeal event – the progression is not a Hegelian *Geist*, and the event to which it is leading is not the Prussian State. If it were so, then there would indeed be nothing dynamic about it. For this reason, although the historical progression of the dynamic genesis is directed towards showing how depths ascend to an incorporeal surface, this history must not be reduced to the claim that corporeal bodies are the 'cause' of incorporeal effects (or vice versa). Rather, the dynamic genesis will show how an evolution unravels through a continually shifting relation between two different realms (the corporeal/incorporeal, states of affairs/pure events, etc.) that indeed remain different despite their own ongoing transmutations. In this respect, I am no more interested in reducing the incorporeal to the corporeal than the contrary. My intention is to instead show how the two collude in the task of creation.[6]

This collusion and the presumption of a creative conception of history, as opposed to historicism, are both supported by the fact that the historical development of the dynamic genesis could also be described as a becoming. But what do I mean here by becoming? Clearly, if the dynamic movement from depth to surface is to be a becoming, it will not be what I have described as static surface becoming. Instead, it will be a form of becoming that could be referred to as *developmental*. To put this distinction briefly, while the former becoming envelops, the latter develops; while the former encloses a surface, the latter unravels into one. Unlike surface becomings, developmental becomings involve an incomplete process, something not yet fully achieved; they are always at some stage of undress, in the process of becoming-other. Surface becomings, it might be noted, are also always becoming-other, e.g. becoming younger and older than one is. But these becomings are never 'at some stage' of a process, for they are at every point and no point at once; in a surface becoming all of the instantiations of an infinitive occur *at the same time* (Aion). For this reason surface becomings are static and sterile, neutral and consistent, already imbued with a particular organisational logic. Such a becoming cannot unfold incrementally, step by step, for it moves at an infinite speed, prosecuting its envelopment simultaneously. The significance of developmental becoming thus lies in its unfinished and dynamically progressive nature, as opposed to the already delimited infinitives of various surface becomings.

The affinity of surface becoming with organisational structures, and static genesis with states of equilibrium, should have already alerted us to the existence of another form or kind of becoming and genesis. Recalling our encounter with thermodynamics in Chapter 1, if a becoming is to avoid explication into a static form then it must not be equalised. By keeping a becoming 'far-from-equilibrium', it can continue to transmute and develop. But as I went on to argue, this form of creation need not be distinct from history. Once we distinguish between two forms of history in Deleuze, one which is equated with historicism and another which more closely resembles developmental becoming, then history is no longer opposed to the future but is that which allows it to remain genuinely open.[7] When so described, we can see that this composite of developmental becoming and progressive history does not at all suggest 'betterment' or realisation of a predetermined ideal. It rather refers to a dynamic movement whereby the new emerges. Put otherwise, it is a form of progression that is Bergsonian and not Hegelian. The dynamic and developmental composite of becoming and history can thus be distinguished from both surface becoming and historicism, the latter two of which, it could be noted, are essentially sterile.

Given that Deleuze's consideration of dynamic genesis will set out an historical study that begins in the depths of corporeality, it is necessary that we first come to know this depth in itself. The most focused series towards this end is the 'Thirteenth Series of the Schizophrenic and the Little Girl'. Appearing and disappearing suddenly as an interlude half way through the first (long) half of *The Logic of Sense*, the 13th series gives depth a proper voice of its own: Antonin Artaud. Deleuze seizes on the antagonism between Artaud and Carroll in order to encapsulate the difference in kind between depth and surface: 'we could say that Artaud considers Lewis Carroll a pervert, a little pervert, who holds onto the establishment of a surface language, and who has not felt the real problem of a language in depth [. . .]' (LS 84). The reason why this encounter is so significant for Deleuze is because Artaud and Carroll both appear to be concerned with the same thing: nonsense and the duality of things/ words. Yet as it turns out, between them everything changes; there is a profound difference in what it is they are doing, how it is they do it and why, leading Deleuze to remark that ultimately that 'they do not compete with [each other] on the same plane' (LS 90).

For Carroll, the escalation of nonsense is a surface game. The play of sense and nonsense 'forms the surface organization upon which Carroll's work plays a mirror-like effect' (LS 86). By contrast, for Artaud *'there is not, there is no longer, any surface'* (LS 86). For Artaud there is no longer any frontier between things and words because bodies no longer have a surface – they are depth entirely. Bodies are like a sieve, their surface in fact a porous skin which 'carries along and snaps up everything into this gaping depth' (LS 87). As Deleuze continues, for Artaud 'Everything is body and corporeal. Everything is a mixture of bodies, and inside the body, interlocking and penetration' (LS 87). This does not mean that there are no frontiers in Artaud, only that the frontiers are of depth and in depth; they are between the infinite foldings and mixtures of bodies rather than between things/words as organised by an incorporeal surface that sets limits. Artaud's nonsense therefore refers to a complete loss of incorporeal sense, an inability to distinguish between 'the action and passions of the body, and an ideational event distinct from its present realization' (LS 87). In Artaud, 'nonsense has ceased to give sense to the surface; it absorbs and engulfs all sense' (LS 91).

We can thus see that unlike Carroll's nonsense, which is derived from an infinite mobility across all sides of the surface simultaneously, Artaud's nonsense is the product of a primal body (the 'body without organs' (BwO)). While Carroll relies upon a dualism of words and things, in Artaud there is no secondary organisation, since the incorporeal is constantly dragged down and split between the dualism of actions and passions:

> It is for this reason that we can oppose Artaud and Carroll point for point – primary order and secondary organization. The *surface series* of the 'to eat/to speak' type have really nothing in common with the *poles of depth* which are only apparently similar. The two *figures of nonsense* at the surface, which distribute sense between the series, have nothing to do with the two *dives into nonsense* which drag along, engulf, and reabsorb sense (*Untersinn*). The two forms of stuttering, the clonic and the tonic, are only roughly analogous to the two schizophrenic languages. The break (*coupure*) of the surface has nothing in common with the deep *Spaltung*. The contradiction which was grasped in an infinite subdivision of the past-future over the incorporeal line of the Aion has nothing to do with the opposition of poles in the physical present of bodies. (LS 91–2)

Does Deleuze side with either Artaud or Carroll? That depends. On the one hand, Carroll is 'the master and surveyor of surfaces', and it is indeed 'on these surfaces [that] the entire logic of sense is located' (LS 93). But as I have pointed out, *The Logic of Sense* will in fact go beyond this logic of sense and surfaces. Deleuze's emphasis on surfaces and 'the incorporeal line of the Aion' must therefore not be pursued to the detriment of depth. To put it one way: 'We would not give a page of Artaud for all of Carroll' (LS 93). Ultimately, what Deleuze will be interested in is how to proceed from one to the other; it is not a question of choosing sides – Carroll's surface becoming or Artaud's abyssal becoming (BwO) – but rather a question of the composite creation they can together form. While Artaud remains consumed by the schizophrenic body, and while Carroll continues to preoccupy himself with little surface games, Deleuze seeks a philosophical reconciliation of the two (which will arguably come to fruition in his work with Guattari). Given this, we must then return to the task of examining the developmental movement between them.

Deleuze principally illustrates this progression by employing a linguistic and psychoanalytic example: namely, how is it that a child is able to assemble a proper language out of what is initially mere noise? Before outlining the stages of this development, it should be noted that although Deleuze chooses in this case to demonstrate the movement from the depths of corporeality to the incorporeal surface by using linguistics and psychoanalysis, this is arguably not necessary; I see no reason why it would not be possible to develop and articulate a Deleuzian theory of dynamic genesis independent of these two paradigms. Deleuze's future work will indeed bear out this possibility, disassociating his theory of the incorporeal event from the context of *The Logic of Sense* in order to employ it in various others. In my analysis below, I will therefore refrain from providing an exhaustive treatment of the philosophy and history of linguistics and psychoanalysis. Instead I will use these fields as contingent examples which 'offer us an expression of the process of dynamic genesis' (Williams 2008: 197–8).[8]

At first there is nothing but noise – the abyss or absolute depths of becoming:

> The depth is clamorous: clappings, crackings, gnashings, cracklings, explosions, the shattered sounds of internal objects, and also the inarticulate howls-breaths of the body without organs which respond to them – all of this forms a sonorous system bearing witness to the oral-anal voracity. (LS 193)

When the child first encounters this sonorous system it is of course entirely new to them. It is, however, approached as something pre-existing. As if entering a conversation mid-sentence, the child does not yet understand but nevertheless has a premonition that something is and has been going on. In this respect, the child 'comes to a language that she cannot yet understand as language, but only as a voice, or as a familial hum of voices which already speaks to her' (LS 229). Although this voice 'has at its disposal all the dimensions of organized language' (LS 193) – denotation, signification and manifestation – it is nevertheless bereft of an organising principle. Because of this, 'one does not know what the voice denotes; one does not know what it signifies since it signifies the order of preexisting entities; [and] one does not know what it manifests since it manifests withdrawal into its [unknown] principle, or silence' (LS 194). Thus while the voice for the child is no longer a noise, it is not yet a language but only the first step towards one: 'from noises as qualities, actions, and passions of bodies in depth, to the voice as an entity of the heights, withdrawn into heights, expressing itself in the name of that which preexists, or rather posing itself as preexisting' (LS 229).

On the one hand, the child comes to a pre-existing language that they do not yet understand. But on the other hand, it is precisely because of this that they are capable of *hearing everything*. For this reason Deleuze privileges 'the child's extreme sensitivity to phonemic distinctions' (LS 230).[9] Paradoxically, it is due to the child's not yet having the whole system of language that the child is able to 'grasp that which we no longer know how to grasp in our own language' (LS 230). More specifically, it is due to the incomplete nature of their incorporeal surface that the child has not yet learnt to disregard those differences in a language that are normally deemed inconsequential. This is why it is invariably the child who gives back to the adult a vibrant language – in their striving to understand, combined with a certain *tabula rasa*, the child creates and reinvigorates language itself. Deleuze will pursue this notion further in his later work, extending it to his philosophy of literature and suggesting that one speak 'like a foreigner in one's own language' (D 4; see also ATP 98). What the foreign speaker shares with the child is the potential to create anew precisely by taking what is *actually* already there, for this is what a native or mature speaker, due to habit, familiarity and laziness, fails to do. Immersed in a prelinguistic system that is not yet refined, the child is free for a moment to make of a language what he/she can or will: 'In the continuous flow of the voice which comes from above, the child cuts out elements of different orders' (LS 230).[10]

It is in this *effort* that speech is brought about. If the first step or transition of dynamic genesis goes from noises to the voice, then the second step progresses from voice to speech (LS 232). Speech, however, is not language. The speech of an infant is still far too base; it consists of too much physicality and not enough abstraction. This means that while the child at the level of speech may be in possession of an organisational structure – a structure, moreover, that contains all the formative elements of language – this structure is not yet language proper: 'we are still in a prelinguistic domain' (LS 232). Deleuze describes this situation by distinguishing between a physical and a metaphysical surface. In ascending from the 'familial hum' of the voice to the sounding of their own speech, 'the child pursues on his own body the constitution of a surface' (LS 201). We may have at this stage a systematisation of depth, but because this system is constituted exclusively on the body of the child, it is a physical surface that is not equal to the metaphysical surface, sense or incorporeal event: 'The organization of the physical surface is not yet sense' (LS 233).

As just alluded to, for the child to progress from a physical to metaphysical surface – the third step of the dynamic genesis – the child must abstract away from the entirely physical system that he/she is currently preoccupied with. To be more specific, the child requires an element that is outside of their own physical surface that can act as an organising principle for that surface. Sonically speaking, this element is the sound of silence. The unspoken is what lies outside the physical system of sound and grounds it. Like Nietzsche's eternal return that was discussed in Chapter 1, this element of silence 'grounds' through its 'universal ungrounding'.

To give an example, young musicians are often noted for their tendency to play too many notes. This is most obvious in gifted protégés who are eager to show off their newly acquired technical prowess. But it is not until such individuals learn to be silent, to use silence and 'play' silent notes, that they can be considered to possess a *mature* musicality. This silence is invariably appropriated from a mentor or inspirational example, who already possesses a 'standard' or 'style' through which their music is channelled. Once the young musician has gained this level of abstraction and a standard/style of their own, they may return to familiar compositions, but when they do so, they will not simply encounter physical notes. This time, the musician will rather 'extract an eternal truth from them' (LS 240), illustrating the existence of a musical sensibility that can now be applied to any collection of corporeal sounds.[11]

It is in this step from an 'intermediary physical surface' (LS 239) to a further metaphysical surface that various incorporeal events, such as language, are made possible. In Deleuze's linguistic example, it is above all the verb that illustrates the arrival of an incorporeal system: 'In the verb, the secondary organization is brought about, and from this organization the entire ordering of language proceeds' (LS 241). As we saw earlier in this chapter, the verb (as opposed to the adjective) refers to an infinitive becoming that is entirely neutral with respect to its various instantiations. Thus unlike the howls which issue from the abyssal depths, the verb is perfectly silent (LS 241). Language is thus engendered when the silent infinitive verb spreads out over the metaphysical surface, in turn supplying an organisational principle by which corporeal noise can be 'made sense of'. The stages of dynamic genesis, charting in this case the 'struggle for the independence of sounds' (LS 240), can therefore be summarised as follows: from noise to voice, voice to speech and speech to the silent verb (which involves the facilitation of a metaphysical surface followed by the projection of language across this surface).

However, having provided a step-by-step elaboration of the process whereby an incorporeal surface is generated, we must stand back from it and ask: from whence does it gain its argumentative force? As it turns out, this impetus is provided by none other than the incorporeal event itself. All of the stages of sonic development can only be understood with respect to the language that they will lead to and that will in turn stipulate their being and order. The final stage of the dynamic genesis therefore sparks an effacement of the dynamic process and its replacement with a static organisation that issues back into the depths at infinite speed from the incorporeal surface. Thus the surface will be seen to produce itself, dictating 'after the fact' the nature of each step that led to it.

Does this turn the dynamic genesis into a sham, nothing more than a teleological tale told by an incorporeal event that was presupposed from the start and never in doubt of realisation? Perhaps. The power of retrospectivity in this process cannot be denied. And if it is emphasised, then the dynamic genesis becomes conducive to a form of history that is synonymous with historicism. I am, however, of the opinion that the historical process Deleuze is describing in the dynamic genesis does not correspond to a standard notion of history but is rather in line with the historical creativity first set out in Chapter 1. I would argue that the retrospective act of effacement that occurs at the end of the dynamic genesis should not be overextended or taken to replace the productive process itself. That an incorporeal event has the capacity to retrospectively account for, understand or make sense of the process that created it should not itself mean that we confer to it the genital power that led to it; a difference in nature must remain between the retrospective power that makes sense of the past and the process by which that power is engendered. This is the difference, in short, between 'making sense of' and the 'making of sense' itself: while the latter leads towards sense, the former issues from it. The necessity of maintaining this distinction is perhaps best put by Bergson:

> But it would be a strange mistake to take for a constitutive element of doctrine what was only the means of expressing it. Such is the first error to which we are exposed, as I was just saying, when we undertake the study of a system. (Bergson 2007: 91)

We will return to this issue in more detail when I discuss the retrospective power of the State apparatus in Chapter 4. But for now, all I wish to point out is that regardless of the retrospective effect of an incorporeal surface, this does not mean that we have to give up on the process that led to it. What came before may be 'repressed or neutralised' by an incorporeal surface, it may even 'exist only as an allusion, as vapor or dust, showing a path along which language has passed' (LS 242), but even this existence is different in kind and irreducible to the incorporeal field that comes to give it sense. In this respect, despite the effects of retrospective identification, the historical progression of dynamic genesis must be reasserted as distinct from, ontologically irreducible to and necessary for the complementary processes of static genesis and surface becoming:

> We have seen the way in which the order of language with its formed units comes about – that is, with denotations and their fulfilments in things, manifestations and their actualizations in persons, signification and their accomplishments in concepts; it was precisely the entire subject matter of the static genesis. *But, in order to get to that point, it was necessary to go through all the stages of the dynamic genesis.* (LS 241, emphasis added)

For every level of surface organisation, for every plane of consistency or plane of immanence (as we will see in Chapters 4 and 5), there is a dynamic process of creation that cannot be wholly reduced to that 'level' of systematicity. Nor can it be reduced to another, since what the dynamic process provides is precisely the 'step' between them – that which connects levels, enabling a *transition* or *movement between* them. If these steps are to remain different in nature to the levels that order them, then the process of developmental becoming and historical progression must not be completely reduced to the surface itself. It is for this reason that I would not go so far as to assert the 'ontological priority' of events over substances.[12] For while it is true that the major concern of *The Logic of Sense* is with the problem of the event, and while it is also true that incorporeal events are irreducible to substances, this does not itself mean that the incorporeal has any more ontological priority than the corporeal. Surfaces may indeed give rise to static objects (actualities), insofar as they allow us to identify them 'as such'. But as Deleuze shows in the developmental and historical process of dynamic genesis, the role of materiality in the production of the incorporeal must also be recognised and reasserted as *no less* important.[13] 'Priority', in other words, will go out the window when it comes to the dualisms of incorporeal/corporeal, virtual events/actual substances, surface/depth, etc. In its place, as this chapter will now go on to suggest, priority must ultimately be given to that which lies between the two: 'the between' itself.

The Herculean surface

This chapter has thus far attempted to complement the analysis of history and becoming in Chapter 1 by exploring Deleuze's reorientation of depth and surface in *The Logic of Sense* and its attendant philosophy of creativity. After describing the logic of surface becoming that drives the majority of the text, we saw how a history is in turn required by Deleuze to complement and complete his analysis of becoming. This history is not merely a string of actualities, nor is it synonymous with the depths of corporeality or the incorporeal surface. Instead, it is a dynamic process of production that develops from one to the other. By inhabiting the space between the ontological dualism of depth/surface, this creative conception of history evades being reduced to either the incorporeal surface/event or the corporeal depth/states of affairs (or as I showed in Chapter 1, virtual becoming or actual history). But in elevating the importance of this 'between' to such an extent, it becomes necessary to ask further after its nature: what exactly is 'the between' in Deleuzian philosophy? Chapter 3 will dedicate itself to addressing this issue. *The Logic of Sense*, however, contains crucial information on 'the between' that can simultaneously cap our examination of depth/surface and foreground our future studies.

As we have seen, the theme of the between arises from Deleuze's investigation of depth and surface, and the relation between them. In *The Logic of Sense*, this between is first located at the surface: insofar as Aion describes the time of an incorporeal event, the event is always 'between' its various instantiations, always yet to come and already past. In this respect, the between is directly associated with the incorporeal surface and forms a dualism with corporeal depth. However, as our investigation of the dynamic genesis illustrated, if the nature of this surface is to be fully understood, then we must acknowledge how incorporeal surfaces are brought about from a movement of transmutation from depth to surface. As such, aside from the between that can be correlated with surface becoming and the Aionic reading of time, there must be another kind of between that corresponds to the movements not 'of' or 'across' the surface but 'towards' and 'away from' it. In other words, there must be a between, a 'movement back and forth', that cannot be exclusively reduced to either Aion or Chronos, the incorporeal event or corporeal states of affairs, virtual becoming or actual history.

Intimations of this between can be found in the 'Eighteenth Series of the Three Images of Philosophers'. This series is interesting and novel for a number of reasons. To begin with, the 18th series is not so much an internal analysis of the logic and ontology of surfaces as it is a positioning of this surface logic and ontology with respect to other alternatives throughout the history of philosophy. More specifically, the 18th series, more so than any other series in *The Logic of Sense*, takes up the discussion of 'images of thought' from the third chapter of *Difference and Repetition* by reorientating that analysis along the surface lines of *The Logic of Sense*. This reorientation, however, is by no means straightforward, given that what is being reoriented is Deleuze's interpretation of the various major orientations of thought. To explain, the analysis of different images of thought in the 18th series is directly informed by the logic and nature of sense and surfaces that *The Logic of Sense* has thus far set out. In this respect, each image of thought explores a relation of life to thought that '*is like* sense which, on one of its sides, is attributed to states of life and, on the other, inheres in propositions of thought' (LS 128, emphasis added). However, it turns out that the surface is also one of these orientations. The surface thus plays a double role in the 18th series: on the one hand, it is what directs (orientates) the analysis into various images (orientations) of thought by distilling their organisational principle; but on the other hand, it is itself one of the three orientations explored, the other two being height and depth.

Highlighting this duplicity allows us to acknowledge that while the 18th series certainly maintains an interest in how an incorporeal surface orients that which is beneath it, the primary objective of the series is to explain how there are various different kinds of orientation of which the surface is only one. In fact, the dominant dualism in the series is not surface and depth but rather height and depth, the surface being that which *moves between* them. As such, the 18th series offers a slight but significant shift in the usage and nature of the surface, whereby the main emphasis is no longer on the dualism that surface becoming forms with that which it envelops but rather on a surface that itself moves in a *dynamic* way between dominant dualisms (such as 'deep' bodies and 'lofty' ideals). If this shift is of importance to our current study, it is because by emphasising the movement back and forth between two realms that are radically different in nature rather than the infinite movement between actualities of the same ontological kind (the Aion between moments of chronology), the surface of the 18th series can in turn suggest to us how the strict opposition of history and becoming might itself be overcome in favour of something in between the two that brings them all together. In other words, the 18th series could be seen to offer us another way of moving that can provide the means for evading the oppositional images of history and becoming in favour of a third image that can be the inspiration for a new philosophy of history – not a historicism or pure becoming shorn of history, but an ontology of historical creativity.

Let us then take a closer look at the three images set out in the 18th series, and in particular their relation, to see how they might aid our understanding of 'the between'. Deleuze begins with a brief description of what he considers to be philosophy's dominant tradition: Platonism. This tradition is defined by its orientation towards the heavens. As Deleuze notes, both the popular image of the philosopher (someone with their head in the clouds) and the technical or scientific image of the philosopher (who cavorts with an intelligible heaven) are given to us by Platonism (LS 127). The Platonic philosopher, as such, is concerned with 'the high principle', with the 'ascent' or 'conversion' of earthly reality into a 'purified' realm of ideas: 'Idealism is the illness congenital to the Platonic philosophy' (LS 127–8).

On the underside of this dominant image and orientation is its counterpart: depth. As we saw in Chapter 1, Nietzsche is for Deleuze the philosopher of depth and subversion par excellence: 'The encased depths strike Nietzsche as the real orientation of philosophy, the pre-Socratic discovery that must be revived in a philosophy of the future, with all the forces of a life which is also a thought, and of a language which is also a body' (LS 129). In this shift of orientation, the Platonic ascent to pure height is replaced with a pre-Socratic emphasis on subversion and descent. Even Nietzsche's eagle is a figure of depth, for unlike the 'beating of the Platonic wings' (LS 129) the bird of prey suspends itself in air before swooping; what is critical for the predator is its dynamic descent.[14] Thus while Deleuze repeatedly praises Nietzsche throughout his career as a philosopher of masks and superficialities, of dancing across a surface with a lightness of foot, for Deleuze Nietzsche must always be returned to the depths via a descent that is coordinate with his biographical trajectory:

> In his own discovery, Nietzsche glimpsed, as if in a dream, at the means of treading over the earth, of touching it lightly, of dancing and leading back to the surface those monsters of the deep and forms of the sky which were left. But it is true that he was overtaken by a more profound task, one which was more grandiose and also more dangerous: in his discovery, he saw a new way of exploring the depth, of bringing a distinct eye to bear upon it, of discerning in it a thousand voices, of making all of these voices speak – being prepared to be snapped up by this depth which he interpreted and populated as it had never been before. He could not stand to stay on the fragile surface, which he had nevertheless plotted through men and gods. Returning to a bottomless abyss that he renewed and dug out afresh, that is where Nietzsche perished in his own manner. (LS 107–8)[15]

Nevertheless, despite Nietzsche's concern for depth, the path that his journey there takes is precisely what leads Deleuze to his third image of philosophy. Aside from the Platonic philosophers of height and the pre-Socratic philosophers of depth, which together form the dualism of the dominant image of thought and its dark side, Nietzsche's reading of the Greeks indicates to Deleuze a third way:

> We have the impression, however, that there arises, in conformity to this method [i.e. Nietzsche's method of 'peering out from the depths'], a third image of philosophers. In relation to them, Nietzsche's pronouncement is particularly apt: how profound these Geeks were as a consequence of their being superficial! These third Greeks are no longer entirely Greek. They no longer expect salvation from the depths of the earth or from autochthony, any more than they expect it from heaven or from the Idea. Rather, they expect it laterally, from the event, from the East – where, as Carroll says, 'all that is good . . ., ris(es) with the dawn of Day!' (LS 129)

Nietzsche's depth therefore *shows the way* to the surface, to a third set of Greek philosophers. These 'third Greeks' – the Megarians, Cynics and Stoics – provide Deleuze with the surface orientation that will direct much of *The Logic of Sense*. It is no longer the Idea above that explains, nor the depths that speak a primal truth. It is rather the surface which now mediates between the two, rendering that which is different in kind through the medium of the surface: 'This is a reorientation of all thought and of what it means to think: *there is no longer depth or height*' (LS 130).

This statement (and others like it in *The Logic of Sense*) must, however, be approached with caution, for despite this rise to the surface, the third orientation of thought still involves and relates to a form of depth – namely, the depths of corporeal bodies. Furthermore, we know that come the 27th series of *The Logic of Sense* Deleuze will return to the depths in order to assert the importance of the dynamic production of surfaces. Given this, although the new surface orientation offered in the 18th series changes what it means to think by overcoming the orientations of height and depth, it must be noted that it does so by instituting a new dualism of depth and surface: on the one hand, 'the devouring Chronos', the corporeality of 'causes-bodies' and their 'infernal mixtures'; and on the other hand, the Aionic and incorporeal event (LS 131–2). Juxtaposing the dualism of Platonic height and pre-Socratic depth (and its surface in-between) with the surface orientation's dualism of depth and surface (corporeal bodies and the incorporeal event) is a revealing exercise, for the clash indicates how there is a subtle yet critical shift of emphasis in Deleuze's surface analysis. As Deleuze articulates the third orientation of thought, what becomes of interest in the surface is not merely its contrast with depth but rather the nature of its relation to height and depth, each of which are orientations of thought. It may well be that depth and surface are also Deleuze's realms of corporeality and incorporeality, but these aspects are distinct from their orientating capacity, the latter of which is the focus of the series. Thus the presiding interest of the 18th series is arguably not so much the Aionic nature of the surface and the way in which events move across the surface but rather the way in which the surface is itself approached – the nature of the *return* to the surface. As Deleuze prefaces in an earlier series: from height to depth, '*everything now returns to the surface*' (LS 7).

An examination of the way Deleuze describes his 'third Greeks' confirms this shift. This discussion is split into roughly two halves. The first explains the thesis whereby 'in the depths of bodies everything is mixture' (LS 130). Of the various examples employed, Seneca's tragedies are forwarded as eminent instances of the Stoic image of thought from their 'discovery of passions-bodies and of the infernal mixtures which they organize or submit to' (LS 131). These same tragedies, however, also provide the counter-side to this *membra discerpta*:

> Let us look now for the antidote or the counter-proof: the hero of Seneca's tragedies and of the entire Stoic thought is Hercules. Hercules is

always situated relative to the three realms of the infernal abyss, the celestial height and the surface of the earth. Inside the depths, he comes across only frightening combinations and mixtures; in the sky he finds only emptiness and celestial monsters duplicating those of the inferno. As for the earth, he is its pacifier and surveyor, and even treads over the surface of its waters. He always ascends or descends to the surface in every conceivable manner. He brings back the hell-hound and the celestial hound, the serpent of hell and the serpent of the heavens. It is no longer a question of Dionysus down below, or of Apollo up above, but of Hercules of the surface, in his dual battle against both depth and height: reorientation of the entire thought and a new geography. (LS 131–2)

Hercules is thus the figure of the surface. But if we look closely at how he is described above, it becomes clear that the focus is not primarily on the way Hercules moves across the surface – his treading over water – but rather on his adventures to the realms of height and depth, and the nature of his return. As such, if Hercules personifies the third image of thought, that of the surface, it is not because he remains on a surface in between height and depth but rather because he is always ascending or descending *to* the surface. Therefore, while it might be said that he belongs to the surface – that he is a proper surface being – this does not preclude him from moving back and forth between height and depth. Indeed, nearly everything interesting about Hercules involves his dealings with height and depth, his clashes and collusions with differences in nature; Hercules would lose much if not all of his singularity if he had forever remained on the surface. In this respect it is the surface itself that delves down into the depths and reaches into the heights, returning with plunder of another kind. When so described, it becomes clear that the Herculean surface must be more than just that which separates dualisms, suspended between the two. Furthermore, this surface-as-between must be more than just that which moves across a surface in an Aionic manner between Chronological actualities. Rather, it must be capable of rendering the dominant dualism of height and depth into an immanent monism or productive composite by the way in which it consistently moves between them all in a dynamic manner.[16]

My emphasis here on Herculean dynamism has perhaps been overplayed. After all, other surface personifications that Deleuze offers in the 18th series – such as the tick and the louse – do not lend themselves as easily to this kind of heroism. Nevertheless, the above description of a surface-as-between that is not even confined to its organisational position between two realms provides us with a useful way of describing the nature of a movement that goes back and forth between dominant dualisms in order to overcome their opposition. For example, once the surface (and its becoming) is liberated from its fixed place between beings, it is no longer the various levels of simultaneous organisation that are emphasised but rather the nature of the steps or dynamic movements between them. This is not to in turn reduce the level to the step, for as I have argued, the choice is not between pure being and pure becoming. Rather the Herculean surface must be both and neither, capable of transgressing and separating alike. It must be a third orientation that is liberated from dualisms due to its ability to both 'be' between, 'move' between and 'bring together' the absolutes on either side.

To achieve this, 'a new geography' will be required. Although Hercules' reconfiguration of the surface shows us the way,[17] it is arguably not until Deleuze's work with Guattari that one is fully delivered. Our next task must therefore consist in following this Herculean image of 'the between' as it departs *The Logic of Sense* and ambulates through Deleuze's future writings. There we will discover how this dynamic and Herculean movement between strict dualisms is of critical importance to Deleuze's development with Guattari of an historical creativity that is irreducible to both pure becoming and historicism.

∗   ∗   ∗

Throughout this chapter and the last, we have explored Deleuze's philosophy of depth and surface to see what it might have to offer our understanding of the relation between history and becoming within a philosophy of creativity. What we have found is that if one goes beyond the crass conception of history that Deleuze is clearly opposed to – history as fixed and uncreative, shackled by teleology and/or the linear law of cause and effect – then there is another history in Deleuze's work that is genuinely productive. While Chapter 1 explored this history through the notion of intensive-depth, in Chapter 2 we have seen how Deleuze advances a dynamic conception of history and historical creativity. This dynamic history is necessitated by the limited nature of incorporeal surface becoming. Although surface becoming is responsible for the extraction of singularities from depth, the static and sterile nature of its infinitive demands that a complementary process of dynamic and developmental production be posited.

This theory of dynamic history, however, requires us to stipulate more precisely what is meant by both history and becoming. On the one hand, the dynamic movement from the depths to the surface indicates a form or kind of creative becoming that is distinct from both pure Aionic surface becoming as well as the primal abyss of fire (Artaud's 'monstrous body' or the Heraclitan 'fire-machine'). And on the other hand, this developmental movement equally indicates a form or kind of history that avoids the extremes of both historicism and generalised relativism. In short, both will be defined by their distaste of the extreme. In this manner, a history and becoming will emerge that is not opposed to one another but aligned in their distinction from pure stasis on the one hand and pure flux on the other; a history and becoming will emerge that is rendered together in order to form a productive composite.

If we are to take this relation or composite seriously, then it demands that we shift our attention away from the extremes of history and becoming to that which lies between – the differential element of 'the between' that is responsible for making their marriage productive. This element of the between is most usefully discussed by Deleuze in his analysis of a surface that moves back and forth between various realms, collecting them together into a surface-as-between. Here we find the wandering figure of Hercules who in the process of transgressing both height and depth in his travels from and to the surface conveys the (often problematic) difference in nature between all three. Insofar as his very being is itself between man and god, Hercules personifies a 'history/becoming' that is simultaneously more than static history and less than eternal becoming. But following the completion of *The Logic of Sense* and the advent of Deleuze's 'new directions' with Guattari (TRM 65), another persona will take up this role of the between: the nomad. It is therefore to Deleuze and Guattari's nomadology that we must now turn.

3

Nomadic History

Deleuze and Guattari's 'Treatise on Nomadology – The War Machine' (ATP 351–423) consists of an elaboration on the relation between the nomad and the State forms. This relation is 'attested to' or described using various models as found in mythology and ethnology, science and mathematics, war and even games. History is another field through which this distinction is played out. This assertion may at first appear inaccurate, for not only is there no dedicated section in the Nomadology plateau to the issue of history, but more importantly it would seem that history is almost entirely dismissed by Deleuze and Guattari. It is, however, for precisely this reason that the project of nomadology has much to offer our understanding of history and becoming. Insofar as Deleuze and Guattari's nomadology is an explicit attempt to provide an alternative ontology and method to the discipline of history, it is arguably the most important work for any investigation into the nature of Deleuze's philosophy of history and its relation to creativity.

This anti-historical inspiration for developing a nomadology is noted by Deleuze and Guattari from the outset. As they say in the introduction to *A Thousand Plateaus*:

> History is always written from the sedentary point of view and in the name of a unitary State apparatus, at least a possible one, even when the topic is nomads. What is lacking is a Nomadology, the opposite of a history. (ATP 23)

How are we to understand this professed opposition? In what does the distinction lie? In addressing these questions, the following initial observation can be made: if nomadology is the 'opposite' of history, it is to a large extent due to its abiding concern for space rather than time. Unlike histories and historical theories that heavily rely upon a philosophy of time in order to explain the past, the important questions for a nomadology focus on territory and topology, ways of moving through and relating to space. Nomadology is *organisational*, whether it is found or deployed in a social field, political or other. In this respect, nomadology could be said to be thematically geographical – that discipline which is often positioned as the foil of history – and as such aligned with becoming: 'We think too much in terms of history, whether personal or universal. Becomings belong to geography, they are orientations, directions, entries and exits' (D 2). This is not to say that Deleuze and Guattari's project of nomadology will be shorn of history, the past or a philosophy of time. Indeed, the Nomadology plateau perhaps more than any other Deleuzian work will employ historical evidence, historical references and historical interpretations. However, the critical point for Deleuze and Guattari is that this engagement with history will occur in contrast to the dominant conventions of historical understanding and practice – so much so that it will be more appropriate in many instances to describe it as spatial and geographical than temporal and historical.

Many instances, but not all, and not necessarily to the detriment or exclusion of history. While the condemnation of history in order to maintain the specificity of nomadology may be preferable in many cases, not least for terminological clarity, such a rendition carries its own confusions and drawbacks. To begin with, it would require us to deny that historians such as Braudel – historians who were eminently geographical – are indeed historians. Although Deleuze does in fact attempt to disassociate certain historical thinkers he is fond of from the practice of history,[1] I am of the opinion that the contrary appropriation would be more beneficial (and accurate) for all concerned: namely, the association of Deleuze with a lineage of historical thinkers that can be defined in part by their attempt to escape the image of history-as-historicism or State history. Presuming that one believes in the possibilities for this alternative path, that one refuses to abandon history en masse to the clutches of historicism, then history must be liberated from its role as State functionary. It is with this justification that I unashamedly seek in this chapter a Deleuzian philosophy of history within the nomadology, despite the fact that it is precisely at this juncture that history appears to be most maligned. For to the extent that I am successful, Deleuze will be shown to help revitalise the philosophy of history and retrieve the practice and conception of history from the dominant historicist image of his day (and arguably still ours).

There will be two main objectives in my prosecution of this task: (1) to explicate what Deleuze and Guattari mean by nomadology; and (2) to show how this nomadology offers significant insights for a philosophy of history. I will begin by establishing the essential dualism of nomadology: the nomad and State forms. In order to explain this dualism, a host of other ontological and ethical dualisms will be introduced and canvassed, including the two multiplicities (heterogeneous/homogeneous, continuous/discrete or non-metric/metric), the smooth and the striated, *puissance* and *pouvoir*, creation and negation, and most importantly, becoming and history. After establishing the nature and position of Deleuze and Guattari's family of dualisms, I will demonstrate how they are complexified through the reintroduction of metamorphosis into their relation. As a result, the critical dualism of the nomad and the State will itself be split or circumscribed by a third term – the phylum – that reconfigures their relation. This reconfiguration will immediately illustrate how it is no longer possible to prioritise one side over the other. The ultimate effect of complexifying the dualism, however, will be to rejoin the two terms, and that which is between them, into a productive whole. From this we will see how despite the many disparaging comments Deleuze and Guattari have on history, nomadology offers us a way of overcoming the dualism of becoming and history in a way that is consistent with their now infamous proclamation:

> We invoke one dualism only in order to challenge another. We employ a dualism of models only in order to arrive at a process that challenges all models. Each time, mental correctives are necessary to undo the dualisms we have no wish to construct but through which we pass. Arrive at the magic formula we all seek – PLURALISM = MONISM – via all the dualisms that are the enemy, an entirely necessary enemy, the furniture we are forever rearranging. (ATP 21)

In this spirit, the following examination of Deleuze and Guattari's nomadology will seek to provide a reorientation of the philosophy of history that can live up to the 'magic formula' of PLURALISM = MONISM, in turn paving the way for a new practice and ontology of historical creativity that could be referred to as nomadic history.

The nomad and the State

Deleuze and Guattari's explication of nomadology begins by separating out the nomad and the State forms in topological terms: if the nomads can be said to be distinct from sedentary dwellers, it is in the first place by virtue of their differing relation to space. Nomads precisely do not 'dwell', but constantly occupy and move across an entire expanse of territory. This spatial distinction has its conceptual

66

roots in one of the earliest and perhaps most enduring dualisms that Deleuze employs in his career: Bergson's separation between differences of nature and differences of degree. As Deleuze explains in his 1956 essay 'Bergson's Conception of Difference', differences of nature are heterogeneous while differences of degree are homogeneous. This little fact, as Bergson would say, is big with meaning: for a difference of nature to be genuinely heterogeneous, it must not merely refer to the difference between two homogeneities, since this would reduce heterogeneity to the identity of homogeneities. Therefore, a difference of nature must differ first and foremost *from itself*: what defines a difference of nature is not merely the way it differs from other external objects, but the way it differs internally, being composed of a heterogeneity on the inside.

The quintessential example of internal difference for Bergson is time, or time-as-duration. Time is that which continually differs from itself: 'In short, duration is what differs, and what differs is no longer what differs from something else, but what differs from itself' (BCD 48). Nevertheless, this does not imply that time is any less material. Indeed, as Deleuze goes on to specify: 'What differs has become itself a thing, a *substance*' (BCD 48). Time-as-duration, in this respect, is no less spatial but rather offers a different way of relating to space.

We already saw this in Chapter 1 when we examined the import of Bergson's two multiplicities for the dualism of intensity and extensity. By the time of *A Thousand Plateaus*, Deleuze and Guattari will have added another way to describe this distinction: smooth and striated. Although these terms are borrowed from the musical composer Pierre Boulez, there is little doubt that Deleuze and Guattari interpret the smooth and the striated through their pre-existing Bergsonism:

> [Boulez] makes palpable or perceptible the difference between nonmetric and metric multiplicities, directional and dimensional spaces. He renders them sonorous or musical. (ATP 477)

Boulez, in other words, provides a very good *intensive* example of Bergson's non-metric multiplicity. He achieves this by distinguishing in his music between a smooth space-time that 'one occupies without counting' and a striated space-time that 'one counts in order to occupy' (ATP 477). These two ways of engaging with sound involve contrasting attitudes towards and experiences of space-time. In a striated space, a 'standard' is imposed onto music, providing an organisational structure to which sounds then correspond. Frequencies of sound are thus distributed within various intervals respective to the breaks that separate them. In a smooth space, on the other hand, frequencies are distributed without breaks; there is no transcendent scale from which to judge the frequency, for the space-time itself continuously modulates. For this reason, smooth space has no boundaries between one interval and another – there is no inside and outside – since it is composed entirely of an alteration that continuously expands or unravels. As Deleuze and Guattari sum up:

> Returning to the simple opposition, the striated is that which intertwines fixed and variable elements, produces an order and succession of distinct forms, and organizes horizontal melodic lines and vertical harmonic planes. The smooth is the continuous variation, continuous development of form; it is the fusion of harmony and melody in favor of the production of properly rhythmic values, the pure act of the drawing of a diagonal across the vertical and the horizontal. (ATP 478; see also 488)

Or again, this time illustrating the connections with Deleuze's intensive spatium of depth as opposed to the extensive organisation of surfaces:

> Smooth space [. . .] is an intensive rather than extensive space, one of distances, not of measures and properties. Intense *Spatium* instead of *Extensio*. A body without Organs instead of an organism and organization. Perception in it is based on symptoms and evaluations rather than measures and properties. That is why smooth space is occupied by intensities, wind and noise, forces, and sonorous and tactile qualities, as in the desert, steppe, or ice. The creaking of ice and the song of the sands. Striated space, on the contrary, is canopied by the sky as measure and by the measurable visual qualities deriving from it. (ATP 479)

Smooth space is thus intensive and non-metric, a continuous heterogeneity as opposed to the striated and homogeneous 'space of *pillars*' (ATP 370). Like the intensive-depth we looked at in Chapter 1, such multiplicities are not observable 'from a point in space external to them', for they can 'be explored only by legwork' (ATP 371); one must therefore place oneself *within* a smooth space itself if one is to appropriately 'know' it.

This type of space, lacking in transcendent structure, can also be described as a *nomos*: 'The smooth is a nomos, whereas the striated always has a logos, the octave, for example' (ATP 478). The use of nomos in this fashion dates back to Deleuze's *Difference and Repetition*. As Deleuze explains it in that work, there are two types of distribution, one 'which implies a dividing up of that which is distributed' and another which is 'a division among those who distribute *themselves* in an open space – a space which is unlimited, or at least without precise limits' (DR 36; see also LS 75). Moving forward to the Nomadology plateau, we find that this 'demonic' (DR 37), 'mad' (DR 224) or 'free' (DR 265) distribution in space is opposed not only to logos, but also the *polis*:

> The *nomos* came to designate the law, but that was originally because it was distribution, a mode of distribution. It is a very special kind of distribution, one without division into shares, in a space without borders or enclosure. The *nomos* is the consistency of a fuzzy aggregate: it is in this sense that it stands in opposition to the law or the *polis*, as the backcountry, a mountainside, or the vague expanse around a city ('either nomos or polis'). (ATP 380; see also 369)

Thus we arrive at the influential dualism of the nomad and the State. The polis or State works to 'reclaim' land by building 'walls, enclosures, and roads between enclosures' (ATP 381). Nomads on the contrary do not so much 'tame' the earth as populate its expanse, inserting themselves into its continually shifting nature. By doing so, the smooth space of the nomads is no longer the outside *of* the inside, for it is outside entirely. Just as with Bergsonian duration, nomadic difference cannot be defined as that which separates zones of control (States), for such striation is utterly foreign to a nomadic sensibility. Instead, nomads, by their way of living – their ontological and ethical essence – make an internal principal of the outside, elevating heterogeneous continuity to the highest order.

One interesting way Deleuze and Guattari articulate this distinction is by contrasting the principles of the line and the point. A line is traditionally defined as the shortest distance between two points. However, as we saw in Chapter 1, it is this reductive definition that is responsible for Zeno's paradox. As long as the line is reduced to the point, it will always be possible to dissect the line between Achilles and the tortoise ad infinitum. But if one frees the line, allowing for a continuous line as opposed to a series of dots, then Achilles' stride will be able to take him past the tortoise. The stride of Achilles, in other words, must occupy the entirety of the space traversed at once, composing a full or indivisible trajectory from one side to the other. As such, this space must be smooth and not striated:

> In striated space, lines or trajectories tend to be subordinated to points: one goes from one point to another. In the smooth, it is the opposite: the points are subordinated to the trajectory. (ATP 478)

It is the nomads who achieve this. Unlike static States who treat 'wild' territories as the (striated) space between polis points, dynamic nomads do the opposite, subordinating points to a trajectory through (smooth) space. This does not mean that sedentaries are incapable of movement, nor does it mean that nomads have no need of or relation to points. In fact, if anything, the contrary is the case. Migrants or transhumants most certainly move across the earth, and to severe effect. The principle of their movement, however, is the point: the transhumant travels on a line in order to arrive at a point. Nomads, on the other hand, pass through points precisely so that they can *remain* on the line. Nomads are thus not without relations to points – the various waterholes and so forth on which their very lives depend. But these points do not define nomadic existence. For example, even if their reference points change over time, both from season to season (different paths) and irrevocably over time (the waterhole which dries up or springs up), the nomad never leaves their smooth space: 'Orientations are not constant but change according to temporary vegetation, occupations, and precipitation' (ATP 493). Paradoxically, therefore, nomads remain where they are. In contrast to sedentaries who move from point to point, nomads are perfectly still:

> We can say of the nomads, following Toynbee's suggestion: *they do not move*. They are nomads by dint of not moving, not migrating, of holding a smooth space that they refuse to leave, that they leave only in order to conquer and die. Voyage in place: that is the name of all intensities, even if they also develop in extension. (ATP 482; see also 381 and DI 259–60)[2]

When so described, the ontological form of the nomad can be said to conform to what I called surface becoming in Chapter 2. As with surface becomings, nomads cover an entire expanse at once: in the same way that Aionic becomings stretch to their infinitive limits, occupying every place in a series at once (as not yet there and already arrived), so nomads populate a smooth space that is irreducible to points of striation. Furthermore, because this occurs instantly, nomadic or surface becoming is in fact still or motionless, like 'the Japanese fighter, interminably still, who then makes a move too quick to see' (ATP 356). In this respect, movement at its absolute is completely stationary. This in turn leads Deleuze and Guattari to distinguish between speed and movement, the former of which indicates an absolute movement that is different in kind from various relative movements:

Immobility and speed, catatonia and rush, a 'stationary process', station as process – these traits of Kleist's are eminently those of the nomad. It is thus necessary to make a distinction between *speed* and *movement*: a movement may be very fast, but that does not give it speed; a speed may be very slow, or even immobile, yet it is still speed. Movement is extensive; speed is intensive. Movement designates the relative character of a body considered as 'one', and which goes from point to point; *speed, on the contrary, constitutes the absolute character of a body whose irreducible parts (atoms) occupy or fill a smooth space in the manner of a vortex*, with the possibility of springing up at any point. (It is therefore not surprising that reference has been made to spiritual voyages effected without relative movement, but in intensity, in one place: these are part of nomadism.) In short, we will say by convention that only nomads have absolute movement, in other words, speed; vortical or swirling movement is an essential feature of their war machine. (ATP 381)

We can thus see how the peculiar nature of nomadic movement corresponds to Aionic or surface becoming: it is a static movement, more accurately described by speed, that gives the nomad the possibility of appearing at any point of actuality within its smooth space (infinitive series).

In order to better illustrate this, Deleuze and Guattari make reference to a Kafka story in which a State citizen describes the sudden appearance of nomadic warriors at the gates of his city: 'In some way that is incomprehensible they have pushed right into the capital. At any rate, here they are; it seems that every morning there are more of them' (Kafka 1983: 416). Like the Mongols who swept into Europe, their arrival is both without warning and completely inexplicable to the sedentary States. Equally so, it might be added, is their sudden disappearance. But if these particular examples of sudden emergence and disappearance are instructive for Deleuze and Guattari, it is most importantly due to the *violent* nature of their movement – the violence of absolute movement or speed. In order to explain, we must now address the second half of the plateau's title: the war machine.

Up till now our discussion has largely consisted of ontological and spatial description. Deleuze and Guattari's nomadology, however, is above all a treatise on *strategy* – of attack and defence, force and resistance. The ontological distinction, in other words, has to do with the way in which the nomad and the State prosecute contrasting strategies via their differing organisational principles. This is evidenced in their comparison of the games chess and Go. These two games not only involve different regulations and uses of space, but they also demonstrate different strategies of combat. In chess, pieces begin in predetermined positions and are endowed with an unalterable nature (movement). In Go, on the other hand, pieces can spring up at any location and have an amorphous nature respective to the location and situation they are thrust into: 'Go pieces are elements of a nonsubjectified machine assemblage with no intrinsic properties, only situational ones' (ATP 353). The relations between chess pieces are thus structural and intrinsic, respective to their predetermined and fixed being, whereas Go pieces form 'extrinsic relations with nebulas or constellations, according to which it fulfills functions of insertion or situation, such as bordering, encircling, shattering' (ATP 353). But most importantly, according to Deleuze and Guattari, the two games differ in the kind of space they purport:

> In Go, it is a question of arraying oneself in an open space, of holding space, of maintaining the possibility of springing up at any point: the movement is not from one point to another, but becomes perpetual, without aim or destination, without departure or arrival. The 'smooth' space of Go, as against the 'striated' space of chess. The *nomos* of Go against the State of chess, *nomos* against *polis*. (ATP 353)

But given the distinction between these two contrasting principles, this raises the following question: how is it that these alternate forms and spaces are created in the first place? As we will see, the nomos is extended by the construction of what Deleuze and Guattari call a war machine, while the power of the polis is extended by the appropriation of one. What then is a war machine? This can be answered in three parts: (1) the war machine is of the nomads and is exterior to the State; (2) the war machine is not the military, for the military is the appropriation of a nomadic war machine; and (3) the war machine may be a weapon directed towards warding off the State, but war itself is not the object of the war machine.

Firstly, the war machine is of the nomads, not the State. Drawing on the work of Georges Dumézil, Deleuze and Guattari claim that there are two poles to political sovereignty, 'the despot and the legislator, the binder and the organizer' (ATP 351). These two heads are not opposed but rather constitute a 'One-Two' by which the State apparatus first appropriates or captures something before administering it. Neither of these powers, however, are the power of creation. Deleuze and Guattari of course use different French words for 'power' to highlight this distinction: *pouvoir* refers to power as domination or control, whereas *puissance* designates power as explosive or energetic force. So put, these are the powers of capture and creation. As we have just seen, States operate by way of *pouvoir*: domination and legislation – the politician, the bureaucracy and their lawyers. But for the State apparatus to carry out this capture, there must be something created in the first place. This initial creation is credited to the nomad. By virtue of their internal affinity with difference, with the heterogeneous multiplicity et al., it is the nomad who exudes *puissance*, the 'power of metamorphosis' (ATP 352). Moreover, because of their need to *continually* transmute, nomads have as their natural enemy those powers of capture and striation. Thus the nomad 'brings a *furor* to bear against sovereignty, a celerity against gravity, secrecy against the public, a power (*puissance*) against sovereignty, a machine against the apparatus (ATP 352). This machine is the war machine – the means by which the nomad breaks State capture in order to remain on or return to the nomos. It is for this reason that the war machine is irreducible to the State: not only is it 'outside its sovereignty and prior to its law', but it is 'of another species, another nature, another origin than the State apparatus' (ATP 352).

Although the war machine is not of the essence of the State, this is not to say that the State does not have a violence of its own. The nature of this violence is, however, telling: appropriate to the power of the polis, the State perpetrates its own brand of violence through the organ of the police. Observation and regulation are the methods of this State organ. Conventional wisdom, however, might respond that this form of control only corresponds to the internal regulation of States, as opposed to a State military which is used for the purposes of waging war on those external to the State. To this, Deleuze and Guattari respond that the military is not itself a war machine but rather the appropriation of one (ATP 355). In this sense, the war machine may be of the nomads, 'but the State learns fast' (ATP 418). This appropriation is, however, fraught with danger. Realising the unrivalled power that the war machine exudes, the State attempts to harness it for its own purposes. But this control is only ever at best tenuous, for there is always a possibility that the war machine might turn on its master.

One way in which this issue has often been discussed throughout history is in the context of how best to manage the immense yet indiscriminate power of the berserker warrior. Although modern State militaries focus their efforts on eliminating unpredictability through drilling, it is nevertheless widely recognised that berserker rages are a continuing fact of battle and can often be partially credited with extraordinary acts of heroism/stupidity. This military problem of harnessing and directing the berserker is the same as the State problem of managing generals (ATP 355): despite the great benefits that such a power can bring to the military and the State, there is nothing they fear more than a war machine gone out of (their) control.

The attitude of State apparatuses towards partisan or guerrilla warfare provides us with an even better illustration of how war machines are always 'of' the nomads despite their appropriation. Because the military institutionalises war, what it detests most are those who fail to 'play by the rules'. The terrain of the military is the battlefield, the front, the rear, and even the home front (in some conflicts). The guerrilla, on the other hand, fights a war 'without battle lines' (ATP 353), where a skirmish or explosion could erupt at any point and at any time. The guerrilla therefore carries out their fight on a smooth space, a space which they are familiar with to the extent that they merge with it; they become one with the forest, the mountains or the ghetto, for they make these spaces no less than they are made by them (ATP 382); the pre-eminent guerrilla is virtually everywhere, everyone. The military is therefore entirely accurate when it coins the term 'asymmetric warfare' to refer to the relation between a State military and an underground guerilla movement, for their rules of engagement and technologies ('conventional' weapons and logistics) are consistent with a striated space that is dissymmetrical or non-symmetrical with that of the partisan group – a group which 'answers to other rules' (ATP 358): the rules of packs, bands or gangs who have a persistence to question hierarchy and engage in blackmail, abandonment and betrayal as part of their 'volatile sense of honour' (ATP 358) – the honour among thieves.

This brings us to the third aspect of the war machine: war is not itself the object. As we have seen, what the nomad seeks is the constitution of a smooth space, meaning 'the occupation of this space, displacement within this space and the corresponding composition of people: this is its sole and veritable positive object (*nomos*)' (ATP 417). To the extent that the nomad is free to realise this objective, the nomad is content. However, when the war machine collides with a State apparatus that attempts to both oppose and appropriate it, war necessarily results:

> It is at this point that the war machine becomes war: annihilate the forces of the State, destroy the State-form. The Attila, or Genghis Khan, adven-

ture clearly illustrates this progression from the positive object to the negative object. Speaking like Aristotle, we would say that war is neither the condition nor the object of the war machine, but necessarily accompanies or completes it; speaking like Derrida, we would say that war is the 'supplement' of the war machine. [. . .] Finally, speaking like Kant, we would say that the relation between war and the war machine is necessary but 'synthetic'. (ATP 417)

In a certain respect, therefore, war does not come from the State (since the war machine is originally nomadic) and nor does it arise solely from the nomad (since war is not the object of the war machine). War is rather that which occurs when the two collide, when the nomad is constricted by State striation. But if war initially comes from the clash between the nomad and the State, it does not remain there. On the one hand, the nomad adopts the task of annihilating the State-form wherever it runs up against it. And on the other hand, after the State has appropriated a war machine, the State makes war the objective of this machine in order to better serve the States' originary directive (control). As such, war becomes profuse, occurring not only between the State and that which is outside it, but also between rival States and even with itself. This is why 'it is at one and the same time that the State apparatus appropriates a war machine, that the war machine takes war as its object, and that war becomes subordinated to the aims of the State' (ATP 418). From this we can see that 'The question is therefore less the realisation of war than the appropriation of the war machine' (ATP 420), for war is in fact only realised when the State attempts to capture an external force for its controlling interests, and it is only multiplied when it successfully does so.

Deleuze and Guattari's insistence that war is not the primary objective of the war machine is crucial because it goes to the heart of their attempt to show how creation and not negation is the ethic of the nomad. If the nomad destroys, it is only as a secondary result of their attempt to escape, a supplement to their act of creation. Every effort thus far in separating out the nomadic and State types has worked towards reinforcing this idea: the nomad cannot merely be defined *in relation to* the State, nomadic existence cannot just be determined by *the negation of* the State, for this would mean that the line is reduced to the point and that difference is only defined as a negation of identity. What we must be after is rather a difference-in-itself, a duration that differs first and foremost from itself, a nomadic existence and a war machine that is irreducible to the State. If ever this genuine difference is lost and nomads are taken to be a force of negation or opposition, then nomadism is a lost cause.

The distinction between creation and negation can be quite easily sourced to Deleuze's early work on Bergson and Nietzsche. What first appears in 'Bergson's Conception of Difference' as the creative power of 'internal difference' is later taken to be the major themes of 'affirmation' and 'active' force in *Nietzsche and Philosophy*, both of which are contrasted by Deleuze with the Platonic and Hegelian dialectic of contradiction, alterity and negation (see BCD 49 and 53 and compare with NP 161–2 and 180–6). However, aside from these two examples, we have now seen this theme in many guises: in nearly all of the major dualisms we have looked at (e.g. intensity/ extensity, the two multiplicities, internal/external difference, smooth/ striated, line/point, nomad/State) what is of most significance is the distillation of a form of creation that is completely expunged of negation. This pursuit for a fully affirmative creativity, crucially, also holds for Deleuze and Guattari's treatment of becoming and history.

The dualism of becoming and history is by no means a mere after-thought to the other dualisms we have looked at. In fact, it could be said that the entire project of nomadology is itself motivated by Deleuze's persistent interest in becoming and history:

> If we've been so interested in nomads, it's because they're a becoming and aren't part of history; they're excluded from it, but they transmute and reappear in different, unexpected forms in the lines of flight of some social field. (N 153)

But whether or not one wishes to make the becoming and history dualism more primary than the others we have discussed, it is not hard to see that this dualism is intimately tied to Deleuze's long-standing ontology and ethics of creation and negation. Time and again history is berated for being uncreative and non-experimental while becoming is afforded invention and liberation (see ATP 296; N 30 and 170–1; WP 96, 110–11 and 113). The historian is thus a State functionary who captures nomadic becomings through a striating procedure: 'History has never comprehended nomadism, the book has never comprehended the outside' (ATP 24). History can certainly speak about nomads, but only from an historical point of view devoid of any creative nomadic essence, since 'history is one with the triumph of States' (ATP 394).[3] It is for this reason that Deleuze and Guattari believe a different way of thinking and speaking is needed to appropriately approach and understand nomadism: a nomadology instead of a history.

Given this, we can now see how becoming and history align with the pure forms of the nomad and State, forms that are themselves aligned with the pure forms of surface becoming and actual being. However, as I argued in Chapters 1 and 2, this is not the final word on the matter but only the first. In each of my two completed investigations, I attempted to show how history is in fact and in principle an integral part of the productive process. This led me to conclude that there is another history in Deleuzian ontology, a history that is not opposed to becoming and does not resemble historicism. But insofar as this other history is itself intensive and dynamic, it can arguably be more accurately described as a composite – what I would refer to as the productive differential of 'history/becoming'. As such, this composite resembles neither pure becoming nor pure history, but is rather between the two, less than both and all the more productive because of it.

Deleuze and Guattari's nomadology, as we will now go on to see, follows this precise development. Despite their strict separation of the nomad and the State, the smooth and the striated, becoming and history, etc., this arrangement only holds in the nomadology for but a moment. Immediately following their setting of the dualism, Deleuze and Guattari begin to complicate the matter by reintroducing metamorphosis. This was perhaps inevitable, given Deleuze and Guattari's Bergsonian and Nietzschean predilection for creative overcoming: how could one ever be satisfied with a becoming that is 'against' history, seeing that the evasion of negation is the goal itself? It is therefore imperative that we continue to follow the undulations of the Nomadology plateau, rather than resting on the initial negative presentation of the dualism.

The phylum and the smith

As the Nomadology plateau progresses, the presiding dualism of the nomad and the State is split by a third element: the machinic phylum that flows between the two and upon which they both depend. However, even before Deleuze and Guattari introduce this third term, we can already find evidence of the breaking up of their initially hardened dualism. Let us then look at this complexification before turning to an analysis of the phylum and its impact on the pure forms of the nomad and the State, becoming and history.

The first thing that can be said about the so-called opposition of the nomad and the State is that they are by no means symmetrical or the inverse of one another. A similar point was made in Chapter 2 when I described how the movement from depth to surface is dissymmetrical to the movement from surface to depth. The translation from one to the other must therefore proceed via different ways and means. It is important to remember, however, that Deleuze and Guattari are not just interested in the different ways that lines are drawn between the two. More profoundly, their concern has to do with the ways in which the smooth *becomes* the striated and vice versa. Their principle interest, in other words, is with the transmutations of form. Citing Boulez, Deleuze and Guattari put it as follows:

> Boulez is concerned with the communication between two kinds of space, their alternations and superpositions: how 'a strongly directed smooth space tends to meld with a striated space'; how the octave can be replaced by 'non-octave-forming scales' that reproduce themselves through a principle of spiralling; how 'texture' can be crafted in such a way as to lose fixed and homogeneous values, becoming a support for slips in tempo, displacements of intervals, and *son art* transformations comparable to the transformations of *op art*. (ATP 478)[4]

In considering these procedures of 'melding' and 'replacement', one might be tempted to think of a smooth space morphing into or taking the place of a striated space (and vice versa). This transmutation, however, can be conceived of in two very different ways: either we can conceive of the smooth and the striated as fixed types, between which movements and transmutations occur, or we can allow the smooth and the striated to *themselves* metamorphise. Put otherwise: either we can subject their relation to a striation, or we can allow it to continually differ from itself, thus reinscribing productive difference back into their relation. As Deleuze and Guattari go about examining the transmutations of striation and smoothing, it is arguably the latter more radical alternative that they have in mind.

To explain this Deleuze and Guattari borrow an example from Paul Virilio: the fleet in being (ATP 387). The purpose of this example is to illustrate how one can spread oneself across the entirety of a smooth space, in this case a vector of sea, at once. Tactically speaking, a fleet of warships can have the effect of extending itself across an expanse of water, simultaneously occupying every crevice of the vector from its ability to appear at any point without prior notice. This capacity is best epitomised by the nuclear submarine, whose power to strike suddenly extends across the globe. By doing so, however, the State navy does not convert the sea – the archetypal smooth space – into a striated space. Rather, the State harnesses the power of the smooth for the purposes of State control. In other words, the smooth is employed by the State *as smooth* for the purposes of striation. The smooth characteristics of the sea are thus maintained, but they are redirected by State powers to achieve a level of control that the State on its own would be incapable of.

What this example emphasises is the precarious and complex relation between the smooth and the striated. Not only does one become the other, but it sometimes does so while remaining the same. Perhaps it is for this reason that Deleuze and Guattari confuse even themselves in some of their examples. As mentioned earlier, Deleuze and Guattari invoke a Kafka story when describing how the nomads appear suddenly due to their absolute movement (speed). It is worth noting, however, that when Deleuze and Guattari previously used this Kafka anecdote in *Anti-Oedipus*, they in fact did so to describe the arrival of the despotic State, not the nomads. And if we look at the Nietzsche quote that Deleuze and Guattari attach to the Kafka quote, this suspicion is confirmed: when Nietzsche says 'They come like fate, without reason, consideration, or pretext', he is referring to the act of violence by which the State emerges, not the nomads who suddenly appear through the violence of their speed. For Nietzsche, this violent act is perpetrated by 'some pack of blond beasts of prey, a conqueror and master race which, organized for war and with the ability to organize, unhesitatingly lays its terrible claws upon a populace perhaps tremendously superior in numbers but still *formless and nomad*' (emphasis added). In other words, given that Nietzsche's point here is to describe how 'these born organizers' mould the 'still formless and nomad' into a State, Deleuze and Guattari's use of this passage in *A Thousand Plateaus* to illustrate the sudden emergence of the nomads is somewhat peculiar. We thus arrive at the following situation: not only is the purpose or problem to which Deleuze and Guattari deploy these quotes contrary between *Anti-Oedipus* and *A Thousand Plateaus*, but that they are used in tandem at all is odd, seeing as one pertains to the sudden emergence of the nomads and the other the arrival of the State (compare AO 191–2 and 195–6 with ATP 353).[5]

Given this shifting deployment of examples, it is perhaps an understatement to say that Deleuze and Guattari complexify the dualism of the nomad and the State. But if anything, these examples only further emphasise the lesson of transmutation. Reality is constantly undergoing processes of striation and smoothing and it is not always so easy to tell which is which. If the sea can be striated *as smooth*, then so too can the very concrete of cities be smoothed out:

> [I]t is possible to live smooth even in the cities, to be an urban nomad (for example, a stroll taken by Henry Miller in Clichy or Brooklyn is a nomadic transit in smooth space; he makes the city disgorge a patchwork, differentials of speed, delays and accelerations, changes in orientation, continuous variations ... The beatniks owe much to Miller, but they changed direction again, they put the space outside the cities to new use). Fitzgerald said it long ago: it is not a question of taking off for the South Seas, that is not what determines a voyage. There are not only strange voyages in the city but voyages in place: we are not thinking of drug users, whose experience is too ambiguous, but of true nomads. (ATP 482)

'True nomads' are therefore not necessarily what anthropologists study. Despite their extensive use of anthropology, Deleuze and Guattari never claim to be anything but philosophers – nomadic philosophers, moreover, who do not even need to leave the city.[6] This demands that the question always be repeated: who are today's nomads, our present-day Nietzscheans, as Deleuze describes them elsewhere (DI 260)? One cannot just gesture to the desert beyond the walls, for while our focus is so directed transmutations occur behind our back. This is also why revolutionary forces and becomings cannot be simply ascribed to those who call for the Revolution and devote their waking lives to its fulfilment (the 'avant-garde'), for not only is it difficult to determine who is a nomad or what is a smooth space by appearance, but the nomad and the smooth are themselves susceptible to appropriation by the State and the striated: 'We say this as a reminder that smooth space and the form of exteriority do not have an irresistible revolutionary calling but change meaning drastically depending on the interactions they are part of and the concrete conditions of their exercise of establishment (for example, the way in which total war and popular war, and even guerrilla warfare, borrow one another's methods)' (ATP 387). It is also why Deleuze and Guattari warn, with their final word on the matter: 'Never believe that a smooth space will suffice to save us' (ATP 500). As the nuclear submarine example acutely illustrates, in some cases it clearly won't, and might even aid in the repression of nomadic tendencies, even when its nature remains unchanged (as smooth). If 'real' nomads are instructive it is therefore only insofar as they can help us discover 'true' nomads – the truth of nomadic becomings in each one of us.

The earlier suggestion that a space was *either* nomos *or* polis was therefore somewhat misleading: it is both, as one becomes the other. In one direction, striated spaces are undone from within as urban nomads redeploy the very constructs of the city to a smoothing. And in the other direction, the power of smooth spaces is harnessed for the purposes of control. In cases of the latter, revolutionary becomings can end up spawning micro-fascisms. But in cases of the former, histories can be intensified *as history* for the processes of smoothing. The pure and fixed dualisms of nomad/State, smooth/striated and becoming/history are thus insufficient for explaining what Deleuze and Guattari mean by nomadology. While it might be initially convenient to abstract the two apart, this is only of use insofar as one goes on to complexify these abstractions. As Deleuze and Guattari say in the conclusion of *A Thousand Plateaus*:

> It is not enough, however, to replace the opposition between the One and the multiple, with a distinction between types of multiplicities. For the distinction between the two types does not preclude their immanence to each other, each 'issuing' from the other after its fashion. (ATP 506)

If the purpose of Deleuze and Guattari's strict separation of the nomad and the State is so that they can in turn be brought back together, the question is: what is it that the two share? As it turns out, between the nomad and the State, the smooth and the striated, there is a third element which renders the dualisms immanent. This is what Deleuze and Guattari refer to as the *machinic phylum*.

The introduction of something between the nomad and the State should cause us to pause, for it raises a paradox: did we not just finish setting out how the nomad was itself the differential element of the between? If the nomad is ontologically and organisationally defined as the between, in contrast to the polis points of States, how can there be a third element between these two that is different in nature to both? To overcome this problem we must again return to the beginning, or, more precisely, the question of beginnings: how it is that something comes about, what is its generative story or explanation? Do genera, collectivities or multiplicities presuppose singularities or produce them? Are pure forms *extracted from* mixtures or *give rise* to them? As I have attempted to demonstrate in each of my analyses of history and becoming thus far, there is no one privileged direction in the process of creation. For example, in Chapter 2 I showed that while incorporeal surfaces extract singularities of sense from the mixture of bodies, these same surfaces rely upon a corporeal dynamism for their very nature. Perhaps this is why Deleuze and Guattari can claim that *de jure* differences determine *de facto* mixes (ATP 475, 410), yet simultaneously maintain that 'the abstract does not explain, but must itself be explained' (D vii; see also WP 7). Following these two sentiments, we can therefore say that, on the one hand, the nomad and State forms are purities that allow us to judge various mixtures, yet on the other hand, these abstractions are themselves what are in need of explanation *precisely through the way they relate in mixture*. In the Nomadology plateau, this relation-in-mixture is described by Deleuze and Guattari using the ontological terms of singularity, assemblage and phyla.

To put it in brief, an assemblage is a constellation of singularities: it is a level of contraction-détente (Bergson), an arrangement of the world according to a single perspective (Leibniz or Nietzsche) or a multiplicity of patches (Riemann). 'What we call an assemblage is, precisely, a multiplicity' (D 132). Each assemblage 'does something' – produces. The effects of an assemblage, however, remain distinct from the productive flows upon which the assemblage arose. This flow is the machinic phylum: the subterranean flow of pure becoming (Nietzsche) or the universal aggregate of action/reaction (Bergson) from which assemblages derive their particular constellation of singularities. On the level of incorporeal surfaces, a singularity is what ties together two different phyla of flow by being prolonged between them. But in the extremities of depth, there is only one 'phylogenetic lineage, a single machinic phylum, ideally continuous [and] in continuous variation' (ATP 406). In a certain respect then, the great phylum is what selects '*through the intermediary of assemblages*' (ATP 398, emphasis added).

We thus have the following situation. Singularities are extracted from the machinic phylum or flow by an assemblage. The assemblages 'differentiate the phyla or the flow, dividing it into so many different phyla, of a given order, on a given level, and introducing selective discontinuities in the ideal continuity of matter-movement' (ATP 406). But while assemblages cut up the phylum, the phylum itself *cuts across* various assemblages, 'taking leave of one to pick up again in another, or making them coexist' (ATP 406). Creation therefore cuts both ways, though not in the same way (as we saw in the movement and communication between the smooth and the striated):

It is thus necessary to take into account the selective action of the assemblages upon the phylum, and the evolutionary reaction of the phylum as the subterranean thread that passes from one assemblage to another, or quits an assemblage, draws it forward and opens it up. *Vital impulse?* [. . .] There is indeed a machinic phylum in variation that creates the technical assemblages, whereas the assemblages invent the various phyla [i.e. *'cuts' from* the machinic phylum]. (ATP 407)

As we can now see, creation occurs at various levels in different ways. Or perhaps more accurately, creation requires the *concerted* efforts of various differences in kind, not just one over the other or 'in the face of' another. This is why Deleuze and Guattari can say in the same paragraph that an assemblage is 'a veritable invention' and that assemblages are also that which 'invent the various phyla' (ATP 406–7).

The significance of this analysis, however, is *not* that it shows a reciprocal and progressive dualism of creation. More importantly, Deleuze and Guattari's recognition of the phylum inaugurates a whole new topology for the nomadology – a topology of three that breaks the dualism. Previously, we noted how Deleuze and Guattari distinguish between two kinds of space – smooth and striated – the former of which was the 'intermezzo' (ATP 380, 478) and the latter of which was polarising. But as it now turns out, these two spaces are themselves derivations from a pure phylum that flows beneath, between and through them. The smooth and the striated, in other words, are *expressions* of a machinic phylum that gives itself to both (ATP 416). Naturally, it does so in different ways, respective to each form, but it is nevertheless the same phylum which 'simultaneously has two different modes of liaison: it is always *connected* to nomad space, whereas it *conjugates* with sedentary space' (ATP 415). For this reason, the phylum, when conceptualised spatially, is neither smooth nor striated but *holey* – the Swiss cheese of space – since it is expressed in some instances as smoothly spread and in others as contracted into a polis (ATP 413–15).[7]

The distinction between the phylum itself and its various expressions is of paramount importance to our current exploration. What is at issue here, as raised in Chapter 2, is a distinction between becomings. It is hard to see, for example, how the flow of the machinic phylum could be synonymous with the incorporeal, sterile and static surface becoming of *The Logic of Sense*. Indeed, the phylum itself is purely *matter*. The significance of Deleuze and Guattari's machinic phylum thus entirely has to do with a becoming specific to matter;

their interest here is not with incorporeal surface becoming, but with a becoming that is also referred to as 'matter-movement', 'matter-energy', 'matter-flow' and 'matter in variation' (ATP 407).

The case study that Deleuze and Guattari select to illustrate this form of becoming is most instructive. In their analysis of how a single matter-movement 'enters assemblages and leaves them' (ATP 407), Deleuze and Guattari consider the example of metal. As they note, far from being fixed, metal has a vitality that allows it to be channelled into various forms. The principle of metallurgy, as such, does not concern a movement between matters but rather the movement of matter itself:

> The difference is that elsewhere the operations occur between two thresholds, one of which constitutes the matter prepared for the operation, and the other the form to be incarnated (for example, the clay and the mold). The hylomorphic model derives its general value from this, since the incarnated form that marks the end of an operation can serve as the matter for a new operation, but in a fixed order marking a succession of thresholds. In metallurgy, on the other hand, the operations are always astride the thresholds, so that an energetic materiality overspills the prepared matter, and a qualitative deformation or transformation overspills the form. For example, quenching follows forging and takes place after the form has been fixed. Or, take another example, in molding, the metallurgist in a sense works inside the mold. Or again, steel that is melted and molded later undergoes a series of successive decarbonations. Finally, metallurgy has the option of melting down and reusing a matter to which it gives an *ingot-form* [. . .] (ATP 410–11)

The metallurgical model thus presents us with a movement that is proper to matter. Rather than reserving movement for that which occurs between thresholds, metallurgy offers a material vitalism that attests not only to the variability of matter but also the matter of variability: 'Matter and form have never seemed more rigid than in metallurgy; yet the succession of forms tends to be replaced by the form of a continuous development, and the variability of matters tends to be replaced by the matter of a continuous variation' (ATP 411).

While this description of variability might appear to align the metallurgical model with the heterogeneous multiplicity and the nomos, Deleuze and Guattari clearly distinguish the two: 'There are no nomadic or sedentary smiths. Smiths are ambulant, itinerant' (ATP 413). At best, therefore, smiths are 'quasi-nomadic' (ATP 372). What is at issue, however, is not so much the attempt to distinguish the smith from the nomad and the sedentary, or the holey from the smooth and the striated. The point is rather to show how the flow of the phylum *transforms itself* into both nomadic and State assemblages. What is key is the following:

> This hybrid metallurgist, a weapon- and toolmaker, communicates with the sedentaries *and* with the nomads at the same time. Holey space itself communicates with smooth space and striated space. In effect, the machinic phylum or the metallic line passes through all of the assemblages: nothing is more deterritorialized than matter-movement. But it is not at all in the same way, and the two communications are not symmetrical. (ATP 413)

It is therefore the *following of immanent flows* that is of most concern to Deleuze and Guattari. If the nomad and the State are formally separated, it is only insofar as we can follow the matter-flow that moves between them and brings them together:

> We always get back to this definition: the *machinic phylum* is materiality, natural or artificial, and both simultaneously; it is matter in movement, in flux, in variation, matter as a conveyor of singularities and traits of expression. This has obvious consequences: namely, this matter-flow can only be *followed*. [. . .] To follow the flow of matter is to itinerate, to ambulate. It is intuition in action. (ATP 409)

To itinerate, to ambulate, to intuit, to intensify, to delve into the depths or place oneself within a movement so that it can be followed on its course through various thresholds and beyond: this is the essential lesson that Deleuze repeats time and again. Satellite imagery and global positioning will never suffice, no matter how advanced, for there is no substitute for 'on the ground' fieldwork. The extraction of constants is not a goal in itself and neither is the uncovering of primary forms. Following from within is rather the business of the phylum and of Nomadology at large:

> Reproducing implies the permanence of a fixed point of *view* that is external to what is reproduced: watching the flow from the bank. But following is something different from the ideal of reproduction. Not better, just different. One is obliged to follow when one is in search of the 'singularities' of a matter, or rather of a material, and not out to discover a form; when one escapes the force of gravity to enter a field of celerity; when one ceases to contemplate the course of a laminar flow in a determinate direction, to be carried away by a vortical flow; when one engages in a continuous variation of variables, instead of extracting constants from them, etc. And the meaning of Earth completely changes [. . .] (ATP 372)

The methodology proposed in Deleuze and Guattari's project of nomadology thus consists of the following of flows. As Bergson and Péguy would say, it involves intuiting or placing oneself within various lines of movement.[8] Not all lines of movement, however, are the same. For example, the flows of metamorphosis that comprise the nomad and the State *and carry them off* (one into the other) occur along dissymmetrical lines. It thus becomes imperative that we articulate more precisely the way in which lines differ in kind.

Deleuze and Guattari's analysis of lines is key to nearly all of their philosophical projects: aside from the nomadology, the diagnosis of lines is also critical for their micropolitics, schizoanalysis and pragmatics, just to name a few (D 125). This, however, does not make the spatial and temporal analysis we have carried out thus far reducible to the analysis of lines. As Deleuze says in an interview:

> We think lines are the basic components of things and events. So everything has its geography, its cartography, its diagram. What's interesting, even in a person, are the lines that make them up, or they make up, or take, or create. Why make lines more fundamental than planes or volumes? We don't, though. There are various spaces correlated with different lines, and vice versa [. . .] Different sorts of line involve different configurations of space and volume. (N 33)[9]

Given this statement, the obvious question would be: what lines correlate to the spaces we have looked at? Encouragingly, it turns out that just as there are three spaces – smooth, striated and holey – so there are three lines – the rigid, the supple and the line of flight. But as we will see, things are not as straightforward as this.

Deleuze's first relevant presentation of the lines occurs in the *The Logic of Sense* series 'Porcelain and Volcano'. This investigation relies heavily on a reading of F. Scott Fitzgerald's *The Crack-Up*. In Fitzgerald's autobiographical piece, he describes a life, much like Gatsby's, which proceeds along fairly normalised trajectories and concerns itself mostly with the superficial – a life in which one may appear to have it all. But then something happens which shatters that happy semblance. This something is the crack-up, the extension of a crack that runs right through us like an old plate, breaking the facade of who we thought we were. This crack, however, plays itself out along two different lines. Respective to the extension just mentioned, the crack occurs 'at the surface, a unique surface Event' (LS 155); it occurs 'at the frontier' or 'at the edge', itself being the extension of this edge. But at the same time, the line of the crack is a charting of *depth*, for its changes in direction are determined by the line of least resistance: one breaks where one's resistance is *thinnest* (the crack being nothing other than the *explication* of this weak/thin intensive quantity). 'What this means is that the entire play of the crack has become incarnated in the depth of the body, at the same time that the labor of the inside and the outside has widened the edges' (LS 155). Or further:

> Though the association may be close, we have here two elements or two processes which differ in nature. There is a crack which extends its straight, incorporeal, and silent line at the surface; and there are external blows or noisy internal pressures which make it deviate, deepen it, and inscribe or actualize it in the thickness of the body. (LS 156)

The first line, for Deleuze, is thus associated with the incorporeal event that extends across the surface, whereas the second line is described as the line which actualises a connective series in depth (LS 156); when the earth cracks open a line scrawls across the surface, but this line is itself produced by a force that shoots from the depths towards the surface. Nevertheless, these two lines are still the same crack – they are the two sides of *the* crack-up. This means that although Deleuze presents two lines in *The Logic of Sense*, he is only discussing the one crack – the crack which occurs *on* the surface but is *of* depth. In this respect, if Deleuze is able to separate the two lines of surface and depth, it is so that he can in turn show how the two are inseparable, together the crack.

Deleuze's ensuing discussion in the 'Porcelain and Volcano' series, in which the significance of actuality is reasserted, emphasises this inseparability. As he says, how can one genuinely speak of an event if one has not felt it in one's depths? Fitzgerald or Lowry cannot speak of the incorporeal event of the crack without the 'gallons of alcohol they have drunk which have actualized the crack in the body' (LS 157). The crack may be on the surface, but one *falls into* a crack, not on it. If one didn't, there would be no danger involved in the breaking to begin with (the danger itself being respective to the extent of the depth).[10] The crack therefore consists in two lines – across the surface and into the depths – but these two lines become 'intertwined' or 'doubled', for it is together, between their play, that the crack is truly extended.

As I pointed out at the close of Chapter 2, the dualism of surface and depth is largely left behind for Deleuze's 'new directions' with Guattari (TRM 65). The crack, however, lives on: insofar as the crack is a combination of two lines, one which spreads across a surface and another which comes from depth, they are together merged in the nomad; it is the nomad who simultaneously strafes an entire expanse while carrying out a smoothing of that space *by the very way they live* (their actual way of life). This association is not entirely surprising, since the nomad, as mentioned earlier in this chapter, has much in common with the surface becoming of *The Logic of Sense*. But when Deleuze returns to discuss the crack (initially) in *Dialogues* with Parnet, he will place this line in between two others.[11] All three lines are again gleaned from Fitzgerald's *The Crack-Up*. As Deleuze and Parnet describe it there, the first kind of line is of rigid segmentarity: those lines which are 'all kinds of clearly defined segments, in all kinds of directions, which cut us up in all senses, packets of segmentarized lines' (D 124). These are the great segments of rich-poor, young-old, health-sickness and so on, which dominate the easily visible and communicable aspects of our social lives (D 126). In contrast to this line of rigid segmentation, the second is supple. These secondary lines are the 'lines of crack' which split through the lines of great segmentary cuts: rather than molar lines with segments, they are molecular fluxes with thresholds or quanta' (D 124). As we can already surmise, these two lines of the rigid/supple (or molar/molecular) form a dualism that accordingly corresponds to the striated/smooth and State/nomad. But there is a third kind of line – a line of flight, or what Deleuze and Parnet call, again citing Fitzgerald, a *rupture* (D 127). On this line, it is 'as if something carried us away, across our segments, but also across our thresholds, towards a destination which is unknown, not foreseeable, not pre-existent' (D 125).

What is this third line? If the first two lines correspond to the State and the nomad, then *who* accounts for the third? The answer, it would seem from subtraction, is the smith. This is most certainly why '*Every mine is a line of flight* that is in communication with smooth spaces' (ATP 412), where 'mine' refers to the metallurgical space of the smith. The line of flight is therefore not nomadic but *phylactic*. War machines, to continue, are not lines of flight per se, but machines that are *constructed upon* such lines: '[W]e define "war machines" as linear arrangements constructed along lines of flight' (N 33; see also ATP 222 and D 141). In this sense, any reference to a 'nomadic line of flight' is a terminological conflation, for nomads more specifically construct and arrange war machines upon a phylactic line of flight. Nomads 'take up' a line of flight that is already flowing through them. What they do with these lines is create: they build, extend and proliferate. But they do so by transmitting a pure becoming *from* the phylum *into* the nomos for the purposes of *escaping* negation and *promoting* creation (ATP 422–3).

From this description we can see that the principle significance of the three lines has to do with the issue of creation. But as one might ask: on which line does creation occur? Can creation be equated with becoming and if so then which line is the line of becoming – the molecular line or the line of flight, the crack or the rupture? If these questions are not so easily answered, it is because the original dualisms of the nomadology have been substantially complexified and broken. To resolve these issues we will therefore have to put the dualism back together again. But in doing so, what we will arrive at is a union that can be more accurately described by two altogether different terms: PLURALISM = MONISM. As we will see, the effect of this equation will be to render each of the initial dualisms we have discussed, including becoming and history, into a productive composite. And insofar as it is the *whole* composite that is responsible for production, we will accordingly arrive at a reorientation of the between: a between which no longer forms a dualism with 'being', but includes even those things that are apparently against it in the process of creation. This between will therefore no longer be a mere synonym for becoming. Rather, it will go beyond this by including history in its becoming and becoming in its history.

PLURALISM = MONISM

As we have seen in our investigation of Deleuze and Guattari's nomadology thus far, creation and capture are initially separated out and apportioned to the nomad and the State, becoming and history. However, following this articulation of their respective singularities, the dualistic character of the nomadology is complexified and broken, leading to a tripartite ontology that seemingly spreads both becoming and being across three kinds. But how does two go into three, and what impact will this have on the ontology and strategy of the nomadology? In the remainder of this chapter, I will show how Deleuze and Guattari themselves struggle to resolve this issue. Subsequently, we are left with two potential readings of nomadology: one which regresses to the initial dualism, and another which resolves this dualism by progressing to 'a new monism' – a monism that in fact equals pluralism.[12] Of these two alternatives, I will argue only the latter is capable of achieving the creative aspirations that Deleuze and Guattari hold for nomadology. But insofar as this latter option involves a rendering together of becoming and history into a productive differential composite, the nomadology will itself promote a creative conception of history – a philosophy of history that does not side with pure becoming or history alone, but always both together for the production of another. In short, a nomadic history.

The difficulty in reconciling the ontologies of two and three is perhaps best illustrated by the peculiar position of the second line within Deleuze and Guattari's schema of lines. This second line is a line of segmentarity, but it is not rigid; it is a molecular line (crack), but it is not the line of pure becoming (rupture). Teasing out the nature of this middle line further would therefore be a good place to start our reorientation of the nomadic process that results in the magical equation PLURALISM = MONISM.

Our initial conjecture, to recap, was that the three lines align with the three spaces of the Nomadology plateau. This meant that the striated-polis matched with the rigid-molar, the smooth-nomos with the supple-molecular and the holey-phylum with the line of flight. This topology in turn allowed us to make a distinction between nomadic and phylactic becoming, as well as nomadic and sedentary being. The *operation* of building a war machine was the process that exhibited these differences par excellence: nomads construct a war machine upon phylactic lines of flight for the purposes of spreading the nomos and escaping the State form. As this arrangement specifies, nomadic assemblages are between the purities of the phylum and the State. On the one hand they are unlike States, yet on the other they are nevertheless assemblages as opposed to pure becoming.

Another way in which Deleuze and Guattari express this middle notion is when they talk about the *drawing of a diagonal*: 'free the line and the diagonal, draw the line instead of plotting a point, produce an imperceptible diagonal instead of clinging to an even elaborated or reformed vertical or horizontal' (ATP 296, 478). As this quote goes on to say, 'When this is done it always goes down in History but never comes from it. [. . .] Diagonal or multilinear assemblages [. . .] have to do with becoming; they are a bit of becoming in the pure state; they are transhistorical' (ATP 296). At first glance, it might appear from this passage that the diagonal falls on the side of becoming in contrast to history. To a certain extent this is true. However, if we look more closely, it will also become apparent that the diagonal is not synonymous with becoming but merely a 'bit' of it. Furthermore, the diagonal is not exclusively a line of flight, since it is also a form of assemblage. The creative diagonal, as such, reinforces one of the original motivations for Deleuze and Guattari's nomadology: not the facilitation of a destructive or disorganising force for its own sake but rather the development of an alternative kind of organisation.[13] Consequently, the diagonal does not ascribe to dualistic separation but if anything provides a means for their union. To put it one way, the diagonal is a *solidus*: it brings together a numerator and denominator (becoming and history) and activates their relation in an assemblage, in a way that horizontal-vertical systems are incapable of. But from this description we can already see that the diagonal assemblage or constructed war machine will be distinguishable from both the punctual system (State history or historicism) and pure becoming itself. As a result, if this assemblage is said to be 'transhistoric', it is not in the sense that it is *devoid* of history (for only pure becoming is), but merely that it is not *reducible* to history *alone*, just as the nomad is not without points but is rather irreducible to them. This is why Deleuze can say in a later text that while the diagonal has to do with becoming, the *drawing* of it is profoundly historical:

> Those who continue to have recourse to History and protest against the indetermination of a concept such as 'mutation' should bear in mind the perplexity of real historians when they have to explain why capitalism arose at such a time and in such a place when so many factors could have made it equally possible at another time and place. 'To problematize series. . .' Whether discursive or not, formations, families and multiplicities are historical. They are not just compounds built up from their coexistence but are inseparable from 'temporal reactors of derivation'; and when a new formation appears, with new rules and series, it never comes all at once, in a single phrase or act of creation, but emerges like a series of 'building blocks', with gaps, traces and reactivations of former elements that survive under the new rules. Despite isomorphisms and isotopies, no formation provides the model for another. The theory of divisions is therefore an essential part of the system. One must pursue the different series, travel along the different levels, and cross all thresholds; instead of simply displaying phenomena or statements in their vertical or horizontal dimensions, one must form a transversal or mobile diagonal line along which the archaeologist-archivist must move. A comment by Boulez on the rarefied universe of Webern could easily apply here to Foucault (and his style): 'He created a new dimension, which we might call a diagonal dimension, a sort of distribution of points, groups or figures that no

longer act simply as an abstract framework but actually exist in space' [Boulez 1966: 372]. (F 21–2)

Distinguishing between the diagonal and pure becoming is therefore not a splitting of hairs, for it is what allows us to acknowledge how the drawing of the diagonal has a bit to do with pure becoming *and* history. It is also what allows us to appreciate how war machines not only need protection from the State (like the Nietzschean 'strong' who need protection from the 'weak'), but they need constructing in the first place; war machines are in no way 'given' – they require building. Therefore, when it was claimed above that smiths are at best quasi-nomadic, perhaps it would have been more appropriate to say that nomads are quasi-phylactic: a bit of becoming in the pure *state*.

The diagonal, however, is not all it appears to be. Although the diagonal is an expression of the attempt to escape from the horizontal and vertical, the diagonal ultimately remains captured, for it is still reducible to the distance between the horizontal and the vertical. The diagonal, as such, is not sufficiently abstracted from being between the horizontal and the vertical; it does not yet have enough of Paul's swagger through the desert.[14] Given this, it is rather the abstract or zigzag line that better encapsulates what Deleuze and Guattari are after:

> [A] *line that delimits nothing, that describes no contour*, that no longer goes from one point to another, but instead passes between points, that is always declining from the horizontal and the vertical and deviating from the diagonal, that is constantly changing direction, a mutant line of this kind that is without outside or inside, form or background, beginning or end and that is as alive as a continuous variation – such a line is truly an abstract line, and describes a smooth space. (ATP 497–8)

As I will point out in Chapter 5, this zigzag line is also associated by Deleuze and Guattari with the line of history as it moves through various planes of immanence. For the moment, however, our attention is drawn to a more immediate discrepancy. At first, we maintained that the second line of the supple and molecular pertained to the nomad, whereas the third line corresponded to the phylactic and metallurgical mine of the smith. But now, the 'truly abstract line' described here is the smooth space of the nomad. How is this possible?

To restate Deleuze and Parnet's analysis in *Dialogues*, an individual, thing or event is composed of three lines: (1) the segmentary

cuts which mark us and concern us 'at a particular time, at a particular place' (D 126); (2) the 'lines of crack' (D 127), those supple
flows 'marked by *quanta* that are like so many little segmentations-
in-progress grasped at the moment of their birth, as on a moonbeam,
or on an intensive scale' (ATP 195); and (3) the lines of flight or
ruptures which correspond to neither 'the great segments, changes
or even journeys which produce this line' nor 'the most secret mutations, the mobile and fluent thresholds, although these approximate
more closely to it' (D 127; see also ATP 203). But where are the
nomads in all of this? Are they an intensive moonbeam, a mobile line
of crack, or are they more pure than this, more still and indistinguishable, like the Pink Panther who paints the world in his own colour
(D 127)? If we look to other discussions of the three lines – the Three
Novellas and Micropolitics plateaus (as well as the Conclusion of
ATP 505–6) – we will find that the nomad is unquestionably aligned
with the pure line of flight. For example, first there is the Roman
State (*pax romana*); then there is the line of the advancing Huns,
with their war machine fully directed towards destroying the peace;
and finally there are the barbarians who are caught between the two,
who pass from one to the other (ATP 222–3). The order of presentation has changed here, but again the nomads are placed on the pure
abstract line that comes 'from the east' (LS 129). How are we then
to reconcile this nomad with the one we have extracted from the
Nomadology plateau?

  An unfavourable reading might simply suggest that Deleuze and
Guattari/Parnet contradict themselves. For example, it is indeed hard
to describe certain sections of the 'Many Politics' essay as anything
but confused. From pages 130–4, the molecular line and line of
flight (crack and rupture) appear to be read together, to the extent
that Deleuze and Parnet even feel the need to defend the apparent
dualism that 'rigid and binary segmentarity' forms with 'molecular
lines, or lines of border, of flight or slope' (the remainder of 'Many
Politics' will often slip between an analysis of three to one of two
(D 141–2)).[15] This merging is then repeated in various parts of *A
Thousand Plateaus*: 'From the viewpoint of micropolitics, a society
is defined by its *lines of flight*, which are *molecular*' (ATP 216,
emphasis added). Other parts of *A Thousand Plateaus*, however, are
unambiguous in their distinction. For example, the brief discussion
of the three lines in the conclusion to *A Thousand Plateaus* clearly
describes the second line as the rhizomatic line in distinction to the
line of flight: 'rhizome lines oscillate between tree lines that segment

and even stratify them, and lines of flight or rupture that carry them away' (ATP 506). Therefore, while the rhizome is described in this passage as the line that 'passes between' and 'belongs to a smooth space', the line that constitutes 'anomalous and nomadic multiplicities', 'multiplicities of becoming, or transformational multiplicities' that are best expressed by 'schizophrenia', this line is nevertheless clearly distinguished from the line of flight that allows for escape.

The situation is also not helped by the fact that Deleuze's appropriation of the three lines from Fitzgerald is rather dubious to begin with. In Deleuze's reading of *The Crack-Up*, the crack is the undoing of our great segments and the rupture is the 'clean break' from the past (see D 127 and ATP 199), the latter of which works much like Nietzsche's untimely (or more specifically Deleuze's reading of the untimely[16]). Deleuze is here referring to the final section of *The Crack-Up*, where Fitzgerald says: 'A clean break is something you cannot come back from; that is irretrievable because it makes the past cease to exist' (Fitzgerald 1945: 81). But as is portrayed by the subtitle of the relevant section of *The Crack-Up* – 'Pasting It Together' – this moment of the crack-up concerns the attempt to *overcome the crack in favour of a new plate*. This new plate, moreover, is detestable in many ways: 'I will try to be a correct animal though, and if you throw me a bone with enough meat on it I may even lick your hand' (Fitzgerald 1945: 84). What Fitzgerald is trying to describe is how he has reached a point where this is the only way to go on, for he can 'no longer fulfil the obligations that life had set for [him] or that [he] had set for [himself]' (Fitzgerald 1945: 81). The 'clean break' is therefore in no way glorious, nor does it appear to be anything but the renewal of complete segmentarity. The burden of 'truth' may be lifted from Fitzgerald's shoulders with this break, but not quite in the same way as Nietzsche's shift from the camel to the child, for Fitzgerald does not bring forth a new world but falls back into the majoritarian one (albeit under a new aegis): 'And just as the laughing stoicism which has enabled the American Negro to endure the intolerable conditions of his existence has cost him his sense of the truth – so in my case there is a price to pay' (Fitzgerald 1945: 84). If expressive happiness comes at the price of enslavement, if the burdens of the past are to be replaced by a 'heady villainous feeling' (Fitzgerald 1945: 82), it is not quite so clear that Fitzgerald's 'Pasting it together' is anything like Deleuze's rupture. In sum, Fitzgerald's 'clean break' is a way to overcome the crack *in favour of the rigid* – a new molar segmentarity unburdened with or oblivious to cracks. As

Deleuze cannot ascribe to this, he claims that it is Fitzgerald's *second* line (the crack) that leads back to the rigid. But this is incorrect, for it is *the complete break from the crack and that which was cracking (the molar)* that allows Fitzgerald to go on, where 'going on' refers to the birth of a new rigid segmentarity. Thus for Fitzgerald, the crack leads to a 'complete break', and rupture inaugurates a new molar. It may be so that this new segmentarity is one where Fitzgerald 'acts like everybody else', but it is a far stretch to suggest that this is the becoming-imperceptible of Deleuze and Guattari.

To an extent, Deleuze is aware of this confused analysis of lines. As he remarks with Parnet: 'Nothing is more complicated than the line or the lines [. . .]' (D 137), for 'All these lines are tangled' (D 128; see also 125 and ATP 223). A more generous interpretation, however, would be to reassert the affinity that the two lines of crack and rupture have for one another. Consider the following passage:

> [W]hat counts is not merely the two opposed [molar] camps on the great line where they confront each other, but also the frontier, through which everything passes and shoots on a broken molecular line of a different orientation. May 1968 was an explosion of such a molecular line, an irruption of the Amazons, a frontier which traced its unexpected line, drawing the segments like torn-off blocs which have lost their bearings. (D 132)

This passage shows us just how close the two lines are. On the one hand, the Amazons are a force of violence, an irruption like May 1968 that is 'not the little crack' (D 131). But on the other hand, this explosion actually *plays itself out* on a molecular line. As such, it is from both the molecular and the abstract lines, *and only together*, that a molar segment is undone: the latter provides the explosive force of rupture that the former pursues in a transformation of the molar. We can then make sense of the statement that 'molecular lines make fluxes of deterritorialization shoot between the segments' (D 131). It is the molecular that makes a flux or threshold of deterritorialisation, just as Ariadne gives being to the eternal return of difference (as discussed in Chapter 1). In a similar way, this also allows us to reconcile the apparent duplicity of quanta, which on the one hand are of the molecular thresholds (see D 124 and ATP 195), yet on the other are what mark lines of flight (ATP 222). Quanta are *markings*, descriptions and expressions of something which is in itself a pure inexpressibility. Unlike the markings of the State, they stand for the grounding of ungrounding, they give their name to becoming. In light of this, they are often mistaken for or combined with that which they 'approximate more closely' (D 127). In the terminology of Deleuze's eternal return, we could say that Theseus (whose name means 'institution') is the great segment, Dionysus is the great becoming and Ariadne is the thread which goes from one to the other. In this respect, the confusion over which line is the line of becoming is no different from the earlier confusion over becoming and the eternal return, as discussed in Chapter 1: pure becoming as the will to power will not suffice on its own, for it needs the eternal return as an adjoining selection principle, it needs a double affirmation which provides for the being of that becoming (the role of Ariadne must not be forgotten). The merging of the molecular line and line of flight is therefore not a side effect but a natural and beneficial development, for it shows the intimate and productive relationship that the two have while maintaining their independence.[17]

Nevertheless, we are still faced with a dilemma: shall we side with the nomad of absolute becoming or shall we side with something more molecular and less pure, more crack and less rupture? The easy answer is to side with the absolute, for this then allows us to neatly slot the nomad back into a binary with the State; when caught in a pinch, it is far easier to fall back on the strict dualisms of becoming/being, becoming/history, nomad/State, etc. However, if the nomadology is to have any great significance, this resolution will not do. As the analysis in this chapter has tried to show, the *development* of nomadology takes the nomad beyond the original limit-dualism that it finds itself a part of. More exactly, the nomad is led 'around the bend' or 'beyond the turn' and *back to the between*.[18] With the advancement of phylactic becoming and the smith, the nomad is reoriented as the figure who 'takes up' lines of flight in the construction of a war machine. As such, while it may be true that the nomad is the 'man of deterritorialization' (D 134) and that 'the nomad can be called the Deterritorialized par excellence' (ATP 381), one must be careful here: what Deleuze and Guattari in fact say is that *if* the nomad can be so called, it is because there is no reterritorialisation afterward *as with the migrant or the sedentary*. This is not to say that there is *no* reterritorialisation, nor that the nomad has no relation to territory. A nomadic organisation, to reiterate, is not a lack of organisation. It is simply a form of organisation that is distinct from the State. If the nomad has an affinity with deterritorialisation, it is therefore due to the particular nature of the nomad's territory and reterritorialisation – the nature of their assemblage; it is due, in short, to the being the nomad makes of becoming rather than the nomad as pure becoming.

In so choosing this arrangement, it should be noted, one does not move away from the nomad as the differential element of the between, but towards it. For example, if the nomad can be described as 'rhizomatic', it is not because rhizomes are becomings but rather because rhizome lines, as stated above, oscillate between arborescent lines and lines of flight or rupture. And as another example, when appraising the topological arrangement of the Romans, Huns and barbarians, we must honestly ask ourselves: who of these three are the true nomads? Who comes closest to the ethic and ontology of transformation? I would contend that it is in fact the barbarians and not the Huns who better fit the bill. The Huns are sure of their task – destruction of the State – but the barbarians, by contrast, have mastered the art of disguise and metamorphosis. Like Hercules, who is constantly moving across the amorphous middle from depth to height, it is the barbarians who are capable of going between the two, becoming one, passing off as another, and then taking up arms against either or both.

In the final analysis, it is always this 'middle' ethic and ontology that Deleuze and Guattari repeatedly aspire towards. And although this between may be initially placed in a binary with being, as soon as Deleuze and Guattari's analysis progresses beyond this dualism it is necessary that we follow the shifting middle. Between the two poles of rigid segmentarity and deterritorialising lines of flight now lies 'a whole realm of properly molecular negotiation, translation, and transduction in which at times molar lines are already undermined by fissures and cracks, and at other times lines of flight are already drawn toward black holes, flow connections are already replaced by limitative conjunctions, and quanta emissions are already converted into center-points' (ATP 223–4). It is in this middle realm – in the midst – where everything happens. This places the middle in a curious position. As Deleuze and Guattari note: 'It is odd how supple segmentarity is caught between the two other lines, ready to tip to one side or the other; such is its ambiguity' (ATP 205). But is not this 'oddity' precisely the essence of metamorphosis and transmutation? Is not this 'ambiguity', as opposed to pure being or pure becoming, precisely what is so 'Interesting, Remarkable, and Important' (WP 82)? Such, in my opinion, is the virtue of this other transformative figure, or second force of nomadism, who moves between the extremities of the formless and the petrified:

What is naturally uninteresting? Flimsy concepts, what Nietzsche called the 'formless and fluid daubs of concepts' – or, on the contrary, concepts that are too regular, petrified, and reduced to a framework. (WP 83)

'Interesting' aside, an examination of Deleuze's more prescriptive moments can easily illustrate how Deleuze is far from a straight philosopher of formlessness or entirely fluid becoming. Invariably, every call for revolutionary becoming is tempered with a precautionary reminder. Witness the conclusion to the 'Many Politics' essay (which is then replicated and developed further in the Micropolitics plateau). Firstly, dissolution of the State and the line of rigid segmentarity is not the point in itself:

> Even if we had the power to blow it up, could we succeed in doing so without destroying ourselves, since it is so much a part of the conditions of life, including our organism and our very reason? The prudence with which we must manipulate that line, the precautions we must take to soften it, to suspend it, to divert it, to undermine it, testify to a long labour which is not merely aimed against the State and the powers that be, but directly at ourselves. (D 138)

Secondly, revolutionary becomings cannot be pursued with free abandon, for they 'produce or encounter their own dangers, a threshold crossed too quickly, an intensity become dangerous because it could not be tolerated. You have not taken enough precautions' (D 138). 'Precaution', 'prudence' – not exactly the words that would support a Deleuzian politics founded on the celebration of deterritorialisation. In fact, in a direct response to those readers who would overly glorify (or attack) his analysis of becoming and deterritorialisation, Deleuze says:

> Some have said that we see the schizophrenic as the true revolutionary. We believe, rather, that schizophrenia is the descent of a molecular process into a black hole. Marginals have always inspired fear in us, and a slight horror. They are not clandestine enough. (D 139)

Such 'marginals', in other words, are a bit too obvious. One should not be able to identify a nomad from their haircut. If it were that easy then genuine creation wouldn't need encouraging or protecting. This is why the question of the revolution is so problematic:

> The question of a revolution has never been utopian spontaneity versus State organization. When we challenge the model of the State apparatus or of the party organization which is modelled on the conquest of that apparatus, we do not, however, fall into the grotesque alternatives: either

that of appealing to a state of nature, to a spontaneous dynamic, or that of becoming the self-styled lucid thinker of an impossible revolution, whose very impossibility is such a source of pleasure. (D 145)

These above passages quite clearly tell us who is *not* a true revolutionary – a 'schizophrenic' or 'marginal'. They also indicate how Deleuze resists oppositional presentations, especially when it comes to 'the question of the revolution'. The choice is not between purities of stasis or movement, being or becoming, the master State or its self-identified antagonist.[19] This is why Deleuze implores us to abandon the above twin image: 'why not think that *a new type of revolution is in the course of becoming possible* [. . .]' (D 147)? This new type of revolution is not entirely sure of the way forward; it is not even always sure where the impediments are or who are the nomads. But it could not be otherwise, since

> we can't be sure in advance how things will go. We can define different kinds of line, but that won't tell us one's good and another bad. We can't assume that lines of flight are necessarily creative, that smooth spaces are always better than segmented or striated ones. (ATP 33)

Thus the radical line of flight cannot be so easily preferred over the rigid or supple lines of segmentarity. Not only do they each carry their own benefits and dangers (none more so than the line of flight, which has the potential to unleash total abolition when left unchecked), but perhaps more importantly, each of them are needed for the ongoing process of life: 'it would be wrong to think that it is sufficient, in the end, to take the line of flight or rupture' (D 139). Any speak of 'priority' or 'dominance' (of one over the other) is therefore almost always misleading. The molecular line, to take another example, may carry out operations that the molar cannot, 'Yet we will not say that it is necessarily better' (ATP 196). It is therefore impossible to prejudge the utility or liability of any of the lines, since all of them are in some way needed for the promotion of creation and life:

> [I]n no sense is [the rigid line] dead, for it occupies and pervades our life, and always seems to prevail in the end. It even includes much tenderness and love. It would be too easy to say, 'This is a bad line', for you find it everywhere, and in all the other lines. (ATP 195)

Or again, this time in more detail on 'what is to be done':

> Staying stratified – organized, signified, subjected – is not the worst that can happen; the worst that can happen is if you throw the strata

into demented or suicidal collapse, which brings them back down on us heavier than ever. This is how it should be done: Lodge yourself on a stratum, experiment with the opportunities it offers, find an advantageous place on it, find potential movements of deterritorialization, possible lines of flight, experience them, produce flow conjunctions here and there, try out continuums of intensities segment by segment, have a small plot of new land at all times. It is through a meticulous relation with the strata that one succeeds in freeing lines of flight, causing conjugated flows to pass and escape and bringing forth continuous intensities for a BwO. Connect, conjugate, continue [. . .] (ATP 161)

Following this lead, it would be too easy to say 'history is bad', for you find it everywhere, including in all the other lines of becoming. Is becoming better than history? Perhaps. But who can be sure that it always is? And even when it is, this does not mean that history is any less integral to the process of creation. As Nietzsche makes clear, both the unhistorical *and* the historical are necessary for a healthy life to be achieved. If Nietzsche appears to favour the untimely over history, it is only because this was the element that historical scholarship had inappropriately ignored, not because he hoped to promote one over the other. For after all, it is the promotion of *life* that is his goal, and history is as much a part of this as the untimely is (Lundy 2009: 189–95).

A tempered position is therefore the most appealing. It is also the most difficult, and in a certain sense the most radical: as the barbarians well know, there is arguably nothing harder than charting one's own path between a binary of oppositional lines. We know that Deleuze often participates in such dualistic decisions, especially when it comes to becoming and history. But in the end, Deleuze always hopes to go beyond these, to itinerate between so that he can both become and defend against its dangers at the same time. This is why it is important to remember that what Deleuze calls the crack refers to the molecular or rhizomatic line *in between* the lines of rigid segmentary and rupture. Only then can we understand the following guideline:

Well then, are we to speak always about Bousquet's wound, about Fitzgerald's and Lowry's alcoholism, Nietzsche's and Artaud's madness while remaining on the shore? [. . .] Or should we go a short way further to see for ourselves, be a little alcoholic, a little crazy, a little suicidal, a little of a guerrilla – just enough to extend the crack, but not enough to deepen it irremediably? (LS 157–8)

Become a little bit, but not too much. Leave the shore, certainly, but do so in order that you may find a new land – do not hope to become irrevocably lost at sea. In other words, extend the crack and connect the rhizome, but do not become the rupture. When you do so, a line will be drawn that is distinguishable from both the inexpressive and the expressions of State segmentarity. That this line is distinct from the line of flight, yet also distinct from the striae that express and organise in an entirely different way (ATP 498), once again reaffirms the middle status of the nomad that has been rearticulated in this chapter.

Following from this analysis, it becomes clear that a dualistic reading of the nomadology that focuses on the opposition of the nomad with the State or becoming with history will only get us so far. And in the subtle shift from two to three, much changes. Since lines of flight are phylactic instead of nomadic, and since nomadic war machines are assemblages instead of absolutes, rhizomes instead of ruptures, the nomadology need not be conceived of as simply promoting becoming against history. While a polarised reading of the relations can certainly get us started, it is only when we reorient this relation into a differential composite, an assemblage that itself produces something, that we get a concept that is more than pure becoming (by being less) and more than State history (by being truly creative).

This rendering of a composite for the production of the new leads us to overcome the dominant Deleuzian dualisms in two simultaneous and synonymous ways. On the one hand, a new monism is born: in place of the dualism of becoming and history, we now have a singular differential composite – 'history/becoming'. On the other hand, however, this singular composite is a pluralism par excellence: not only does the composite continually produce others, but it is capable of transmuting itself, as we have witnessed throughout this chapter. And thus we arrive at a version of Deleuze's magical formula PLURALISM = MONISM. This equation is not against dualisms any more than it relies upon them. It is similarly not against history any more than it requires one – a creative conception of history, a nomadic history, that plays its part in the production of the new.

*   *   *

As we have now seen, nomadology is Deleuze and Guattari's alternative to the dominant form of social and political analysis that relies upon historical explanation. Because of this, the Nomadology plateau is indispensable for any attempt to elicit the relation between history and becoming and its accompanying philosophy of historical creativity. But what exactly is nomadology? Through a close investigation of the manner in which the Nomadology plateau unfolds – Deleuze and Guattari's own practice of nomadology, as it were – it becomes evident that nomadology consists of three moments or movements. At first, there is the setting of two. This is the extraction or abstraction of *de jure* purities from the *de facto* mixture; it is the ridding or cleansing of pure becoming of any traces of history (and vice versa), the nomad from any reducibility to States, etc. A second moment, however, moves from this two to three: 'It is certainly no longer a matter of a synthesis of the two, of a synthesis of 1 and 2, but of a third which always comes from elsewhere and disturbs the binarity of the two, not so much inserting itself in their opposition as in their complementarity' (D 131).[20] The binary is broken by the between, showing how if the between is itself elevated to the level of a limit principle, then it is in turn returned to the fold by processes of transmutation that change its nature and objective. A new middle emerges, underneath which pure becoming flows, and from which tertiary arrangements spring forth – Hercules and the nomad as always between that which is above and below. However, if there are three levels/lines, it is because this negotiation or experimentation – this *play between two* – has the result of producing another. A final moment therefore returns us from three to one. This one is the one that is said of a new monism, the open whole, the eternal return of difference, the dice throw, crowned anarchy or the univocity of Being; it is the one that allows for the unknown, affirms that which is outside by making it immanent and ensures that the game goes on.[21] In each case: from one and its other, to another, repeat – from two to three to one.

My intention in this chapter has been to show how the distinction of different levels and kinds of creation in the nomadology can have significant ramifications for how we understand history and becoming. It may indeed be true that Deleuze and Guattari employ history and becoming as limit concepts within their greater philosophy of creativity, epitomised in this instance by the State historian and the nomad devoid of history. But if we acknowledge that this is only the first and not final word on creation in the nomadology, that 'Dualism is therefore only a moment' (B 29), then it allows us to see how the 'history/becoming' differential also plays itself out at a more advanced level: the middle that is their monistic-pluralistic composite.

Accounts of history and becoming which fail to follow this

're-formation' miss out on the possibility of a productive nomadic history. To take an example, Jay Lampert's reading of nomadic history involves identifying two forms of history – a 'good' and 'bad' form – that are synonymous with pure becoming and historicism (Lampert 2006: 7). This leads him to claim that 'revolutionary history' is something 'which Deleuze and Guattari generally call "becoming", but sometimes call "history"' (Lampert 2009: 72). But which becoming is this? The molecular or the line of flight? The rhizomatic or the rupture? Or is it the phylum? If anything, we have seen in this chapter how it is necessary to specify more precisely the nature of becoming and history in each circumstance, if one is to articulate the implications of nomadology for a philosophy of history and a philosophy of creativity. Furthermore, we have seen how it is necessary to go beyond the oppositional dualism of history and becoming, including its accompanying associations with 'good' and 'bad', in order to go back to the between, where a new monism and pluralism can be pursued that brings about continual creativity. Lampert may be willing to allow for two different senses of 'history' in Deleuze's work, but it is doubtful whether a philosophy of history worthy of Deleuze's name can be extracted from their opposition.[22]

When forced to choose between becoming and history, the response is immediate: '"Becomings" are much more important than history' (N 30). But one need not dig far under the surface to see that things are more complicated than this. Just as Deleuze and Guattari warn that the smooth will not always save us and that the molecular is not always better, so too we must be careful with becoming and history. For once we begin to crack the dualism, a philosophy of historical creativity begins to emerge that can be instructive to both those who have become enamoured with pure becoming and those who still cling to State history. This nomadic history may at times appear to contradict clear dualisms, but surely it is the hope of Deleuze and Guattari's nomadology to liberate us from declarations of allegiance ('are you with us or against us') so that we can get busy bringing forth the new.

4

From Prehistory to Universal History

As this book has now made clear through the investigation of three separate works, a Deleuzian philosophy of history and becoming will revolve around the ontological distinction and relation between capture and creation: intensive becomings emerge from their depths into explicated beings; dynamic developments result in a surface that orientates actual bodies and states of affairs; and nomadic creations are captured by State apparatuses. In each of these studies, we have seen how the initial segregation of history on the side of capture and becoming on the side of creation can be misleading if not mistaken, for not only can history and becoming be shown to exceed these allocations, but each will require the other for their very nature. This in turn led me to conclude that there must be *another* history in Deleuze, a history that does not lack vitality but is an integral part of it, a history that is not at odds with becoming but is in productive relation with it.

In exploring the nature of this other history, the initial segregation of capture from creation was itself complexified. This was perhaps inevitable, given that their preliminary relation itself harboured much causal-linearity. To illustrate, the notion of capture would seem to definitionally presuppose that which it captures, obliging us to draw a causal-linear connection from one to the other: first something is created then it is captured. Even if we allow for capture to have an impact back upon that which nomadically or intensively creates, this bifurcating relation arguably fails to adequately contest standard accounts of linearity and sequential causality. It is therefore necessary that we push our investigation of capture and creation farther, showing not just how we go 'from one to its other, to another, repeat', but how this process can be said to occur in both a simultaneous and non-linear fashion.

It is towards this end that Deleuze and Guattari themselves ask: how is it that the State form emerges, and *when*? This case study is of the utmost importance, for as we saw in Chapter 3, 'History', according to Deleuze and Guattari, 'is always written from the sedentary point of view and in the name of a unitary State apparatus' (ATP 23). In asking after the birth of the State, Deleuze and Guattari are therefore quite literally inquiring into the *prehistorical*: is there a prior set of events that leads to the birth of the State form at a particular date in chronological time, and if so, what is the relation between this prehistory and the birth of the historical method/apparatus of capture that is one with the State? Are we to understand this relation historically, prehistorically or other? As we will see, Deleuze and Guattari's analysis of the emergence of the State apparatus and the question of its prehistory demonstrates how virtual formations of society must coexist with each other in various mixtures of actuality. In this respect, even the prehistory of the State will be shown to exist simultaneously with its history, despite the appearance of their successive relation.

But to the extent that Deleuze and Guattari are successful in showing how apparent progressions are made up of simultaneous encounters, where does this leave history? Must history be confined to the concrete and the actual, to the chronological and the causal-linear, and separated from simultaneity? Aside from the intensive, dynamic and nomadic alternatives that I have explored in this book thus far, Deleuze and Guattari suggest to us another method for ameliorating the presumed opposition of successive history and simultaneous becoming: *universal history*. Describing this alternative history as universal might seem ill-advised, given that most universal histories reduce all of history (and often the future) to a necessary guiding force, such as *Geist* or *Being*. Such histories, as we have seen, are 'historicist', for they do not allow for a succession that is genuinely creative, reducing it to a static simultaneity which institutes a radical mechanism or finalism (teleology). Deleuze and Guattari's universal history, however, differs from such accounts, for it employs a conception of the universal that is defined by contingency rather than necessity. Their universal history, as such, is both a history of contingent occurrences and itself subject to contingency.

Due to its contingent nature, this universal history will not gain its impetus by asserting the 'true meaning' of history or determining its origins and ends, limits and possibilities, 'once and for all'. Its purpose will rather be to show how history need not be merely fixating, representational and/or revisionary, but might instead be open, creative and non-linear. Accordingly, my investigation of Deleuze and Guattari's universal history will follow these three lines of contingency: (1) the ability to remain open to the future and thus open to change; (2) the possibility for history to be created by a presently existing power; and (3) the insistence that history be approached in a non-linear fashion, so that it can continually change and have a vital influence on what it is that becomes. From my elaboration of these three contingencies, Deleuze and Guattari's universal history will be shown to unite succession and simultaneity in a manner that doesn't reduce one to the other, but promotes a form of historical creativity. I will therefore conclude this chapter by questioning the capitalist roots of this universal creativity and comparing it with its schizophrenic alternate. As with previous chapters, we will see from this analysis how Deleuze's philosophy of creativity cannot be so easily apportioned to schizophrenic becoming and opposed to paranoic history, since between the two there is a productive differential composite.

The prehistory of the State apparatus

Deleuze and Guattari's 'Apparatus of Capture' plateau is the companion piece to their 'Treatise on Nomadology'. Whereas the Nomadology, as we saw in Chapter 3, concentrates on how the nomad escapes State capture and State history, the 'Apparatus of Capture' plateau carries out a more detailed analysis on the nature of the State apparatus or State form. Although this analysis includes an insightful history of the State from one instantiation to another, what is arguably of more significance for Deleuze and Guattari is their evaluation of when and under what conditions the State apparatus is born, including its accompanying form of State history. How is it, in other words, that the State apparatus first gains its nature, and when? Insofar as this investigation concerns what precedes the State and its attendant history, determining the nature of the State apparatus depends in part on its *prehistory* – those processes of simultaneous becoming that Deleuze and Guattari claim are then captured in a history of causal-linear succession. Let us then begin our exploration of the State apparatus and its form of history by analysing the nature of its prehistory.

As with the Nomadology, Deleuze and Guattari begin their exploration of the State apparatus by describing the two poles of the State (the magical-emperor and the jurist-priest king, the binder and the organiser) and the nomadic war machine that is exterior to them. In this initial presentation, the 'between-ness' of the war machine is explicitly placed in between the two State apparatuses. Furthermore, the between term is acknowledged to be the creative force between the two poles, capable of engendering movement between them. This in turn gives rise to 'a tempting three-part hypothesis: the war machine is "between" the two poles of political sovereignty and assures the passage from one pole to the other' (ATP 426). But as Deleuze and Guattari are quick to point out, such a hypothesis would suggest a basic causal-linear relation of the three terms – a '1-2-3' – that is ontologically dubious.

Deleuze and Guattari give three reasons for why they reject this hypothesis. Firstly, the middle term cannot be assumed to explain the States on either side, since the middle term is either utterly exterior to the States it is between or already a part of them. If the middle is truly exterior then it cannot explain what it is between, but if what is in between already belongs to a State, then it is the State that explains its middle rather than the other way around. The second reason this causal-linear account is misleading is because the two poles of the State must be in resonance with one another to begin with. It would therefore be inaccurate to suggest that one comes after the other, since it is always 'necessary for each State to have both poles' (ATP 427). The third reason a causal-linear story will not suffice is because the State always appears as pre-accomplished. States always posit their own causes and as such 'beg the question' (ATP 427). All three of these reasons indicate the difficulty in answering the question of 'which came first'.

In order to illustrate this, Deleuze and Guattari analyse in detail the relation between primitive society and the archaic State. The first State is the archaic State – the State of the emperor-despot that comes prior to private property and is associated by Marx ('the historian') with the 'Asiatic formation' (ATP 427–8). Deleuze and Guattari note how for Marx this archaic State presupposes a certain level of development within primitive societies, specifically the development of a potential surplus from which a State stock and specialised classes can arise. But as they go on to show, this reading of historical development is arguably a fabricated causal-linear account that covers over a much more complex and non-linear set of relations. Not only is it contestable whether the archaic State presupposes a certain level of primitive development, but it could be that the contrary is the case. For example, is it agriculture that gives rise to a State stock, or is it rather a stock of uncultivated seeds that produce, 'at first by chance', mixings and hybridisations from which agriculture becomes possible? This reversal has profound implications:

It is no longer the stock that presupposes a potential surplus, but the other way around. It is no longer the State that presupposes advanced agricultural communities and developed forces of production. On the contrary, the State is established directly in a milieu of hunter-gatherers having no prior agriculture or metallurgy, and it is the State that creates agriculture, animal raising, and metallurgy; it does so first on its own soil, then imposes them upon the surrounding world. It is not the country that progressively creates the town but the town that creates the country. It is not the State that presupposes a mode of production; quite the opposite, it is the State that makes production a 'mode'. The last reasons for presuming a progressive development are invalidated. Like the seeds in a stack: It all begins with a chance intermixing. (ATP 428–9)

From this it is clear that Deleuze and Guattari are opposed to the standard account of the archaic State's genesis. But more significantly, Deleuze and Guattari are not simply interested in replacing an accepted causal-linear account with another – their motive is not to carry out a 'revisionary' history. Rather, their point is that a standard conception of historical progression will not suffice; the archaic State did not come 'before' the primitive development of a potential surplus, nor the opposite, for they both *coexist*. But what does this mean? In order to answer this we will need to establish more clearly what Deleuze and Guattari mean by coexistence and progression, or simultaneity and succession.

In order to break with the standard causal-linear account of history, Deleuze and Guattari first note that the basic evolutionary account upon which it rests has itself been challenged in many significant ways, e.g. 'zigzag movements, stages skipped here or there, irreducible overall breaks', etc. (ATP 428). Deleuze and Guattari, however, wish to go beyond these critiques by not only questioning the manner of an evolutionary movement, but whether there is any evolution to speak of in the first place. Although ethnology is critical for making this argument, archaeology is arguably more significant for Deleuze and Guattari. This is because archaeological excavations show how different ethnological states of reality *exist together in the same stratum*. At any particular archaeological depth, what we will find is evidence as to how different communities and *types* of communities coexist and relate to one another: 'The self-sufficiency, autarky, independence, preexistence of primitive communities, is an ethnological dream: not that these communities necessarily depend on States, but they coexist with them in a complex network' (ATP 428). The reality of this network shows that primitive societies are not superfluous to, pre-existent to or unable of comprehending the State. If anything, as we saw in the last chapter, they know it all too well and thus attempt to ward it off. Conversely, the State is never a 'result' that 'puts an end' to primitive societies, for not only do such primitive societies continue to exist in their own right, but there are always attempts from within a State to release nomadic movements. Indeed, as Deleuze and Guattari claim, this is precisely what nomadism is: not a state of existence which precedes sedentarisation, but the ever-ongoing attempt to escape settlement in a polis (ATP 430). Furthermore, as Deleuze and Guattari make clear on numerous occasions, all that exists *in fact* (*de facto*) are mixtures (ATP 474; see also BCD 45). The suggestion that pure societies must exist in relation to one another is therefore itself slightly inaccurate, for every single society is made up of various heterogeneous components. As Deleuze and Guattari put it elsewhere when distinguishing one regime from another: 'There is such mixture within the same period or the same people that we can say no more than that a given people, language, or period assures the relative dominance of a certain regime' (ATP 119). In light of this, it is erroneous to ask the question 'which came first', for 'everything coexists, in perpetual interaction' (ATP 430).

By 'everything', Deleuze and Guattari specifically mean machinic processes. For Deleuze and Guattari, social formations are defined not by their modes of production but by the different social machines that produce these modes (ATP 435). Deleuze and Guattari thus outline a social topology which categorises the different types of societies according to their principle of power: 'Thus primitive societies are defined by mechanisms of prevention-anticipation; State societies are defined by apparatuses of capture; urban societies, by instruments of polarisation; nomadic societies, by war machines; and finally international, or rather ecumenical, organizations are defined by the encompassment of heterogeneous social formations' (ATP 435). But most importantly, these types of social formation do not exist in isolation but in constant relation to one another. This coexistence occurs 'in two fashions: extrinsically and intrinsically' (ATP 435). For example, extrinsically, primitive societies anticipate and ward off the archaic State which forms 'a part of their horizon' (ATP 435; see also AO 217). Similarly, if a State is said to capture something, then what is captured must clearly coexist *in its own right* – the State cannot appropriate something that ceases to exist. In such a case, however, it is also true that what is captured has an effect on the capturer. As we saw in Chapter 3, striated spaces *and the power of striation itself* are constantly subjected to smoothings (e.g. urban nomads). Concomitantly, it is always possible that smooth spaces, *as smooth*, can be converted into a striation (e.g. the nuclear submarine). Thus 'Each process can switch over to other powers, but also subordinate other processes to its own power' (ATP 437). From this we can see that both extrinsically and intrinsically, the machinic processes that define social formations do not follow one another successively but exist simultaneously.

But how is it that Deleuze and Guattari can deny the before and after of history's transpiring, for does not the word 'primitive' itself indicate a sense of 'occurring prior'? As it turns out, Deleuze and Guattari will not deny that history transpires. What they will do, however, is appeal to two different readings of time.[1] As we saw in Chapter 2, these two times are Chronos and Aion. Chronos naturally proceeds in a chronological fashion: moments come and go, emerging and elapsing one after the other as they are successively presented. Aion, on the other hand, is not bound by such a successive account: for Aion, not only is the present always already split into 'the essentially unlimited past and futures' (LS 61), but this freedom from the present means that Aion is able to strafe the entire past and future simultaneously. As a result, when we refer to the before and after of time, we must be clear *which* time it is we are referring to. For example, tomorrow will come after today just as surely as Alice will age corporeally as the days go by, but this is only true according to Chronos. In Aion, the incorporeal past is simultaneous with the incorporeal future and Alice cannot grow without shrinking, becoming larger *at the same time* as she becomes smaller than she will be (LS 1).

Although this theory of coexistence (and in particular the example of Alice) might seem to be nothing more than a play on words, Deleuze and Guattari point out that this challenge to traditional cause-effect accounts is by no means unscientific or merely linguistic:

> And it is true that the human sciences, with their materialist, evolutionary, and even dialectical schemas, lag behind the richness and complexity of causal relations in physics, or even in biology. Physics and biology present us with reverse causalities that are *without finality* but testify nonetheless to an action of the future on the present, or of the present on the past, for example, the convergent wave and the anticipated potential, which imply an inversion of time. More than breaks or zigzags, it is these reverse causalities that shatter evolution. (ATP 431)

These reverse causalities do not so much suggest that we can go back in (chronological) time, as if yesterday was just around the corner. What they rather refer to is how something that has not yet arrived can still have an impact upon what has by forming an effective limit. Thus Deleuze and Guattari argue that '[the archaic State] was already acting before it appeared, as the actual limit these primitive societies warded off, or as the point toward which they converged but could not reach without self-destructing' (ATP 431).

As is clear from this quote, Deleuze and Guattari's promotion of reverse causalities is tied up with their thoughts on critical points of change. For a critical point of change to exist, there must already be a threshold of consistency on the other side of that point. This means that before a critical point is reached and crossed, what lies awaiting on the other side must in some sense already exist. This sense is most commonly associated by Deleuze (and Deleuzians) with the virtual. It is also commonly explained by using the example of temperature: on either side of the critical point 0 °C lie the consistencies of ice and water. When considered virtually, both thresholds exist simultaneously, but when considering the actual state of a particular body/substance, there is at most an ongoing succession of one after the other, a process whereby coexisting virtualities are consecutively actualised by crossing a critical point of change.[2]

By adopting this ontology, the paradox of something existing before it does dissolves. As long as a sharp distinction is maintained between the two kinds of time – Aion and Chronos – and the two kinds of existence – virtual and actual – then there is no conflict between Deleuze and Guattari's anti-evolutionism and their account of the State's evolution. The former refers to the State apparatus or State form that exists simultaneously with other social machines, while the latter refers to the particular ways in which these virtual machines are actualised in a chronology. When put in this manner, we can see why Deleuze and Guattari argue that: 'All history does is to translate a coexistence of becomings into a succession' (ATP 430). History is defined in this statement as a progression or string of actual occurrences that is distinct from the simultaneous existence of virtual machines.

In their analysis of different regimes of signs, Deleuze and Guattari make the same point: the designations of first and second are not given 'from the standpoint of an abstract evolutionism' (ATP 117). As they stipulate, although the various semiotics and their mixtures may appear in a history, 'We are not suggesting an evolutionism, we are not even doing history' (ATP 119). In this study of signs, what is crucial is the distinction between an abstract machine and a concrete assemblage. An abstract machine is defined as follows:

> [A]n abstract machine is neither an infrastructure that is determining in the last instance nor a transcendental Idea that is determining in the supreme instance. Rather, it plays a piloting role. The diagrammatic or abstract machine does not function to represent, even something real but rather constructs a real that is yet to come, a new type of reality. Thus when it constitutes points of creation or potentiality it does not stand outside history but is instead always 'prior to' history. Everything escapes, everything creates – never alone, but through an abstract machine that produces continuums of intensity, effects conjunctions of deterritorialization, and extracts expressions and contents. (ATP 142)

As we can see here, if an abstract machine is not a force of historicism, this is primarily because an abstract machine comes prior to history itself. In this sense it belongs in the domain of prehistory: abstract machines are prehistorical or unhistorical formations that guide or pilot a history that will come.[3] When such a history does unfold, it does so in the form of concrete assemblages, within which various abstract machines exist simultaneously. These assemblages are therefore mixtures *of* machines, which is why they are also referred to as machinic assemblages – the 'properly machinic' (ATP 146). Machinic assemblages put into play or effectuate in history the abstract machines that coexist prior to and beyond history. Put otherwise, assemblages convert an abstract diagram into an actual programme that can 'distribute everything and bring a circulation of movement with alternatives, jumps, and mutations' (ATP 146–7). It is in this spirit of separation between the abstract and the concrete, the untimely and the historical, the diagrammatic and the programmatic, that Deleuze and Guattari provide the following suggestion: 'Perhaps we must say that all progress is made by and in striated space, but all becoming occurs in smooth space' (ATP 486).

But as we saw in Chapter 3, the rigid aligning of history with the striated and becoming with the smooth is by no means the final word on history or becoming: on the one hand, the progression of history need not be homogeneously measured or confined by teleology, but can be open, unpredictable and nomadic; and on the other hand, becoming need not already reach its infinitive limits, but can proceed in a more cautious and incremental fashion. Chapters 1 and 2 came to similar conclusions: creation cannot be solely attributed to an enveloping surface becoming, since this surface is itself dynamically produced; intensity cannot be divorced from history, insofar as history is not synonymous with explication but is rather an intensive movement from depth itself that is distinct from the extensive series explicated on the surface. In light of these analyses, the relatively straightforward explanation of the State in which its virtual and simultaneous form is separated from its actual and historical instantiations can be shown to be inadequate.

This can be highlighted if we compare Deleuze and Guattari's virtual/actual ontology with its Bergsonian source. When Bergson first developed his virtual/actual ontology, he specifically used it to distinguish between a past that no longer exists as the present but nevertheless continues to coexist with it in some capacity.[4] This means that for Bergson the critical point is not so much between virtuals (e.g. ice on one side and water on the other) but between a virtual past and an actual present (e.g. a present sonic note and the past progression or phrase that led to it, and thus exists in it virtually). As such, *the past is essentially virtual*, separated in kind from the present it moves towards as it is actualised.[5] Bergson thus does not distinguish between two versions of the past – Aionic/virtual and chronological/actual – that are in turn correlated with becoming and history. Rather, what becomes is our history as it continually surges from the past to meet the present. History is not just a reading or representation of the virtual past, in the same way that Chronos has its own present interpretation of becoming (LS 164). Rather, history *is* the movement of the virtual past. For instance, as we saw in Chapter 1, Bergson claims that if we are to truly come to know something then we must be able to look beyond its superficial present and see it *in depth*. But what is this depth if not the history of its present moment? Bergson's point is that this historical past cannot be 'forever done with', since it forms a continuum of duration that reaches towards and joins with the present in order to make it 'thick' (Bergson 2007: 106). History is thus not in conflict with the virtual or consigned to the concrete and actual. If bled of its virtuality, it is little wonder that history appears anaemic and lifeless. But when its virtuality is reasserted, as Bergson would have it, history is shown to play a vital role in the production of life.

In light of this reappraisal, it is somewhat misleading to suggest that the virtual and the actual correspond to two opposing or isolated readings of time. As it turns out, the virtual and the actual are two sides that *together* provide the productive circuit from which time gains its enduring nature. If there is a simultaneity in Bergson it is therefore this: two successive moments are rendered simultaneous by contraction-détente not specifically for the purposes of bringing out their incorporeal and atemporal nature but so that time may indeed be allowed to *elapse*. Furthermore, the successive moments that are rendered simultaneous need not be immediately adjacent, but can be brought forth from the farthest recesses of the virtual past to resonate with the critical point of present actuality. For example, when a note is actualised in a melody, it brings forth or *accentuates* tonic notes that were 'long past', while simultaneously mitigating the importance of the 'just past'. This means that while the nature of the note actualised is dependent upon the past progression that leads to it, so too is the past progression dependent upon the demands of the present: one cannot be exclusively reduced to the other, since they are mutually presupposing. Thus while all of the past may be said to coexist with the present (we carry all of it along at every moment), this does not occur at the expense of time's succession or even in contrast to it. Rather, the succession and simultaneity of time are two sides of the same coin called duration: duration corresponds neither to the simultaneous/Aionic nature of becoming nor the successive/ chronological image of history, for it is more than either of them. It is a prolongation or continuity of a heterogeneous moment, a moment *in* which time endures or transpires by pulling together two differences in kind – succession and simultaneity, the virtual and the actual, the past and the present, history and becoming.

This point can be further explained by taking an example from economics. According to classical political economy, the four stages of production, distribution, exchange and consumption progressively proceed from one to the other in a causal-linear fashion. But as Marx shows in the introduction to the *Grundrisse*, this account is for the most part a fabrication, since each of the four elements must be mutually determined; not one of them can be considered or defined independently. This leads Marx to state the following:

> The conclusion we reach is not that production, distribution, exchange and consumption are identical, but that they all form the members of a totality, distinctions within a unity. [. . .] Mutual interaction takes place between the different moments. This the case with every organic whole. (Marx 1975: 99–100)

On the one hand, this mutual determination clearly suggests an ontology of simultaneity; production, for example, does not happen before consumption, for 'Production is also immediately consumption' (Marx 1975: 90). On the other hand, however, this ontology is developed by Marx for the explicit purpose of combating the ahistorical idea of human nature that the classical account relies upon. Marx's primary objective, in other words, is to *put history back in the process and the process back in history*. As Jason Read astutely summarises:

> It is against this conception of the social, of the anthropological foundation of the social, that Marx presents a fundamentally different relation between production, distribution, exchange, and consumption that is thoroughly historical. Or, put differently, rather than maintaining the simple and linear causality of natural needs and historical mediations, Marx develops a thought of the complex relations of production, distribution, exchange, and consumption in which all act on and determine each other and, to a certain extent, produce each other. (Read 2003b: 50)

The simultaneity of mutual determination must therefore not be taken to be contrary to the historical but if anything its affirmation. The 'unity' or 'organic whole' which Marx speaks of above, moreover, quite clearly resonates with the Bergsonian organic and open whole that we have touched on: a whole that indeed renders a multiplicity of elements simultaneously, but does so precisely so that time may be allowed to pass (successively endure) and that historical contingency may be asserted. The implication that simultaneity occurs at the expense of succession is thus false, for as the examples from Bergson and Marx have shown us, each is rather an enabler for the other within the organic whole that they together form – the 'new monism' or pluralism which I advanced in Chapter 3.

Returning to Deleuze and Guattari's example of the prehistory of the State apparatus, we can now see that this prehistory need not be in opposition to a history that follows, insofar as the two will require one another for their very nature. But more importantly, Bergson's philosophy demonstrates how any designation of the former as virtual and the latter as actual will arguably still fail to address the paradox we began with. Our task, if we remember, was to locate the emergence of the State apparatus and explain how its prehistory could coexist with its subsequent history. Deleuze and Guattari's response to this paradox was to distinguish between the virtual and the actual, and subsequently show that while actual States emerge chronologically (see ATP 448–60), the virtual State form has always existed. This response, however, does not exactly answer the question of when and how the State apparatus first emerged, for it merely displaces it by hiving off succession/progression in the realm of the actual. The paradox thus persists, despite Deleuze and Guattari's evasive manoeuvre, since the question of succession must still be put to the virtual itself, regardless of its own simultaneous pretensions: Have all virtualities always existed? If so, then how (and how many), and if not, then which came first, followed by what and why? The State form may appear to be immemorial, but is it really, and if so why and how? Simply because it is virtual? Or is there some other particular and limited reason? Such questions are necessitated by the fact that the virtual, as we can now see from our return to Bergson, is not a realm in which to hide from temporality, but is a part of duration itself. Virtualities have a history, and not just of actuality or in actuality, for history is also virtual. We must therefore ask after this history of virtuality.

As this history can clearly not be the history-as-actual that Deleuze and Guattari criticise, it must be admitted that there is another history at work in their ontology – a history that is not opposed to the virtual but a part of it. This other history should be able to better respond to the unresolved questions regarding the birth, succession and simultaneity of virtual machines such as the State apparatus. To the extent that this history will differ from a standard causal-linear history, it will also require a new name. Whereas I nominated 'nomadic history' in Chapter 3, there is another worthy candidate in the work of Deleuze and Guattari: *universal history*. Universal history makes a composite out of succession and simultaneity from its ability to array an entire successive progression simultaneously. It is indeed only with respect to this universal history that Deleuze and Guattari are able to define the archaic State and distinguish it from the other forms that will follow (see ATP 459); it is none other than universal history, in other words, that illustrates how various social formations lead to and interact with one another. But what is universal history and how is it responsible for determining the various relations between succession and simultaneity, history and becoming? And more fundamentally, how can Deleuze and Guattari espouse a universal history at all when they are so firmly against historicism?

The universalism of capitalism

The notion of a universal history comes to prominence in Deleuze and Guattari's work within the context of their machinic history, spread throughout the two volumes of *Capitalism and Schizophrenia*. In explaining the relation between the three great social machines – the primitive territorial machine, the barbarian despotic/imperial machine and the civilised capitalist machine – Deleuze and Guattari present a sequential account that forms a kind of history. First there is the primitive territorial machine, which carries out a coding of the earth; then there is the imperial machine, which overcodes these various codes, diverting them all to a despot; and finally there is the capitalist machine, which proceeds by decoding every instance of coding and overcoding in order to allow for their exchange and continual reinscription. While this appears to present a neat and tidy historical causal-linear progression from one to the other, Deleuze and Guattari insist that such is by no means the case: for example, not only are primitive machines eminently contemporary, but so too has the capitalist machine always existed. As such, if a progression exists from the primitive to the capitalist machines, it is specifically with respect to the universal history that the capitalist machine produces: 'capitalism determines the conditions and the possibility of a universal history' (AO 140). Of the three machines it is thus capitalism that brings about a universal history. Let us then look more closely at the nature of this machine and its universalism, so that we may see how it contours Deleuze and Guattari's understanding and use of universal history, and furthermore, the historicity of virtualities.

For Deleuze and Guattari, there are two defining features of the capitalist machine: (1) its superior power of decoding/ deterritorialisation; and (2) its axiomatic structure. The former facet is responsible for breaking down existing codes in a society. Unlike the despotic machine which reinscribes a social field by subverting productive flows into a surplus of code, the capitalist machine achieves this by specialising in the *exchange* and *flow* of capital: capitalism transforms code into flux (AO 228). For example, it makes no difference to a capitalist 'what' is inscribed in each code (as well as what kind of society produces it), for all that matters is the translation of those codes into capital flow so that differences between them can be *capitalised* on. In today's world it is perhaps the futures-trader that best illustrates this activity. As codes travel across a computer screen, the trader is not so much concerned with its actual value as he/she is with its *differential* value – the difference between two actual values. Given this ethic and ontology, the process of capitalisation does not even make any intrinsic claims on efficiency: it matters not to capitalism whether the capital produced is done so by the most advanced means or the most antiquated; a place will be found for all, provided it contributes to the increased production of capital flow. If capitalism is thought of as a modern phenomenon, it is therefore only insofar as it is *anachronistic*; capitalism does not kill off the past, but puts it to work.

This characterisation of capitalism, whereby capitalism is equated with the ongoing and amorphous decoding of flows, aptly describes what Marx might have meant by his dictum: 'all that is solid melts into air'. As the social machine that trades in codes and proliferates vectors of deterritorialisation, capitalism can be said to exert the nomadic force of a war machine. Indeed, the capitalist and the nomad have much in common. Both, for instance, resist the regulations of the State apparatus: the nomad constructs a war machine directed towards breaking State striation, while the capitalist measures their worth by how effectively loopholes can be found, created and exploited.

Nevertheless, it must be remembered that this aspect of capitalism only accounts for one half of its nature. Aside from its tendency to decode and deterritorialise, capitalism is also defined by its tendency to axiomatise decoded flows: '[Capitalism] axiomatizes with the one hand what it decodes with the other' (AO 246).[6] By axiomatic, Deleuze and Guattari explicitly mean that as defined and used by modern mathematics:

> If it is true that we are not using the word axiomatic as a simple meta-phor, we must review what distinguishes an axiomatic from all manner of codes, overcodings, and recodings: the axiomatic deals directly with purely functional elements and relations whose nature is not specified, and which are immediately realised in highly varied domains simultane-ously; codes, on the other hand, are relative to those domains and express specific relations between qualified elements that cannot be subsumed by a higher formal unity (overcoding) except by transcendence and in an indirect fashion. The *immanent axiomatic* finds in the domains it moves through so many models, termed *models of realization*. (ATP 454)

Thus axioms do not offer their own exegeses but rather provide the formal system and operational field in which differential relations and capitalisations occur. Because of this, the axiomatic axis of capitalism is uniquely positioned to interface with the processes of becoming that define its other side. As the pure immanence of flow continues to evade codes and overcodings unabated, the capitalist machine can appropriate any and all of these escaping lines of flight by simply adding on a new axiom or subtracting an old one. This gives capitalism an unrivalled flexibility and multiple realisability. Changes in the social field lead to the addition of new axioms, which in turn generate a new structure from which further decodings escape, only to then be reabsorbed by the addition of new axioms that 'capitalise' upon the newly generated difference: 'How much flexibility there is in the axiomatic of capitalism, always ready to widen its own limits so as to add a new axiom to a previously saturated system' (AO 238). In this manner, capitalism continually displaces its own limits in the very same moment (or movement) that it realises them. This is indeed the 'deepest law of capitalism: it continually sets and then repels its own limits, but in so doing gives rise to numerous flows in all directions that escape its axiomatic' (ATP 472; see also N 171 and AO 231). As this quote indicates, what defines capitalism is not simply the subordination of deterritorialisation to axiomatisation – the domination, as it were, of capture over creation – since capitalism is equally defined by its ability to produce new flows. Capitalism thus cannot be reduced to either of its two tendencies, for it is more precisely constituted and defined by the complementary way in which its processes of axiomatisation and deterritorialisation, or repression and release, interact.

Throughout the history of capitalism, this insurmountable strength, in which 'its axiomatic is never saturated [since] it is always capable of adding a new axiom to the previous ones' (AO 250), has been exhibited on numerous occasions:

> After the end of World War I, the joint influence of the world depression and the Russian Revolution forced capitalism to multiply its axioms, to invent new ones dealing with the working class, employment, union organization, social institutions, the role of the State, the foreign and domestic markets. Keynesian economics and the New Deal were axiom laboratories. Examples of the creation of new axioms after the Second World War: the Marshall Plan, forms of assistance and lending, transformations in the monetary system. (ATP 462)

The more recent 'global financial crisis' of 2008 could be seen as another axiom laboratory. As new regulations and ways of doing business are implemented by various institutions and capitalists, the capitalist machine progresses, making an unfortunate mockery of those who saw the crisis as a crisis *of* capitalism. On the contrary, capitalism is not itself in crisis or meltdown, for capitalism feeds on such crises: capitalism *is* crisis. If the term 'meltdown' is still an appropriate way of describing the events of the recent financial crisis, it is therefore because it explains how the capitalist machine melts down various axioms through intensified flows of evasion, and as a result institutes new axioms based on those escaped flows. Furthermore, as soon as new axioms are established, whether it be the creation of a new regulatory body or amendments to the financial codes of conduct, new decodings and deterritorialisations are released which both take advantage of the new system and evade it.[7]

This ability to continually meet and overcome its own limits brings out a key aspect of the capitalist machine: there are no sacred axioms in capitalism.[8] Capitalism exhibits a profound heterogeneity, a willingness if not need to incessantly change what it 'is'. This is why Deleuze and Guattari claim that capitalism is *isomorphic* as opposed to homogeneous: the capitalist machine does not make everything the same in kind but rather trades in all kinds. Although capitalism instantiates an axiomatic nexus (the capitalist world market) that in a way limits or conditions international relations, this limit is not foundational or final. Indeed, the capitalist machine *requires* a peripheral polymorphy of heteromorphic social formations that enable the capitalisation of difference to continue. Far from homogenising the world, capitalism 'gives rise to and organises the "Third World"' (ATP 437). Thus capitalism welcomes its others and enemies, since its very strength is drawn from those forces that are outside it and resist it. There is nothing better for the capitalist machine than a good healthy recession, for this creates instability, driving down wages and increasing the *rates* of profit. Wars and taxes are other good ways to clear out room for capitalist *growth*. Combined with the abilities of technology and consumer society, the capitalist machine can practically find aid anywhere in its proliferation of and capitalisation on flow surplus – like a Nietzschean sickness, its strength resides precisely in the manner of its afflictions:

> The dysfunctions are an essential element of its very ability to function, which is not the least important aspect of the system of cruelty. The death of a social machine has never been heralded by a disharmony or a dysfunction; on the contrary, social machines make a habit of feeding on the contradictions they give rise to, on the crises they provoke, on the anxieties they *engender*, and on the infernal operations they regenerate. Capitalism has learned this, and has ceased doubting itself, while even socialists have abandoned belief in the possibility of capitalism's natural death by attrition. No one has ever died from contradictions. And the more it breaks down, the more it schizophrenizes, the better it works, the American way. (AO 151)

None respected and marvelled at the force of capitalism more than Marx. But as we can see in this analysis, Deleuze and Guattari's version of capitalism, where even its contradictions make it stronger, provides us with a theory that better corresponds to the formidable reality capitalism has become. It further explains how capitalism is not exactly 'in league' with the State apparatus nor opposed to it. Our discussion of the two sides of capitalism – decoding/deterritorialisation and axiomatisation – makes this clear. While it is true that an axiomatic is 'a stopping point' and that '[t]he great axiomaticians are the men of State', Deleuze and Guattari also point out that creation and contingency are in part produced by axiomatisation: 'It is the real characteristics of axiomatics that lead us to say that capitalism and present-day politics are an axiomatic in the literal sense. *But it is precisely for this reason that nothing is played out in advance*'. To oppose axiomatisation to decoding/deterritorialisation or creativity is thus mistaken: 'an axiomatic is not at all a transcendent, autonomous, and decision-making power opposed to experimentation and intuition'. This is because not only must the two work in concert to produce anything, but also because even axiomatics 'has its own gropings in the dark, experimentations, modes of intuition' (above quotes from ATP 461, emphasis added).

When so described, Deleuze and Guattari's capitalism takes on a unique flavour. On the one hand, capitalism is clearly repressive and reactive, constituting a system of subjugation far more pervasive than the despotic machine (AO 254). But on the other hand, capitalism is the quintessential machine of decoding and deterritorialisation. Indeed, it is due to this aspect that Deleuze and Guattari, far from advocating that capitalism be stopped or 'brought under control', call for the further *intensification* of capitalism:

> But which is the revolutionary path? Is there one? – To withdraw from the world market, as Samir Amin advises Third World countries to do, in a curious revival of the fascist 'economic solution'? Or might it be to go in the opposite direction? To go still further, that is, in the movement of the market, of decoding and deterritorialisation? For perhaps the flows are not yet deterritorialized enough, not decoded enough, from the viewpoint of a theory and a practice of a highly schizophrenic character. Not to withdraw from the process, but to go further, to 'accelerate the process', as Nietzsche put it: in this matter, the truth is that we haven't seen anything yet. (AO 239–40)

As this passage shows us, Deleuze and Guattari do not necessarily advocate the acceleration of capitalism because they wish to spread misery to the point of system failure (i.e. classical communism), and nor do they do so because they believe capitalism brings justice and wealth to all. If the increased intensification of capitalism provides a 'revolutionary path', it is by virtue of its great capacity for change. But as we have seen above, change is not only attributable to deterritorialisation. While the axiomatic of capitalism may be a force of conjunction distinct from deterritorialisation, it is no less a trigger for change. As Paul Patton reminds us: '[T]he axioms of the capitalist social machine do not simply repress a natural state of free and undirected social existence. They are also constitutive of new social forces and forms of life' (Patton 2000: 105). In this respect, capitalism, as defined by Deleuze and Guattari, cannot be so easily dismissed as being exclusively repressive or reactive, nor can it be venerated solely for its superior deterritorialisation, for it also creates, and creates through the relation of *both* its sides. To suggest that the creativity of capitalism is attributable to only its side of deterritorialisation, whereas its axiomatic side inhibits this process, is thus mistaken. If the capitalist machine is creative in a way unlike all others, it is due to its ability to productively combine its superior deterritorialisation with an axiomatic of equal stature.

When capitalism is so described, it becomes impossible to perfectly define the form of the capitalist machine from the outset, for capitalism itself is constantly breaking down – it is by no means a well-oiled machine, but a beautiful disaster. Capitalism is characterised by anachronism, by fits and bursts, ebbs and flows, axiomatisation and deterritorialisation. This nature allows capitalism to incorporate all that has come before it, forming nothing less than 'a motley painting of everything that has ever been believed' (AO 34, 267).[9] And it is in doing so that capitalism gives rise to a universal history. Capitalism is able to occupy every point in history, for it has no point of its own; it is able to interpret every coding and overcoding throughout history, for it has no essential code or sign of its own. Like a spectre or faceless ghost, capitalism haunts all previous forms of society 'as their terrifying nightmare, [. . .] the dread they feel of a flow that would elude their codes' (AO 140). But given that this universalisation of history is brought about by the complete lack of essential code or overcoding, it becomes clear that Deleuze and Guattari's universal history will differ markedly from those forms of universal history that subordinate history to a guiding spirit, essence or endpoint. In a word, Deleuze and Guattari's universal history will not be defined by a *necessary* outcome, analytic process or eternal truth, but by the *contingency* of all things: 'universal history is the history of contingencies, and not the history of necessity' (AO 140, 195 and 224). But what do Deleuze and Guattari actually mean by this statement, and in particular by contingency? As I shall now demonstrate, how one understands the meaning of contingency can have significant ramifications for Deleuze and Guattari's conception of universal history and the philosophy of historical creativity it is a part of.

The contingency of universal history

The nature of contingency in Deleuze and Guattari's account of universal history can be broadly interpreted in three different ways: forward-looking, retrospective and continuously non-linear. To begin with, one could say that something is contingent insofar as it need not have occurred – things could have been different: 'For great accidents were necessary, and amazing encounters that could have happened elsewhere, or before, or might never have happened, in order for the flows to escape coding and, escaping, to nonetheless fashion a new machine bearing the determinations of the capitalist socius' (AO 140). As we can see here, even the emergence of that machine which universalises the past (in a way distinct from other machines) was due in part to contingent encounters and unforeseen accidents. In this sense, any history, including universal history, is a history of things that could have occurred differently or not at all.

As Jason Read rightly points out, Deleuze and Guattari's emphasis on the contingent nature of capitalism's emergence is lifted from Marx's early writings (Read 2003a: §4). Capitalism arises, according to Marx, from an encounter between free labour and capital-money. This encounter, however, is not sufficient by itself, for it need not lead to capitalism. Marx illustrates this by using a Roman example:

> Thus one fine morning there were to be found on the one hand free men stripped of everything except their labor power, and on the other, the owners of all the acquired wealth ready to exploit this labor. What happened? The Roman proletarians became not wage laborers but a mob of do-nothings more abject than those known as 'poor whites' in the South of the United States, and alongside them there developed a mode of production which was not capitalist but based on slavery. Thus events strikingly analogous but taking place in different historical surroundings led to totally different results. By studying each of these forms of evolution separately and then comparing them one can easily find the clue to this phenomenon, but one will never arrive there by using as one's master

key a general historico-philosophical theory, the supreme virtue of which consists in being supra-historical. (Marx and Engels 1955: 294)[10]

This example emphasises the role that contingency and appropriateness play in Marx's conception of history: there is no 'master key' that exists prior to the unfolding of history, for even necessary principles must obey the contingency of history (rather than the other way around). Deleuze and Guattari will reiterate this point every time they echo the question of capitalism's contingency: 'Why capitalism in the West rather than in China of the third or even the eighth century' (WP 95–7; see also AO 197, 224, ATP 452 and F 21)? Deleuze and Guattari proffer their own answer to this question, largely lifted from the historians Etienne Balazs and Fernand Braudel.[11] The specifics of this response are, however, irrelevant to the point that I am making: to take such a question seriously is to demonstrate how there is no necessary relation between a set of structural elements and a *particular outcome*. What is contingent in this case is thus the *outcome* of an encounter. Because of this, it must be noted that if Deleuze and Guattari's questioning of capitalism's emergence employs a sense of contingency, it does so to illustrate how the *future* of an encounter is contingent. The contingency that is being emphasised in Marx's example above, for instance, is not whether an encounter will occur, but the *result* from two encounters that are strikingly analogous (i.e. one encounter that results in capitalism and another, similar in kind, that results in slavery). The lesson from Marx's Roman example is therefore that we cannot fully know the future of an encounter in advance, even if we are completely aware of its principle elements, since what will arise from the encounter cannot be solely deduced from its structural form. Although this lesson is drawn from an analysis of the past, Marx's point here is not to suggest that the past *as past* is changeable but rather that when the past *was present*, it need not have happened as it did. As such, even when this treatment of contingency is carried out through an analysis of the past, it is essentially forward-looking, for its ultimate value is found in the way it liberates the future for us. One might in turn suggest that the past is itself dependent upon the way in which the present posits it. But insofar as this is true, it indicates that we will require another sense of contingency, a sense that is not only forward-looking but *retrospective*.

This brings us to a second sense or way of using contingency: universal history is contingent *with respect to* that force which universalises it. Unlike the first sense of contingency, which merely indicates how any given occurrence 'need not have happened, or happened in the way it did' (since the future is open, to a certain extent), this second sense addresses how eventualities are *contingent upon* certain forces. Deleuze and Guattari offer two main examples of this. The first reprises the power of the State apparatus and despotic social machine. As we have seen, the despot's power is derived directly from those who serve under him or her; the despot redirects, overcodes and captures the productive forces of others. Once captured, this power itself becomes the cause of servitude, but only on the condition that it provides a convincing tale of its origins in order to justify its continued appropriation of productive power. Thus every despot retrospectively generates its origins. If an origin tale is to be effective, it must cover over the contingency of the status quo. But once a State apparatus is made indisputable, it also gives off the appearance of emerging fully formed, since the inevitability of its *complete* realisation is presumed to exist from the outset. This is why the first, archaic or Asiatic State is also the primordial *Urstaat*: 'the eternal model of everything the State wants to be and desires' (AO 217; see also ATP 359). In this way, the State apparatus not only makes the past contingent upon its power of capture, but it also teleologically reduces the future to its eternal image. Or put otherwise, the *Urstaat* not only finds itself fully formed at the beginning of time, but also at the end, from where it carries out a retrospective of all that has occurred and finds itself in every frame:

> [The despotic State or *Urstaat*] appears to be set back at a remove from what it transects and from what it resects, as though it were giving evidence of another dimension, a cerebral ideality that is added to, superimposed on the material evolution of societies, a regulating idea or principle of reflection (terror) that organizes the parts and the flows into a whole. What is transected, supersected, or overcoded by the despotic State is what comes before – the territorial machine, which it reduces to the state of bricks, of working parts henceforth subjected to the cerebral idea. In this sense the despotic State is indeed the origin, but the origin as an abstraction that must include its differences with respect to the concrete beginning. (AO 219)

As a second example, Deleuze and Guattari note, again following Marx, that capitalists carry out a similar procedure on the past. On the one hand, capitalism is said to arise with the combination of capital and workers, but on the other hand it is none other than capitalism that gives rise to 'capital' and 'workers' to begin with. In order to resolve this paradox, capitalism must therefore tell a story about how an *original* accumulation of capital occurs that in turn allows capitalism to 'get off the ground'. This is traditionally done by appealing to the virtue of 'thrift': due to their unique thriftiness, as the story goes, the first proto-capitalists were able to generate their own productive difference upon which they rightfully capitalised. Such a story, however, is told after the fact by those who benefited, precisely so that they may legitimately continue to do so. As Marx puts it:

> This primitive accumulation plays approximately the same role in political economy as original sin does in theology. Adam bit the apple, and thereupon sin fell on the human race. Its origin is supposed to be explained when it is told as an anecdote about the past. Long, long ago there were two sorts of people; one the diligent, intelligent, and above all frugal elite; the other lazy rascals, spending their substance, and more, in riotous living. (Marx 1977: 873)

Moreover, as with State power, capitalism is retrospectively contingent not only because it creates its beginnings but also because it places itself at the end of history. In the case of capitalism, what occurred prior to it is defined in relation to its particular power to decode: 'It is the thing, the unnamable, the generalized decoding of flows that reveals *a contrario* the secret of all these formations [of coding and overcoding]. [. . .] Whence the possibility of a retrospective reading of all history in terms of capitalism' (AO 153). Capitalism thus gives rise to a universal history (in part) because it projects its origins *and* those of previous social formations (which now culminate in capitalism): 'If capitalism is the universal truth, it is so in the sense that makes capitalism *the negative* of all social formations' (AO 153). Marx famously describes this situation in his *Grundrisse*:

> Bourgeois society is the most developed and the most complex historic organization of production. The categories which express its relations, the comprehension of its structure, thereby also allows insights into the structure and the relations of production of all the vanished social formations out of whose ruins and elements it built itself up, whose partly still unconquered remnants are carried along with it, etc. Human anatomy contains a key to the anatomy of the ape. The intimations of higher development among the subordinate animal species, however, can be understood only after the higher development is already known. The bourgeois economy thus supplies the key to the ancient, etc. (Marx 1975: 105)[12]

Because of this retrospective power, the genital accounts which Marx, Deleuze and Guattari give of capitalism's emergence must be taken with a grain of salt. In some locations, capitalism is said to arise due to the encounter of flows of labour with flows of money-capital, whereas in others 'the capitalist machine begins when capital ceases to be a capital of alliance to become a filiative capital' (Deleuze and Guattari 1984: 227).[13] But regardless of which response is given to the question of capitalism's emergence (or whether there is an intrinsic relation between the two), my point here is that its truth or accuracy is itself dependent upon the universal history that posits it. For example, in order to identify the particular conjunction of naked labour and pure wealth as the catalyst for capitalism, or alternatively constant and variable capital, we must already be in possession of the virtual form of capitalism – that form which defines capitalism by its ability to constitute an axiomatic of decoded flows. Thus when Deleuze and Guattari specifically locate the origins of capitalism in a particular differential conjunction, this tale is only valid from the *retrospective* angle of a universal history. Put otherwise, where we happen to find the 'concrete beginning' of the capitalist machine (as with the ideal or abstract *Urstaat*) will depend upon the precise definition of the virtual machine that we begin with. The retrospective nature of contingency is thus insufficient on its own in answering how virtual machines such as capitalism arise, for it does nothing more than show us how origin tales are contingent upon the power that retrospectively posits them. If universal history is to be truly contingent, it must therefore have more to offer than mere retrospectivity.

Before I go on to suggest what this might be, it would perhaps be prudent to expand on my last claim, given the tendency within the secondary literature on Deleuze and Guattari's universal history to focus on its retrospectivity.[14] There are a few notions that might be of help to us here. The first is 'quasi-causality'. A quasi-cause, to explain in short, causes itself as an effect. Capitalists, for example, make a quasi-cause of themselves when they cause the process that leads to them. The capitalist machine can furthermore be described as the quasi-causal machine par excellence, since it is not beholden to any one quasi-cause but on the contrary proliferates and trades in them, so long as it is to 'the benefit of the capitalist system and in the service of its ends' (AO 233) – namely, capitalisation. Capital is thus the ultimate quasi-cause, not only in the sense that existing capital is used to create future capital (filiative capital), but also in the sense that existing capital is used to retrospectively create the *past* of that capital.

The concept of immanent-causality would be another way of explaining this capacity. According to this concept, an effect cannot be said to transcend its cause, since the two must be immanent to one another. As Althusser remarks when critiquing the 'two-level reality' of inside/outside that is pervasive in Marx studies: 'The effects of the structure of the whole can only be the existence of the structure itself' (Althusser and Balibar 1979: 191). There is thus no disconnect between an interior pure essence and an outside phenomenon, for the two are entirely immanent to one another. Or as Deleuze puts it:

> What do we mean here by immanent cause? It is a cause which is realized, integrated and distinguished in its effect. Or rather the immanent cause is realized, integrated and distinguished by its effect. In this way there is a correlation or mutual presupposition between cause and effect, between abstract machine and concrete assemblages [. . .] (F 37)

This idea of an immanent relation between cause and effect is a mainstay of Deleuze's philosophy and goes back to his understanding of the correlation between a problem and its solution. A solution, Deleuze observes, is always immanent to the problem it is a part of. To 'find' a solution we must therefore go back to the problem, *evaluate* its singularities and *state* them properly. As Deleuze remarks in the opening paragraph of his *Nietzsche and Philosophy*: 'We always have the beliefs, feelings and thoughts that we deserve given our way of being or our style of life' (NP 1). As it happens, this point is also the starting place for Deleuze's take on Bergsonism:

> [T]he problem always has the solution it deserves, in terms of the way in which it is stated (i.e., the conditions under which it is determined as a problem), and of the means and terms at our disposal for stating it. In this sense, the history of man, from the theoretical as much as from the practical point of view, is that of the construction of problems. (B 16)

In this text Deleuze quotes at length directly from Bergson's essay 'Stating of the Problems', demonstrating that his reading of Bergson is not idiosyncratic (on this point) but rather straightforward. In this passage, the key sentence, according to Deleuze, is the following: 'The stating and solving of the problem are here very close to being equivalent: The truly great problems are set forth only when they are solved' (B 15–16; for the original see Bergson 2007: 37). However, if there is something particularly novel and interesting about Deleuze's reading of this Bergsonian idea, it is the further connection he draws to Marx:

> We might compare the last sentence of this extract from Bergson with Marx's formulation, which is valid for practice itself: 'Humanity only sets itself problems that it is capable of solving'. In neither example is it a case of saying that problems are like the shadow of pre-existing solutions (the whole context suggests the contrary). (B 16)

It is therefore unsurprising that when Deleuze reiterates this point again in *Difference and Repetition*, it will be in aid of confirming Althusser's reading of capitalism's immanent causality:

> Althusser and his collaborators are, therefore, profoundly correct in showing the presence of a genuine structure in *Capital*, and in rejecting historicist interpretations of Marxism, since this structure never acts transitively, following the order of succession in time; rather, it acts by incarnating its varieties in diverse societies and by accounting for the simultaneity of all the relations and terms which, each time and in each case, constitute the present: that is why 'the economic' is never given properly speaking but rather designates a differential virtuality to be interpreted, always covered over by its forms of actualisation; a theme or 'problematic' always covered over by its cases of solution [see Althusser and Balibar, *Reading Capital*, London: New Left Books, 1970: 174 ff., 212 ff.]. [. . .] The famous phrase of the *Contribution to the Critique of Political Economy*, 'mankind always sets itself only such tasks as it can solve', does not mean that the problems are only apparent or that they are already solved, but, on the contrary, that the economic conditions of a problem determine or give rise to the manner in which it finds a solution within the framework of the real relations of the society. [. . .] More precisely, the solution is always that which a society deserves or gives rise to as a consequence of the manner in which, given its real relations, it is able to pose the problems set within it and to it by the differential relations it incarnates. (DR 186)

This passage in fact draws together several of the major themes that I have discussed in this book. The 'structure' which Deleuze is referring to in Althusser's work is ahistorical, universal and synchronic (in keeping with Althusser's brand of structuralism). It furthermore consists of relations that move at infinite speed or simultaneously, thus adhering to the logic of surface becoming that I set out in Chapter 2. This reading of Marx distinguishes itself from historicist interpretations that attempt to explain capitalism by a necessary historical succession, but it does so on the grounds that capitalism, as the social formation that is *presently* in power, retrospectively posits its origins and incarnates itself in prior formations – previous varieties of society are understood *with respect to it*. The past, as such, is covered over with a history that issues backwards from capitalism, just as explicated extensities cover over productive intensities (see Chapter 1) and State forces capture nomadic creations (see Chapter 3). Today's capitalist reality is therefore not merely the effect of an historical cause but rather a 'quasi-cause' or 'immanent cause' of itself, due to its retrospective power and the requirement that all solutions or effects be contoured by the problem or social machine that poses it. In this sense, the capitalist machine works much like the incorporeal event and its surface becoming that we explored in Chapter 2, insofar as it retrospectively 'causes' the chain of actual states of affairs that lead to it via the operation of static genesis.

In his later work, Althusser amends this reading of capitalism's retrospectivity by elaborating further on its prehistory.[15] As he acknowledges, any synchronic logic that purports universal and fixed laws is itself produced by an incremental and developmental process of becoming. There is thus no such thing as necessity, for the concept of necessity can at best only apply to a reading of the past:

> [N]o determination of these elements can be assigned except by *working backwards* from the result to its becoming, in its retroaction. If we must therefore say that there can be no result without its becoming (Hegel), we must also affirm that there is nothing which has become except as determined by the result of this becoming – this retroaction itself (Canguilhem). That is, instead of thinking contingency as a modality of necessity, or an exception to it, we must think necessity as the becoming-necessary of the encounter of contingencies. (Althusser 2006: 193–4)

To label a present fact as necessary is thus somewhat misleading, according to the late Althusser, for it was not always necessary but only *becomes* so. Althusser is attempting in this essay to insist on the contingency of factual occurrences that appear necessarily irrefutable: 'every accomplished fact [. . .] is only a provisional encounter, and since every encounter is provisional even when it lasts, *there is no eternity in the "laws" of any world or any state*' (Althusser 2006: 174, 195–6). Note the resonance of this passage with Deleuze's final chapter of *Difference and Repetition*: laws of nature cannot explain creativity on their own, since they are themselves the extensive manifestation of an intensive process that produces them. Althusser will furthermore agree with Marx, Deleuze and Guattari (and Braudel) that in the case of capitalism, the encounter that leads to its emergence (whether it be between labour and capital-money or constant and filiative capital) was not always necessary but became so 'after the fact' (Althusser 2006: 197–8). Before the encounter, a particular social system was in place – meaning in relative equilibrium. The encounter, however, acts like a tipping point, itself brought about by what Althusser refers to as a 'swerve', shattering that equilibrium and eventually bringing about a new system with its own systematicity. Once settled, this new system in turn redefines necessity, specifically *what is necessary for it*. But most importantly, this necessity need not have happened, for it owes its very nature to a contingent swerve and encounter. Necessity is thus projected backwards over the course of an historical event (Althusser 2006: 169).

Interestingly, Bergson makes precisely the same argument in his essay 'The Possible and the Real'. As his famous quote reads: 'Backwards over the course of time a constant remodelling of the past by the present, of the cause by the effect, is being carried out' (Bergson 2007: 84–5). Bergson is here attacking the same notion of necessity as Althusser but through its companion conception of the possible. As commonly understood in its Aristotelian form, something must be possible before it is realised, like the oak tree whose very possibility is contained in the acorn prior to its realisation. Everything that occurs thus must pre-exist itself as its own possibility. But for Bergson, something which is possible can only *have been* possible:

As reality is created as something unforeseeable and new, its image is reflected behind it into the indefinite past; thus it finds that it has from all time been possible, but it is at this precise moment that it begins to have been always possible, and that is why I said that its possibility, which does not precede its reality, will have preceded it once the reality has appeared. The possible is therefore the mirage of the present in the past; and as we know the future will finally constitute a present and the mirage effect is continually being produced, we are convinced that the image of tomorrow is already contained in our actual present, which will be the past of tomorrow, although we did not manage to grasp it. That is precisely the illusion. (Bergson 2007: 82)

What all these examples have in common is the way in which a present power itself retrospectively posits contingency. Noting this, however, alerts us to their shared limitation: the retrospective sense of contingency is not on its own a genuinely productive and open contingency. In each case, what is being described is the way in which a static sense or being envelops or captures that which is beneath or before it. Whether it be the hardened explication of an intensity, the static summation of a dynamic development or the State capture of a nomadic production, in each case the retrospective form of contingency has more to do with *pouvoir* then it does *puissance* – it has more to do with the static history of contingency than it does the dynamic contingency of history. In the language of Bergson, it has more to do with the Aristotelian possible than it does with the open virtual. And in the language of Althusser, it has more to do with necessity than the becoming (swerve and encounter) of necessity. In such retrospective accounts of creativity, 'Everything is accomplished in advance; *the structure precedes its elements and reproduces them in order to reproduce the structure*' (Althusser 2006: 198). It is for just this reason that each of my studies in this book have sought to get *between* the dualism of historicist succession and simultaneous becoming in order to locate an historical process that is indeed intensive, dynamic and nomadic. The critique of historicism proffered by Marx, Bergson, Althusser, Deleuze and Guattari is most certainly effective in demonstrating how reality and truth is an illusion posited by a presiding power: 'The *retrograde movement* of the true', as Deleuze puts it in his book on Bergson, 'is not merely an illusion *about* the true, but belongs *to* the true itself' (B 34). But it is nevertheless questionable whether this critique is itself capable of advancing a genuinely creative alternative, for the power of retrospectivity will clearly be inadequate.

Given that this retrospective capacity is ultimately a force of capture, it is not surprising that Deleuze and Guattari are also able to affiliate universal history with the *Urstaat*: 'Being the common horizon for what comes before and what comes after, it conditions universal history only provided it is not on the outside, but always off to the side, the cold monster that represents the way in which history is in the 'head', in the 'brain' – the Urstaat' (AO 220–1, translation modified). But in recognising this character trait, we are forced to reappraise the examples of contingency that we have thus far touched on: if 'original accumulation' and 'original sin' are both retrospective, it is in the sense of State-sanctioned histories or 'authorised' biographies (gospel or secular); if Marx's capitalist example of an effect that causes itself is of significance, it is only insofar as it resembles the power of the archaic State or despotic machine, in which '*He* is the sole quasi cause, the source and fountainhead and estuary of the apparent objective movement' (AO 194). This does not mean that such retrospectives are outright unproductive – as Jason Read puts it, 'a misrecognition of the source of production [. . .] is in turn productive, producing obedience and docility' (Read 2003a: §21). But for the same reason that this latter productivity is described by Read as a 'displacement' of the former, and for the same reason that capitalism is the *negative* of all social formations, it must be noted that a retrospective power ultimately pertains more to the power of capture than creation.

In light of this, we must be cautious when discussing the retro-spective contingency of universal history, for it is essentially synony-mous with the *synchronic* power of the despotic machine, a power which freezes time in order to give an ideal description – namely, the description of the *Urstaat* throughout all time. The universal history that ensues from this cannot be solely attributed to the capitalist machine, for what distinguishes capitalism from the synchronic State is its *diachronic* nature, which concerns an *historical development*. This is indeed the 'great difference' between the two: '[T]he despotic machine is synchronic while the capitalist machine's time is dia-chronic. The capitalists appear in succession in a series that institutes a kind of *creativity of history*, a strange menagerie: the schizoid time of the new creative break' (AO 223, emphasis added).

If we are after a genuine contingency, a non-linear contingency, then we must promote a universal history that does not just retro-spectively create history in its image, but allows for a 'creativity of history' itself. This outcome could have perhaps been easily foreseen: that history is written by the victors, and that this history will in turn give rise to various further effects, including the way people act, think, desire and perceive, is by no means a radical claim. In response, it might be argued that new readings of the past can have very real effects on the present (and future). But while this is most certainly true, such a claim does not directly challenge the causal-linear or teleological ontology that this study has been attempting to problematise. Nor does it fit with the particular universalism of capitalism. According to the specifications of the capitalist machine, universal history must be *more* than just that history which is 'written from the standpoint of a present which provides a privileged point of view on the past' (Patton 2000: 96), for capitalism cannot be confined to a single standpoint let alone the present. In short, universal history must *also* be a history in which the past is allowed to have a vital impact upon the present *as itself* in a non-linear fashion.

This brings us to the third way in which universal history is contingent: what is universal is the *continuity* of contingency, meaning that which *continues to be contingent*. In this sense of contingency, the past is not merely shown to 'have been' contingent (so that the future can become so), nor is our 'understanding' of the past merely shown to be contingent upon the forces that posit it. More profoundly, the past is contingent because it is *itself* never done with. The past continues to change ontologically, but not because one static image is replaced by another. It changes because it is vital and alive, *continually coexistent* with the present. The movement of history, when so understood, is not cinemagraphic (like a slideshow) or foregone (gifted by a present), but continuously creative and contingent.

By 'continues' I do not mean well-measured or homogeneous but rather what Bergson calls a continuous and heterogeneous multiplicity. As such, this continuity is full of abruptness and unpredictability. Paradoxically, it might even be more accurate to characterise this continuous multiplicity by 'ruptures and limits, and not continuity' (AO 140). For example, although the history of the French Revolution can be described as a singular trajectory that is continuous and heterogeneous, it can equally be said to be composed of nothing other than accidental encounters (in varying degrees of accidentality). The encounter and the continuum of history, when both understood heterogeneously, are thus not opposed but if anything indistinguishable (as a productive composite). State powers may recast an event in order to break or capture an existing continuity (for example, the contrasting ways in which the French Revolution is captured by the First Empire and the Third Republic, the former reducing the event to Napoleon and the latter to Republicanism), but they only do so by conjoining a new one and becoming in turn a part of future ones. This means that it is not a question of what comes first – the caesura or continuity, the instant or duration, Bachelard or Bergson – nor is it a question of which one is made up of the other, for lingering on such a dichotomy is misleading: they are together one, the differential composite or new monism = pluralism.

Althusser's rendering together of the swerve and the encounter demonstrates this compositionality most capably. As he says, a swerve induces an encounter of one atom 'with the atom next to it, and, from encounter to encounter, a pile-up and the birth of a world – that is to say, of the agglomeration of atoms induced, in a chain reaction, by the initial swerve and encounter' (Althusser 2006: 169,

191). We can thus see how a swerve and an encounter combine to produce a world – a world, moreover, that is in no way necessary but instead always contingently becoming necessary (and becoming unnecessary, it might be added). This becoming, however, is clearly *not* the surface becoming or pure becoming of Deleuze. The swerve-encounter, as a becoming, is not an Aionic organisation of simultaneity, but a 'chain reaction' that more closely resembles what I have termed 'developmental becoming': a world is born from an *unravelling* continuity of heterogeneity, a succession or progression of dynamic and intensive encounters. This becoming does not occur all at once, nor are previous encounters in the chain ever fully done with, since they make themselves felt *as themselves* in the present encounter under consideration (as well as every swerve-encounter in between).[16] As Bergson says when remarking on the process of falling asleep, it is not just the last tick of the clock that causes one to fall asleep. Rather, it is the accumulation of time – the previous ticks heard as it were – that collectively make themselves felt in a present moment that is *rich* or *laden* with them:

When the regular oscillations of the pendulum make us sleepy, is it the last sound heard, the last movement perceived, which produces this effect? No, undoubtedly not, for why then should not the first have done the same? Is it the recollection of the preceding sounds or movements, set in juxtaposition to the last one? But this same recollection, if it is later on set in juxtaposition to a single sound or movement, will remain without effect. Hence we must admit that the sounds combined with one another and acted, not by their quantity as quantity, but by the quality which the quantity exhibited, i.e. by the rhythmic organization of the whole. (Bergson 2001: 105–6)

Deleuze and Guattari's account of the encounter has much in common with Bergson's last tick of the clock and Althusser's tipping point. As Deleuze and Guattari note, the most important point in a series is the penultimate point – the last point before the point of change. The significance of this penultimate point is that it gives consistency to the series that leads up to it; it marks the limit beyond which a new threshold of consistency is engendered. As an example, the most important drink for an alcoholic is the one *before* the one that will force them to discontinue drinking. The ideal alcoholic is thus the one who reaches for the penultimate drink but never for the one after, since to do so would hamper their ability to continue their way of life (ATP 438). Put otherwise, the art of alcoholism consists in knowing how to align the last drink with the penultimate one, for knowing where this penultimate point lies is essential to warding off a change in kind.[17]

My point is, however, the following: it is not *just* the penultimate moment that is responsible for the series leading to it, for the penultimate moment *is itself produced (in part) by that very series.* As Deleuze says of Fitzgerald's and Lowry's alcoholism, their disintegration is in part brought about by the gallons of alcohol already in their body – the body laden with past drinks (LS 157); their crackup may appear suddenly (bearing in mind that the crack line, as I showed in Chapter 3, is the one before the ultimate rupture), but it is certainly not disconnected from the life that has been lived leading up to it, regardless of one's powers of denial. But to be rich with the past is not merely to retrospectively posit it or to 'recollect' it in a certain way, for this would be nothing more than a form of presentism or State subjugation. Rather, for a penultimate moment to be rich or laden with the series that leads up to it means that the past moments of the series must themselves be alive and vital, effective of and within the present. The past series, in other words, must be intensive and dynamic, nomadic and irreducible to the present and the penultimate – a veritable past-in-itself.

It is for this reason that a continuously contingent event is marked by breaks and resumptions, encounters and swerves, and need not always be presented as present. Indeed, it never fully is. As Deleuze reiterates throughout all of his writings, there is always a virtual excess that cannot be fully exhausted by actuality; there is always something of the event that exceeds its various instantiations in states of affairs. It would, however, be incorrect to equate the actual with history, and what exceeds and evades being actualised with virtual becomings, for as we saw above, history has just as much right to virtual status. Furthermore, as I have argued throughout this book, the virtual is itself in part historical – its very nature produced and defined in part by the creative history that it is laden with. If the continuity of contingency is never fully present, it is therefore not only because it flees into an unknown future, but also into a past that is equally unknown and in the ongoing process of modulation. Without this maintenance of a continually changing and effective past, contingency collapses on linearity, whether forward-looking (in which the past is unchangeable as opposed to the open future), retrospective (in which the past is rendered inert and manipulable by a present power) or both. But with it, contingency is allowed to form a heterogeneous continuity that finds itself in the middle and at every part of an emerging present and a vital past. Contingency, in short, is allowed to be properly non-linear.

This non-linear form of contingency may go beyond what Deleuze and Guattari originally had in mind, giving rise to not only a universal history of contingency but also a *contingency of* universal history. Nevertheless, it would appear to be necessary if we are to think 'not only the contingency of necessity, but also the necessity of the contingency at its root' (Althusser 2006: 187). It would furthermore appear to be needed if we are to avoid inappropriately conflating the retrospective capacity of the capitalist machine with the overcoding of the despotic machine. For while the contingency of capitalism may be retrospective, it could also be said to be much more than this: capitalism is not universal 'once and for all' but is rather continually universal 'again and again'. This continuity is not cinemagraphic or a mere succession of State powers, but neither can it be said to be opposed to such powers since it requires them for its very nature: for every flow that escapes capitalism a new axiom emerges.

However, in positioning capitalism as the social machine capable of effectuating such a radical form of contingency, two significant and interrelated problems are raised. Firstly, what of schizophrenia? Is not the schizophrenic, as opposed to the capitalist, the quintessential persona of radical contingency and creativity for Deleuze and Guattari, and thus of universal history? And secondly, if there is indeed a positive contingency and creativity in capitalism distinct from that characterised by the schizo, what normative or prescriptive claims can be derived from Deleuze and Guattari's critique of capitalism? To address these concerns we must look more closely at the relation between capitalism, schizophrenia and universal history.

The creativity of universal history

In his excellent discussions on capitalism, schizophrenia and universal history, Eugene Holland suggests the following interpretation of their relation: whereas capitalism 'offers the key to universal history' (Holland 2005a: 38), schizophrenia is 'the potential hope of universal history' (Holland 2005b: 237) and 'the true end of universal history' (Holland 1999: 115). By this, Holland means that capitalism provides for the *possibility* of universal history, but that universal history is only *realised* by schizophrenia (Holland 2009:

154, and Holland 1999: 92, 94–5, 109). If this reading is attractive, it is principally due to its apparent compatibility with Deleuze and Guattari's description of capitalism as the relative limit of all societies as opposed to the absolute limit that schizophrenia forms:

> [C]apitalism is indeed the limit of all societies, insofar as it brings about the decoding of the flows that the other social formations coded and overcoded. But it is the *relative* limit of every society; it effects *relative* breaks, because it substitutes for the codes an extremely rigorous axiomatic that maintains the energy of the flows in a bound state on the body of capital as a socius that is deterritorialized, but also a socius that is even more pitiless than any other. Schizophrenia, on the contrary, is indeed the *absolute* limit that causes the flows to travel in a free state on a desocialized body without organs. Hence one can say that schizophrenia is the *exterior* limit of capitalism itself or the conclusion of its deepest tendency, but that capitalism only functions on condition that it inhibit this tendency, or that it push back or displace this limit, by substituting for it its own *immanent* relative limits, which it continually reproduces on a widened scale. (AO 245–6)[18]

But if capitalism is the relative immanent limit of every society and schizophrenia the absolute exterior limit, does this mean that we only arrive at a proper universal history with schizophrenia? Put otherwise, is it true to infer from the above description that capitalism takes us only halfway to universal history, each time thwarted by its capturing axiomatic, and that we must wait for a schizophrenia liberated from this axiomatic to fully realise a universal history?

There are reasons to think otherwise. To begin with, the fact that schizophrenia is the absolute exterior limit of capitalism need not itself mean that universal history is only realised in schizophrenia. Deleuze and Guattari may indeed stipulate that 'the universal comes at the end – the body without organs and desiring production – under the conditions determined by an apparently victorious capitalism' (AO 139), but they do not actually say that universal *history* arrives with schizophrenia. Rather, universal history is repeatedly shown by Deleuze and Guattari to be a working part of the capitalist machine, as the textual evidence in my above analysis has demonstrated. It could be noted in response that Deleuze and Guattari also associate schizophrenia with the 'end of history'. But even in such cases, it is not at all clear that 'universal history' and the 'end of history' are the same thing.[19] Thus although the schizo 'consumes all of universal history in one fell swoop' (AO 21), and as such brings it to an end, this is not to say that the schizo renders history universal by consuming it. Instead, it is capitalism that universalises history and the schizo who consumes all of *universal* history.[20]

If a universal history is already fully present in capitalism, this is by virtue of the universalism appropriate to capitalism. Unlike the absolute universal that is schizophrenia, an absolutism that can only be brought about through a liberation from the capitalist axiomatic, the capitalist machine is universal precisely *because of its axiomatic*. More accurately, capitalism universalises the world and its history from the relation it forms between its axiomatising and decoding/deterritorialising tendencies, which together enable capitalism to account for all previous societies. Capitalism produces a universal history, in other words, *because of its relativity*, as opposed to the absolutism of schizophrenia.

One way in which the relative universalism of capitalism is explained by Deleuze and Guattari is through the notion of self- or auto-critique. Although it might be thought that self-critique is the sole prerogative of the schizophrenic due to the unique ability of the schizo to fracture and disperse their own subjectivity, capitalism, as it turns out, has its own brand of self-critique that is no less significant. In the words of Deleuze and Guattari: '[C]apitalism is without doubt the universal of every society, but only insofar as it is capable of carrying to a certain point its own critique – that is, the critique of the processes by which it re-enslaves that which, within it, tends to free itself or to appear freely' (AO 270). As we can see here, capitalism is universal by virtue of the self-critique that it carries out. This self-critique, moreover, is described through the way in which capitalism simultaneously captures decoded/deterritorialised flows and in doing so gives rise to new ones that escape its axiomatic. Self-critique is thus the mechanism by which capitalism is able to continually displace its *own* limits in the very act of meeting them, and thus form a universal that encompasses the world and its entire history.

This pivotal link between the universalism of capitalism and self-critique is borrowed by Deleuze and Guattari from Marx. As Marx says in the *Grundrisse*: '[B]ourgeois economics arrived at an understanding of feudal, ancient, oriental economics only after the self-criticism of bourgeois society had begun' (Marx 1975: 106). Although Deleuze and Guattari's notion of self-critique may be more loaded than what Marx has in mind here, this brief quote nevertheless indicates to us several things: (1) self-critique is a facet of the capitalist machine; (2) this critical characteristic is distinct from the retrospectivity of capitalism; and thus (3) the universalism of capitalism and history involves a form of contingency that cannot be reduced to retrospectivity or continual critique alone, since it requires them both for its nature.

It light of this analysis, it must be concluded that the universal history of contingency, and furthermore the contingency of universal history, need not wait for schizophrenia, since capitalism is already fully capable of giving rise to one due to the nature of its universalism. It may be true that the task of schizoanalysis is to 'seize control of the conditions of [universal history's] contingent, singular existence, its irony and its own critique (AO 271), but this should not be taken to suggest that the capitalist machine was not already in possession of a fully functioning universal history imbued with contingency. The fact that the capitalist machine has its own kind of self-critique pays testament to this. If this self-critique differs from the absolute annihilation of the self that the schizo carries out, it is because the axiomatic is an integral element in its operation. And correspondingly, if the universalism of capitalism differs from that as found in schizophrenia, it is due to the complementary partnership it forms between axiomatisation and deterritorialisation, not the subordination of one to the other. Universal history, as such, need not wait for the ascendency of deterritorialisation over axiomatisation, for if anything this will bring an end to universal history, not mark its realisation.

Although this assessment of universal history might appear somewhat technical and inconsequential, significant implications can be drawn from emphasising the contingent and creative capacities of the universal history of capitalism. Foremost of these is a recognition that the notions of contingency, creativity and capture cannot be uniformly assigned in Deleuze and Guattari's work. While the capitalist axiomatic is a repressive instrument, it is also the source of much experimentation and creativity. And while schizophrenia proliferates an absolute freedom liberated from the axiomatic, this freedom can be as destructive as it is creative. It is perhaps for this reason that generating a normative reading of capitalism and schizophrenia (and many other elements of Deleuzo-Guattarian philosophy) is such a tricky business. There is no question that Deleuze and Guattari are critical of capitalism, and there is no question that they are Marxists. But regardless of this, to overly valorise schizophrenia and/or demonise capitalism is to do a disservice to the complexity of their analysis. For every line they write on the insidious nature of capitalism there is a reminder that it 'pales by comparison' to the line of flight converted into a line of death (ATP 229–31). For every description of schizo-phrenia as 'the wilderness where the decoded flows run free', there is another that refers to it as 'the end of the world, the apocalypse' (AO 176).

Given this, what conclusions or prescriptions, if any, can be taken from Deleuze and Guattari's investigation of the universal history of capitalism and schizophrenia? What is to be done, in other words, in light of their descriptions? One common response revolves around the reiteration of Deleuze and Guattari's 'Marxist' credentials. According to such a view, the capitalist axiomatic is unambiguously negative and in need of 'bringing down' so that freedom can reign.[21] Such a position, however, is not Deleuze and Guattari's (or at least not by the time of *A Thousand Plateaus*). For starters, it is to a certain extent futile: throwing a spanner in the works of the capitalist machine will not bring about its demise, for capitalism is precisely defined by its always breaking down and starting up again. But more tellingly, as I demonstrated in Chapter 3, although Deleuze and Guattari attempt to limit their prescriptive recommendations to a minimum, what few there are very often take the form of warnings against the absolute becoming and deterritorialisation of schizophrenia.

Processes of stratification, conjugation and reterritorialisation are not the enemy, or at least not always, even if they may be some-times. It is also a mistake to summarily exise them from the process of creation. 'Connect, conjugate, continue' – this is the formula for creativity, since the process of creation occurs through the continu-ous *interplay* of connection and conjugation (ATP 161). Freedom and creativity are not synonymous with deterritorialisation and constricted by reterritorialisation, since de- and reterritorialisation are both part of the *same* productive act (lest deterritorialisation fail to create a new territory and degenerate into pure destruction). Thus while Deleuze and Guattari are clearly in favour of fostering creativity and promoting freedom, it must be remembered that this is not necessarily at the expense of the relative, molar strata or his-torical processes. Nor can it necessarily be achieved by facilitating an absolute universality of schizophrenia or predominance of deterrito-rialisation over axiomatisation. On the contrary, what we are shown here is the immense importance of historical processes and relational mechanisms that link strata with lines of flight in order to produce 'a small plot of new land' (ATP 161).

* * *

Throughout this chapter I have attempted to subject the ontology of capture and creation to a fresh analysis. Recognising that the two categories implicitly suggest a causal-linear relation, this investigation has provisionally shown how capture and creation must occur in a simultaneous fashion. Taking an example from Deleuze and Guattari's 'Apparatus of Capture' plateau, this study began by asking: how is it and when is it that the archaic State first appears? The simple response was that it depends. According to historical actuality, a progressive series of occurrences eventuates in the emergence of a social formation that can be identified as the archaic State. But when considered in their virtuality, primitive society cannot be said to occur before the emergence of the State form, for they have always coexisted in perpetual interaction. In this respect, an answer to the question of when the State apparatus emerges cannot be found in history, for it pre-exists and outlasts history itself – it is suprahistorical.

Such a response, however, has the effect of merely reconstituting the original problem in a new location. Whereas before we wondered how actualities emerge and elapse, now we are faced with providing a genetic justification for coexisting virtualities. From whence do they come? We know that they cannot directly issue from actual occurrences in a causal-linear fashion, for actualities are themselves dependent upon the virtual for their sense. But by the same token, it is equally implausible that actualities directly issue from virtual machines, since these virtualities cannot all have always existed – virtuals are not eternal. They can, however, be universal. This universality is explained not only by the way virtualities instantly reach the limits of their infinitive (Aion), but also by the way they provide sense to the history below their incorporeal surface – virtualities give a reading of history with respect to their singular rubric. When this occurs, the immediate question is always: *which* virtual is reading the past or the states of affairs beneath it? Or w*ho* is it that is sense-making in each case and on what good authority? The nature of this authority, as it turns out, is consistent with the *retrospective* power of the State: *pouvoir*. It may be that this power does not insist upon a particular actuality or grants itself the option of altering its dictates, thus allowing history to remain openly contingent to a certain *degree*, but this good grace does not extend to its virtuality in the same way (i.e. the virtual machine and its source of power is not itself directly challenged). Because of this, the becoming and contingency that the universal-virtual allows for

142

will require a further amendment if it is to be genuinely creative and open.

This amendment can be sourced from Bergson. Bergson gives us a virtual that is not above time or atemporal, a virtual that does not come from nowhere and is not 'without history'. Bergson's virtual is if anything *in* time, eminently temporalised. When history is put back in the virtual and virtuality in history, the limitations of a universal history that is merely retrospective or forward-looking are broken or accelerated in order to give us a universal history that is not defined by a State power but is properly creative – a universal history, in other words, that is not merely an ongoing procession of necessities but is continually contingent. By insisting upon this contingency, what we end up with is not just a universal history *of contingency*, but a *contingency of* universal history. Only then do we become able to think 'not only the contingency of necessity, but also the necessity of the contingency at its root' (Althusser 2006: 187).

If there is something important in Deleuze and Guattari's universal history, it therefore must include, if not revolve around, this third sense of contingency. For aside from the most hard-nosed of determinists, no serious thinker of history today claims that events could not have been different. And aside from the most naive of thinkers, no one denies the capacity for history to be bent respective to a retrospective power. But by allowing the past, at every level, to itself continually impact upon the present as a vital, intensive, dynamic and nomadic history, we approach a sense of contingency that appropriately includes non-linearity. In so doing, contingency no longer refers to merely the unknown status of the future and/or the ongoing manipulation of the past by the present, for the past too will be allowed to manipulate us, since it is in fact and in principle inseparable from our present selves to begin with. History, in short, will be genuinely allowed to become and evade what it is, rather than being consigned to the dustbin of what was.

Where then do we locate a beginning if it is impossible to pin it down actually or completely release it virtually? Inevitably it will be in the middle, between the two. For example, in answering from whence does a virtuality arise, we must say that it is born from other virtualities *and* actualities; it arises via the rendering together of a particular virtual/actual composite. Actual entities, it might be noted, arise in the same way, being influenced by all kinds of virtualities as well as coexisting actualities. But this is to be expected, seeing as the two are mutually presupposing. This does not make them identical or the same in kind anymore than life is identical with death: despite their tandem nature, the difference in direction and movement between the two ensures that their difference in kind is as strong as ever. But it does mean that when we look for one we will also find the other: in every actuality lies virtual ideas/machines, and in every virtuality resides a composition of actual events (or other virtualities that are similarly composed). If we were to track these various movements running from an actual to all of its virtual levels, to every other actuality that each of these levels of virtuality touches, and so on, then such an activity might be described as the making of a contingent universal history of contingency. So long as we attempt to explain an origin (of either an actual or virtual) by using *either* a teleological/causal-linear history *or* a strict ontology of simultaneous becoming, we will continue to come up short every time. But if we allow for a history that opens itself to the future, acknowledges the role of a present power and promotes the ongoing metamorphosis of the past-in-itself, then we will have a form of history that is sufficiently non-linear and creative to be called Deleuzian.

What is History in *What Is Philosophy?*

We have now seen how there is another conception and use of history in Deleuze and Guattari's work that differs from the image of historicism or State history. This history is intensive and dynamic, nomadic and universal-contingent. It is not confined to the actual, but neither is it exclusively virtual. It is not opposed to becoming but rather promotes a differential composite of history *and* becoming – both together for the production of another. In short, it is creative. For the final study of this book, I will investigate how this philosophy of historical creativity appears in Deleuze and Guattari's last monograph, *What Is Philosophy?* This text is particularly instructive on what Deleuze and Guattari mean by history, not only because it contains several curt remarks on the nature of history, but more importantly because it exhibits the role that history plays in their definition of philosophy itself. Because of this, Deleuze and Guattari's act of defining philosophy provides an excellent case study for illustrating their philosophy of history. My analysis of this text will therefore simultaneously address Deleuze and Guattari's comments on the nature of history in *What Is Philosophy?* as well as analyse the historical ontology that their project depends upon.

Deleuze and Guattari define philosophy in three parts: the concept, the plane of immanence and conceptual personae. Following the articulation of these *de jure* elements of philosophy, Deleuze and Guattari then consider the significance of certain *de facto* conditions that not only facilitate the emergence of philosophy (*as philosophy*), but continue to direct the development of its nature. It is at this point that history has its most obvious say in the matter, making possible a rearticulation of philosophy as an historiophilosophy. However, as I will attempt to show, history is required by philosophy not just due to contingent *de facto* circumstances, but necessarily so. To this end, my investigation will follow Deleuze and Guattari's definition of philosophy from within, pointing out at every stage both the methodological role history plays in their analysis as well as the historical nature that is a part of philosophy's principle. From this we will see, once again, that far from being 'against' history, Deleuze and Guattari in fact possess an important philosophy of history that is an integral part of their philosophy of creativity.

Historical concepts

First definition of philosophy: 'philosophy is the art of forming, inventing, and fabricating concepts' (WP 2, 5). Although this answer is often taken as a conclusion to what Deleuze and Guattari mean by philosophy, it is in fact where they begin. Indeed, as the sentence following their above definition tells us: 'But the answer not only had to take note of the question, it had to determine its moment, its occasion and circumstances, its landscapes and personae, its conditions and unknowns' (WP 2). Immediately we can see that creation will not only be under the purview of a productive untimely that escapes the present, but must also involve a significant contribution from existing conditions, particular landscapes and contingent occurrences. In order to see how this relation between conditions and unknowns works, let us begin by looking at Deleuze and Guattari's understanding of the concept.

Deleuze and Guattari start this investigation by employing an ontology already familiar to us: a concept is a multiplicity (WP 15). More specifically, a concept is a multiplicity of components: 'Every concept has components and is defined by them. It therefore has a combination' (WP 15). A concept's combination is the order of its difference – the differential constellation of components that defines each singular concept. From this we can see that although a concept is a multiplicity, it is also a 'whole' due to its singular combination. This description is unambiguously indebted to Bergson. Throughout his writings Bergson repeatedly shows how heterogeneous multiplicities form a whole: in *Time and Free Will*, time must be considered in whole durations rather than discrete portions (if time is to indeed be allowed to transpire); in *Matter and Memory*, habitual memory operates by the 'decomposition and then recomposition of a whole action' (Bergson 2004: 89–90), while attentive memory, in its process of contraction-détente, calls upon and is 'laden with the whole of the past' (Bergson 2004: 220), and as we see in *Creative Evolution*, it is through intuition and the impulse of the *élan vital* that this 'condensation of the history we have lived [. . .], as a whole, is made manifest to us' (Bergson 1998: 5). Each time, a multiplicity is made whole, its parts connected into a continuity. For Deleuze and

146

Guattari, concepts and their components follow this ontology: the concept 'makes-whole' a combination of components in the same way that Bergson's 'properly philosophical multiplicities [were a] "multiplicity of fusion", which expressed the inseparability of variations' (WP 127). A concept is thus a continuous or heterogeneous multiplicity.

As an example, Descartes' concept of the self makes a whole of the components 'doubting', 'thinking' and 'being'. What defines this concept is not so much the particular components per se but rather the nature of the relations within the (whole) concept, the way in which the components are linked together and the particular story that this linkage tells. In the case of the cogito, the three components are arranged in what Deleuze and Guattari call 'zones of neighborhood or indiscernibility that produce passages from one to the other and constitute their inseparability' (WP 25). As they go on to spell out: 'The first zone is between doubting and thinking (myself who doubts, I cannot doubt that I think), and the second is between thinking and being (in order to think it is necessary to be)' (WP 25).

Such compositional arrangement into zones or fields indicates how Deleuze and Guattari's definition of the concept borrows from the logic of surfaces that I discussed in Chapter 2. There we saw how surfaces or orders of sense can on the one hand stretch to infinity but on the other hand are themselves limiting in nature. Deleuze and Guattari's concept, like an infinitive verb, works in the same way: it is defined by the way an infinitive becoming determines the parameters of its relations. Just as each surface becoming is an infinitive reading of depth, so concepts must 'circumscrib[e] a universe that explains them' (WP 15) – a universe which is not 'chaos pure and simple' (WP 15) but is the sense which determines the unique nature of their difference and multiplicity. However, as I went on to point out in Chapter 2, this surface becoming is only one half of the story, for what it (intentionally) leaves out is history.

As it happens, Deleuze and Guattari broach the issue of history in the initial pages of their analysis of the concept. In a short paragraph they tell us that 'every concept always has a *history*, even though this history zigzags, though it passes, if need be, through other problems or onto different planes' (WP 18). This remark is, however, left unexamined at this point, as is the precise role this history plays in the ontology of the concept. Instead, Deleuze and Guattari immediately focus their investigation on the other side of a concept: its becoming. As they explain, aside from the history of a concept, a concept also has a *becoming* that involves its relationship with concepts situated on the same plane. Here concepts link up with each other, support one another, coordinate their contours, articulate their respective problems, and belong to the same philosophy, even if they have different histories. (WP 18)

Deleuze and Guattari are here foregrounding what they will call the 'exoconsistency' of a concept. Along with the zones of neighborhood or indiscernibility that describe the 'endoconsistency' of components within a concept, concepts are connected to one another or rendered exoconsistent via the construction of bridges between them (WP 19–20). Looking ahead, endo/exoconsistency will be absolutely crucial to Deleuze and Guattari's definition of philosophy. But neither of these, it must be said, specifically address the zigzag movements between planes, instead referring exclusively to the internal and external relations within and between concepts on a plane. This point cannot be overly stressed, for as Deleuze and Guattari's account of the nature of philosophy continues, it will often rely not only on the relations of becoming within a single concept and/or plane, but also the zigzag movement between planes that has been associated with, if anything, the history of a concept.

To elucidate what is at stake here, consider Deleuze and Guattari's 'Example 2'. The purposes of this example are twofold. First of all, the example is intended to illustrate the ontological mechanics of concepts – their various relations of becoming. Thus Plato's concept of 'the One' is shown to be made up of 'two components (being and nonbeing), phases of components (the One superior to Being, equal to being, inferior to being; the One superior to nonbeing, equal to nonbeing), and zones of indiscernibility (in relation to itself, in relation to others)' (WP 29). This concept is furthermore related externally to other concepts such as 'the Idea', which in turn have their own internal components (the quality possessed or to be possessed; the Idea that possesses it first, as unparticipable; that which lays claim to the quality and can only possess it second, third, fourth; and the Idea participated in, which judges the claims) and zones of neighbourhood (time in the form of anteriority) (WP 30). However, aside from illustrating the ontological structure of concepts through their relations of endo/exoconsistency, the more significant purpose of this example is to demonstrate how concepts are *created*. For example, even when 'truth is posed as presupposition' (WP 29), as in the case of Plato, this very concept, Deleuze and Guattari point out, needed to be created in the first place (the creation of the uncreated).

The crucial question for Deleuze and Guattari is therefore: *how* is it concepts are created, *from whence* do they arise? As 'Example 2' unravels, it becomes clear that an answer to this is provided not only by the ontological structure of becoming but also the *history* of philosophy. Following their explanation of the endo/exoconsistent relations of Platonic concepts, Deleuze and Guattari go on to show how these concepts are subsequently altered in the work of Descartes and Kant. The novelty of concepts, as well as 'the power of their becoming when they pass into one another', is thus demonstrated through an *historical evaluation* (WP 32). But as I have queried throughout this book, what is the nature of this evaluation? Is it merely a form of explanation that 'captures' the creative process of becoming or is it not itself a part of creation?

Evidence taken from 'Example 2' would appear to suggest the latter. Although this example is concerned with the relation between concepts on a plane (e.g. the concepts of 'the One' and 'the Idea' on the Platonic plane), what is of greater interest in this example is the way in which concepts relate to one another on *different* planes (e.g. Plato's 'Idea' and Descartes' 'cogito'). On the one hand, this movement between planes is clearly a creative movement – the creation of a new concept that diverges from the former. But on the other hand, 'Example 2' clearly maintains relations between the new and old concepts, indicating how the past continues to play an active part in the creation of the new. Put simply, the novelty that is engendered by Descartes – his creative act – specifically occurs *with respect to* Plato's creation. As Deleuze and Guattari say, Descartes' cogito is 'prepared' by the Greek plane that precedes it, even if it cannot be 'fully accomplished' (WP 30). Descartes' creation is thus distinct from Plato's – a genuine creation – but nevertheless related to it in a productive manner (*puissance* and not *pouvoir*). The same point is made again in the case of Kant:

> The fact that Kant 'criticizes' Descartes means only that he sets up a plane and constructs a problem that could not be occupied or completed by the Cartesian cogito. Descartes created the cogito as concept, but by expelling time as *form of anteriority*, so as to make it a simple mode of succession referring to continuous creation. Kant reintroduces time into the cogito, but it is a completely different time from that of Platonic anteriority. This is the creation of a concept. (WP 32)

As we can see here, concepts are created (in part) by altering, adding to or subtracting the components of previous concepts. But as I pointed out in Chapter 2, creation cannot be exclusively attributed to the level of ontological and logical organisation, for it must also consist in the mounting of steps between such levels. Between the various planes of Plato, Descartes and Kant, each of which are defined through relations of surface becoming, is thus a zigzag line that moves according to an entirely different nature.

One way that we could describe the nature of this movement is nomadic. As we saw in Chapter 3, nomadology proceeds via connections and conjunctions that not only define the structure of machines, assemblages and singularities, but also chart the various movements of flow between them (de/reterritorialisation). In this manner, Deleuze and Guattari's tracking of Plato's Idea through Descartes and Kant could be usefully compared with their nomadology of the sabre. In each case there is a 'line of innovation': while 'Example 2' follows Plato's creation on a Platonic plane to new planes and new creative manipulations, Deleuze and Guattari's nomadology of the sabre runs from the metallurgists who invented crucible steel towards the various social machines and assemblages (e.g. the Chinese empire and the Scythians) who implement, express and transmute this matter-flow in different ways (ATP 404–5). My intention here is not to suggest that the two examples are identical – Descartes and Kant, for instance, are not exactly the nomad and the State. However, despite the different problems to which these examples are directed (the creation of concepts in one case and technological innovation in the other), the ontology of becoming and history that they employ is arguably consistent in an insightful way: becomings may contour the structure of a constellation of singularities (each of which is itself a particular multiplicity of components), but the prolongation of singularities across such constellations attests to an historical lineage that continues to have a vital influence on what is, was and will be (continual contingency).[1]

To this end, the nature of the relation between Descartes' creation and Plato's could be equally well described as an intensive and dynamic movement that ambulates from the depths towards the surface. As Plato's concepts move from the past towards Descartes and vice versa, a trajectory is formed between the two that cannot be reduced to one or the other, for it arises out of their compositional relation. The trajectory or flow is thus always *between* the two – itself the between. Using Bergson we could say that there is a duration or double movement, whereby the past surges towards the present as the present turns to meet it. Or employing Nietzsche's imagery, we could say that Descartes embraces Plato's creation like the oracular voice of the past – a voice that inspires but does not enslave. But either way, what is clear is that creation cannot be entirely given over to becoming, for history must also play an active part in the production of the new; one need not flee from the past in order to create, for returning to it in the appropriate manner can also be highly productive. As Paul Atkinson says when commenting on the history of Bergsonism: 'Bergson's heritage, like his philosophy, is dynamic, and to return to the past should always result in the extension of new lines of differentiation beyond the turn of experience' (Atkinson 2009: 255). The logical organisation of surfaces or the virtual structure of an incorporeal event/machine are thus insufficient on their own to bring about the production of the new, for a concomitant history is also required that evades historicism and embraces an ontology of historical creativity.

An examination of Deleuze and Guattari's discussion immediately preceding 'Example 2' confirms this significance of historical creativity. As they correctly note, if a concept is to be new, let alone worthwhile, then it must go beyond and be irreducible to the old: 'If one concept is "better" than an earlier one, it is because it makes us aware of new variations and unknown resonances, it carries out unforeseen cuttings-out, it brings forth an Event that surveys [*survole*] us' (WP 28). A new concept thus brings forth an Event in a way that the past was incapable of. Nevertheless, even if a new concept is to be 'of our time' (or 'a time to come'), as opposed to a past time, this is not to say that it occurs in isolation from the past: 'If one can still be a Platonist, Cartesian, or Kantian today, it is because one is justified in thinking that their concepts can be reactivated in our problems and inspire those concepts that need to be created' (WP 28). To insist that the new is irreducible to the past is thus not to deny that the past has a continual affectivity. While it is true that 'Nothing positive is done, nothing at all, in the domains of either criticism or history, when we are content to brandish ready-made old concepts like skeletons intended to intimidate any creation' (WP 83), it is no less true that neither critique or history need be confined to this State image. If we look to Nietzsche's early work on history, as I noted in Chapter 1, an alternative image can be located in the historian of youth – he or she who uses their ignorance and arrogance (ahistorical and suprahistorical power) to promote a history for life. And if we look to Deleuze's early work on Nietzsche, we can see how it is Deleuze himself who is attempting to promote an alternative notion and method of critique and history: instead of brandishing ready-made values that are used to proliferate conformism and submission, Deleuze's 'Nietzschean inspiration' consists in the practice of *evaluation* – that differential element in Nietzsche's genealogy which is 'both critical and creative' (NP 1). Having a critical relation to the past thus need not preclude the act of creation, for as Deleuze and Guattari note: 'Criticism implies new concepts (of the thing criticized) just as much as the most positive creation' (WP 83). And if Deleuze and Guattari are willing to allow for a creative form of critique as opposed to the 'critic of their day', why should an alternative form of history not also be so allowed? Without such a history, without such a way of relating to the past, how would we ever be capable of *following* Deleuze and Guattari in the manner they stipulate:

> What is the best way to follow the great philosophers? Is it to repeat what they said or *to do what they did*, that is, create concepts for problems that necessarily change? (WP 28)

In summary, Deleuze and Guattari's discussion of the relation between Plato, Descartes and Kant emphasises how the creation of concepts involves a relation to the past whereby the past continues to be alive and vital, capable of inspiring *new* creations. This is demonstrated not only by what they say, but more importantly by what they do: if we follow the movements of Deleuze and Guattari's demonstration, their analysis of the nature of concepts can be shown to involve not only a becoming, but an historical ontology of creativity. At this point, however, it must be admitted that our analysis of the concept, as with Deleuze and Guattari's, has relied upon notions that have yet to be fully explained – namely, the plane of immanence. We must therefore examine in more detail the nature and role of Deleuze and Guattari's plane in their definition of philosophy. In doing so, we will see once again how history relates to becoming in a continually creative way.

Historical planes

As we have just seen, concepts are determined by their relations of endo/exoconsistency. These concepts, however, are themselves made intelligible by the plane in which they exist. The definition of philosophy as the creation of concepts is therefore incomplete, for this act of creation must itself be grounded. Hence Deleuze and Guattari's amended definition of philosophy: 'Philosophy is a constructivism,

152

and constructivism has two qualitatively different complementary aspects: the creation of concepts and the laying out of a plane' (WP 35–6).[2]

For Deleuze and Guattari, a plane is 'a table, a plateau, or a slice; it is a plane of consistency or, more accurately, the plane of immanence of concepts, the planomenon' (WP 35). Put more simply, a plane is the field in which the creation of concepts must occur; it is the absolute horizon to which created concepts must always correspond (WP 36). Without this horizon, concepts cannot be created, since the plane is what gives concepts their consistency with respect to others. But the plane should not be thought of as a static framework, for if nothing else it is a living movement: 'Concepts are the archipelago or skeletal frame, a spinal column rather than a skull, whereas the plane is the breath that suffuses the separate parts' (WP 36). The plane is the breath of air or force which picks up concepts, gives them their direction and sets them in motion.

In order to help us better understand this distinction between concepts and planes, Deleuze and Guattari call upon several dualisms that we have come across throughout this book. As illustrated by the following quote, the relation between concepts and planes borrows from the ontology of surfaces, events, machinic assemblages and nomads that we have already looked at:

> Concepts are absolute surfaces or volumes, formless and fragmentary, whereas the plane is the formless, unlimited absolute, neither surface nor volume but always fractal. Concepts are concrete assemblages, like the configurations of a machine, but the plane is the abstract machine of which these assemblages are the working parts. Concepts are events, but the plane is the horizon of events, the reservoir or reserve of purely conceptual events: not the relative horizon that functions as a limit, which changes with an observer and encloses observable states of affairs, but the absolute horizon, independent of any observer, which makes the event as concept independent of a visible state of affairs in which it is brought about. Concepts pave, occupy, or populate the plane bit by bit, whereas the plane itself is the indivisible milieu in which concepts are distributed without breaking up its continuity or integrity: they occupy it without measuring it out (the concept's combination is not a number) or are distributed without splitting it up. The plane is like a desert that concepts populate without dividing up. (WP 36–7)

The plane is thus an orientation, or more precisely orient*ing*, of thought; it is diagrammatic rather than intensive, an impetus that moves thought but which it must not be confused with (WP 39–40).

The plane does not itself create concepts, but it 'shelters their seeds' 'in an intuition specific to them', allowing them to grow and become what they are and might be (WP 7). In this respect, a plane of immanence is 'like sense' or the various images of thought I analysed in Chapter 2, all of which exude an orientation or organisational principle that guides the relations between things and thought (LS 128).

Despite the explicit distinction between concepts and planes ('the plane of immanence is neither a concept nor the concept of all concepts' (WP 35)) it must be admitted that the two nevertheless share some important traits. For example, just as a concept is a multiplicity (with respect to its components) yet singular (with respect to its incorporeal infinitive), so there are a multiplicity of planes which are each an 'unlimited One-All' (WP 35). This means that while planes may have an absolute or infinitive nature – an unlimited becoming much like an incorporeal surface or virtual event – a plane is by no means *the* absolute infinity itself.[3] If there is such an absolute beyond the plane – a 'set of all sets' – it is chaos. By definition, chaos is neither a set nor an order but on the contrary that from which orders are derived and that to which orders return: 'Chaos makes chaotic and undoes every consistency in the infinite' (WP 42). Every order that arises from and returns to chaos is therefore a slice or plane of chaos: 'The plane of immanence is like a section of chaos and acts like a sieve' (WP 42, 43). As observed in Chapter 1, if these slices of chaos that order difference differently were to be stacked on top of one another, they would form a diagram akin to Bergson's cone of virtual memory. Each slice of the cone is a plane of immanence that circumscribes chaos according to the singular curvature of its conic section. Although each conic section is itself infinitive and contains the whole of reality, since it does so in varying degrees of difference each plane is but one among a plurality: 'There are innumerable planes, each with a variable curve' (WP 76). Each conic section can also be said to act like a sieve, sifting through difference according to a particular level of contraction-détente. In this way, each plane regulates (resonates) difference respective to the level of specificity required. Thus the extraction of any particular concept is dependent upon which plane we delve to in order to locate it, which plane it is that lays it out.

However, as I demonstrated in Chapter 4, although all the levels of virtual difference could be said to simultaneously coexist, this does not mean that they are atemporal – after all, the cone is a model for the *passing* of time, not its death. Thus while the cone may show us different orders of difference simultaneously, these orders of 'inseparable variability' are most certainly in and susceptible to the succession of time. It is therefore significant that when Deleuze and Guattari note how planes are both singular-absolute but also one among a multiplicity, they do so by referring to the multiplicity of planes and their relations *in time and history*:

> But if it is true that the plane of immanence is always single, being itself pure variation, then it is all the more necessary to explain why there are varied and distinct planes of immanence that, depending upon which infinite movements are retained and selected, succeed and contest each other in history. The plane is certainly not the same in the time of the Greeks, in the seventeenth century, and today. (WP 39)

As this passage indicates, Deleuze and Guattari are not simply concerned with showing how planes relate to one another in an atemporal or static sense; their analysis rather concerns how planes come into and pass out of existence in time. Just as was the case with *The Logic of Sense*, from this point on it becomes clear that the *logic* of planes will require a complementary *history* of planes, if we are to understand their nature and how it is they come about.

Thus we return to the question of history. This question is addressed in two interrelated ways: (1) by examining the relation of planes to one another; and (2) by focusing on how it is one moves, like Hercules, towards a plane and between planes. It might initially seem that such movements are the prerogative of becoming, not history. For example, as the above quote states, the variation of planes 'succeed and contest each other in history'. This would appear to suggest that while movements may necessarily 'return' to history, they are 'of' becoming, not history. In other words, the above construal would seem to contrast simultaneous virtual becomings with successive actual history. But as I have now established through the course of this book, such a strict separation is neither final nor entirely accurate. This can be most effectively highlighted in our present study of *What Is Philosophy?* by noting Deleuze and Guattari's heavy reliance upon Bergson's theory of multiplicities for their ontology of planes and concepts.

Bergson's pre-eminent multiplicity of fusion, as I pointed out in Chapter 1, is duration – that multiplicity which demonstrates the continually ongoing variation of time. Deleuze and Guattari will acknowledge this when they later distinguish between 'scientific types of multiplicity' and 'properly philosophical multiplicities *for which Bergson claimed a particular status defined by duration*' (WP 127, emphasis added). Although duration is initially forwarded by Bergson as an alternative to the spatialisation of time, by the time of *Creative Evolution* it will also be deployed as an effective protagonist to historicism, of which there are two varieties: radical mechanism and radical finalism. In radical mechanism, reality is subjected to an a priori systematisation that is causal-linear and fixed. The essence of mechanical explanation is therefore 'to regard the future and the past as calculable functions of the present, and thus to claim that *all is given*' (Bergson 1998: 37, 39). Radical finalism, on the other hand, is teleological. In Bergson's words:

> This doctrine of teleology, in its extreme form, as we find it in Leibniz for example, implies that things and beings merely realize a programme previously arranged. But if there is nothing unforeseen, no invention or creation in the universe, time is useless again. As in the mechanistic hypothesis, here again it is supposed that *all is given*. Finalism thus understood is only inverted mechanism. It springs from the same postulate, with this sole difference, that in the movement of our finite intellects along successive things, whose successiveness is reduced to a mere appearance, it holds in front of us the light with which it claims to guide us, instead of putting it behind. (Bergson 1998: 39)

When so put, both radical mechanism and finalism could be said to capture a creative movement – to render the movement of duration inanimate. But if the pre-eminent multiplicity of fusion is distinguished from historicism, does this mean that it is opposed to history? Such a conclusion was arguably not Bergson's intention. For example, when Bergson applies his theory of duration to the evolution of life as a whole, he remarks how 'this evolution constitutes, through the unity and continuity of the animated matter which supports it, a single indivisible history' (Bergson 1998: 37). Most importantly, this is *not* to say that the 'single indivisible history' comes *after* evolution – the trajectory of duration does not come after duration, for it *is* duration. Duration is thus not opposed to history, for history is a part of it. This theory of an unfolding and emerging history is further confirmed in one of Bergson's most infamous examples:

> Though our reasoning on isolated systems may imply that their history, past, present, and future, might be instantaneously unfurled like a fan, this history, in point of fact, unfolds itself gradually, as if it occupied a duration like our own. If I want to mix a glass of sugar and water, I must, willy nilly, wait until the sugar melts. This little fact is big with meaning.

For here the time I have to wait is not that mathematical time which would apply equally well to the entire history of the material world, even if that history were spread out instantaneously in space. It coincides with my impatience, that is to say, with a certain portion of my own duration, which I cannot protract or contract as I like. It is no longer something *thought*, it is something *lived*. (Bergson 1998: 9–10)

The representation of actual things into a successive order may therefore be historicist, but history need not be condemned to historicism. Indeed, as Bergson shows above, if we are to successfully combat historicism, we will need to recognise how history *itself* has a duration.[4]

In light of this reconnection of history with multiplicities of fusion, let us then return to Deleuze and Guattari's explication of planes. Earlier in this chapter, it was noted how concepts connect with one another across different planes. This in turn gave the impression of distinct 'One-All' planes that can be separated and detached from one another according to the particular way each composes difference – their singular constellation. However, although planes are distinct from one another, this is not to say that they are unrelated. As Deleuze and Guattari stipulate, planes of immanence are *interleaved* (WP 50). Planes thus do not lack relations to one another, but are immanently composed of such relations. If a plane is the breath or gust of air that gives movement and direction to concepts, this breath is therefore itself a confluence of others, the culmination of which forms a trade-wind that pushes concepts on their way.

Given this multiplicity of planes, each of which is criss-crossed by others, Deleuze and Guattari's earlier analysis of the creation of concepts is rendered significantly more complex. Previously, Deleuze and Guattari asserted that 'concepts can only be assessed as a function of their problems and their plane' (WP 27). This point is of course a further development of Deleuze's 'problematic' philosophy that I addressed in Chapter 4, where solutions and effects are always immanently related to the problems and causes they are a part of. As we follow the life of a concept in its movement through planes, the transmutation of that concept and creation of new ones is attributed in part to the distinctiveness character (singular combination) of each plane. But as it turns out, it is not just concepts that can be related across distinct planes, for planes are *themselves* so interwoven:

When comparing particular cases it is no doubt difficult to judge whether there is a single plane or several different ones: do the pre-Socratics have the same image of thought, despite the differences between Heraclitus and

Parmenides? Can we speak of a plane of immanence or image of so-called classical thought that continues from Plato to Descartes? (WP 50)

How then do we distinguish one plane from another, given that in some cases Plato's plane is distinct from Descartes' and in others it is not? The simple answer is that it depends on one's perspective, the 'more-or-less close or distant points of view that would make it possible to group different layers over a fairly long period or, on the contrary, to separate layers on what seemed to be a common plane' (WP 50). The problem with such a solution, however, is that it risks collapsing evaluation onto a 'historicism' or 'generalized relativism' (WP 50). In order to avoid these two alternatives, Deleuze and Guattari return us again to familiar territory: 'In all these respects, the question of the one and the multiple once again becomes the most important one, introducing itself into the plane' (WP 50). But what do Deleuze and Guattari mean by this, and how does it help?

If we look at the passage immediately following this claim, we will see that the question of the one and the multiple is in fact pursued by Deleuze and Guattari through the question of how the new relates to the old:

> In the end, does not every great philosopher lay out a new plane of immanence, introduce a new substance of being and draw up a new image of thought, so that there could not be two great philosophers on the same plane? It is true that we cannot imagine a great philosopher of whom it could not be said that he has changed what it means to think; he has 'thought differently' (as Foucault put it). (WP 51)

Insofar as a philosopher is truly creative, they give rise to a plane that is their's alone, utterly different from what has come before. Nevertheless, even these planes are not disconnected from the past, for 'every plane is not only interleaved but holed, letting through the fogs that surround it' (WP 51). As such, a plane of immanence is not entirely smooth, as one might have thought, but is rather a holey space (as I described in Chapter 3). Insofar as a plane is holey, it is not cut off from the past but allows past planes to rise up like a fog, immersing themselves with the new. In this way, a present plane is made up of more than itself – it lives and breathes the past. But it does so through its *own* lungs, its unique suffusion of difference. Thus at one and the same time the past is both subjected to the present and the air which allows the present to breath.

To illustrate how these relations occur in an historical manner, consider Deleuze and Guattari's 'Example 4' (WP 51–7). After noting how Descartes makes 'error' a diagrammatic feature of his plane of thought, Deleuze and Guattari chart how this feature wanders from one plane to another, thus indicating the interleaved and holed nature of planes. For instance, on the one hand, 'error' can 'be traced back to Socrates, for whom the person who is wicked (in fact) is someone who is by right "mistaken"' (WP 52). But on the other hand, 'A major change occurs' in this feature between Plato's plane and Descartes', 'when ignorance and superstition replace error and prejudice in expressing what by right is the negative in thought' (WP 52). Thus at one and the same time, the feature of 'error' is both unique to a plane and dependent upon others. Kant similarly takes up the feature of 'error', yet completely reorientates it by showing how 'thought is threatened less by error than by inevitable illusions that come from within reason' (WP 52). As such, 'A feature cannot be isolated' (WP 53) from the plane that gives it voice – 'the breath that suffuses the separate parts' (WP 36). But *that* the feature of 'error' mutates from one plane to the next nevertheless attests to a lineage that runs between them. This lineage may be heterogeneous as opposed to homogeneous, emphasising how Kant inherits from the past 'at the price of a profound mutation' (WP 53–4), but as we know from Deleuze's Bergsonism, this heterogeneity need not come at the cost of continuity. On the contrary, what threads Deleuze and Guattari's analysis in 'Example 4' together, from Descartes back to Plato and forward to Kant (and beyond), is a continuous heterogeneity, a multiplicity of fusion or 'single indivisible history', that carries out a particular contraction-détente of the past with the present. In this manner, while Deleuze and Guattari's objective is to no doubt stress the distinctiveness of various planes of thought, to do so they will require a notion of historical creativity that can (in part) allow for the appropriate lineage (trajectory/duration) to be drawn.

As may have become apparent, this example of the relation of planes is quite similar to Deleuze and Guattari's previous example of how concepts relate. Both concern the ways in which various durations can be drawn, rendering together a heterogeneous continuity that fosters creativity. But as we have seen, this process is not foreign to history, if by history we mean an historical ontology of creativity that is distinct from historicism. Both involve the determination of appropriate durations and intuitions, contractions and trajectories, directions and diagrams; both involve historical progressions that are distinct from (though not opposed to) surface or planar becomings and display what I have referred to as developmental becomings.

These determinations and developments are the 'complex and relative assessments' (WP 58) that separate or conjoin planes together.
Sometimes these planes are composed of minimal parts, or have
minimal impact on the world (minimal importance). Other times,
'they join together at least to cover fairly long periods' (WP 57).
But these same determinations and developments are no less at play
when historical 'ages' and 'civilisations' are rendered together and
sundered apart: the long nineteenth century and the short twentieth,
for example, are in part determined by a relative contraction-détente
of history, and Europe, to give another example, is defined not only
by its geography (e.g. its ever moving eastern border) but also by its
historical links (e.g. how close or far, foreign or familiar, it is to the
Ancient Greeks and Romans).

But again, it could be argued that despite their similarities, this
method of historical determination cannot follow the philosophical
assessments of planes, since the latter requires a non-linear consideration of time. Deleuze and Guattari make this point at the close of
their analysis on planes. There they say that in order to determine
what 'the requirements of the age mean', we must 'give up the narrowly historical point of view of before and after in order to consider
the time rather than the history of philosophy' (WP 58). But in what
exactly does this distinction lie? What it requires is an acceptance
that whereas time can proceed in a non-linear and sporadic fashion,
history is necessarily linear, causal and chronological. This requirement, however, is exactly what I do not accept. Why must history
proceed in this way? Why can it not be akin to what Deleuze and
Guattari describe as *stratigraphic* time, a 'time where "before" and
"after" indicate only an order of superimpositions' (WP 58)? The
critical aspect of this time is that the past is never done with: 'very old
strata can rise to the surface again, can cut a path through the formations that covered them and surface directly on the current stratum to
which they impart a new curvature' (WP 58–9). When this happens,
the strata or superimpositions are altered and given a new order. But
why must this aspect be exclusive to the 'infinite becoming of philosophy' and opposed to a linear history that it cross-cuts (WP 59)?

As I have maintained throughout this book, this claim can only be
made if we consign history to historicism. There are indeed numerous history books in which the virtual is reduced to actual reality,
the incorporeal event is reduced to presented states of affairs or
concepts are reduced to propositions; one can certainly find 'many
histories of philosophy in which solutions are reviewed without ever

determining what the problem is (substance in Aristotle, Descartes, Leibniz), since the problem is only copied from the propositions that serve as its answer' (WP 80). But there is another kind of history, a kind which, as we saw in Chapter 1, can be associated with Péguy's engendering of the Republican *mystique*, or Nietzsche's bringing to life of Greek culture in *The Birth of Tragedy*. A history that doesn't shackle us to the past, but allows us to engage with a past that, if nothing else, can help us see 'how in the past individuals succeeded in transcending their own past' (de Jong 1997: 273). Deleuze and Guattari's 'Example 4' is the perfect example of this kind of history. These histories are not radically mechanistic, the mere procession of propositions; nor are they radically finalistic, reducing life to a teleology. They also do not 'conform to the ordinary laws of succession', for they allow proper names to 'coexist and shine either as luminous points that take us through the components of a concept once more or as the cardinal points of a stratum or layer that continually come back to us, like dead stars whose light is brighter than ever' (WP 59).

Thus when an historian engenders an historical event or culture (as opposed to 'passively observe' historical 'facts'), they do so in relation to others; their event is linked to other events in the same way as concepts are, and their culture is as interleaved and holed as a plane of immanence is. For example, when the historian of republicanism composes their particular stratum of study, various events and encounters, such as the French Revolution and National Socialism, 'cut a path' from whatever other strata they were lodged in to 'impart a new curvature' to the surface they are now also a part of. Similarly, other strata, from the Kantian plane to the modern image of thought, dissect their particular strata in meaningful and continually ongoing ways.

Given Deleuze's fondness for Foucault, such a possible compatibility of history with stratigraphy is not altogether surprising: when Foucault brings an historical event from a stratum of archaeological depth to our attention, the event is so visceral that one cannot but help feel its impact upon one's own stratum. Foucault's histories, furthermore, do not subject the indeterminacy to a causal-linear image of History, but are rather consistent with a stratigraphy that superimposes various strata of coexistence, while continually dissecting these levels with flows or tangents that dynamically move between. I already referred to this passage in Chapter 3, but it is worth quoting again:

Whether discursive of not, formations, families and multiplicities are historical. They are not just compounds built up from their coexistence but are inseparable from 'temporal reactors of derivation'; and when a new formation appears, with new rules and series, it never comes all at once, in a single phrase or act of creation, but emerges like a series of 'building blocks', with gaps, traces and reactivations of former elements that survive under the new rules. [. . .] One must pursue the different series, travel along the different levels, and cross all thresholds; instead of simply displaying phenomena or statements in their vertical or horizontal dimensions, one must form a transversal or mobile diagonal line along which the archaeologist-archivist must move. (F 21–2)

History, as such, turns on the construction and multiplicity of planes just as much as philosophy, for these planes of consistency are as much historical as they are philosophical: the two 'are inseparable'. The following of transversal lines that cut across various levels and thresholds, moreover, is the remit of the 'archaeologist-archivist' – those people who are also referred to in this passage as 'real historians'. We can thus conclude the following: (1) history is entirely compatible with stratigraphy, if understood in the appropriate manner; and (2) this historical-stratigraphy emphasises the significance of lines that move between planes of coexistence according to an ontology of historical creativity – what I have variously described as an intensive emergence, a dynamic development, a nomadic construction and a universal-contingent process of continual creation.

Nevertheless, we are still faced with difficult questions: is there not a critical difference between an historical field and a philosophical plane, or an historical person and a philosophical concept? To fully address these issues, we will need to examine the third element in Deleuze and Guattari's definition of philosophy: conceptual personae.

Historical personae

Up till now this chapter has attempted to show how when philosophers create concepts and lay out a plane, they do so in consultation with a past that is alive in them. When Descartes creates the cogito and institutes the Cartesian plane, for instance, he does so partly with respect to Plato's constructions. The Platonic plane, furthermore, is not entirely detached from Descartes', even if it is distinct, since the two are interleaved and holed. However, when Descartes the phi-

162

losopher engages with Plato, who, precisely, is Plato? What is Plato's ontological status with respect to Descartes?

According to Deleuze and Guattari, when Descartes engages with Plato to create concepts and lay out his plane, he does so not by conversing with Plato the historical person (as 'represented' in and by Plato's writings) but rather with Plato's conceptual persona (e.g. Socrates). Conceptual personae, put simply, personify concepts; they are the means by which philosophers converse with concepts, present or past. If these personae are significant, however, it is not merely because they allow us to put a face to a concept. Rather, it is because they bring concepts to life *in us*. Thus while planes shelter concepts like seeds in the ground, it is conceptual personae who cultivate and disseminate their vitality (WP 7). As Deleuze and Guattari admit, the ontological nature of conceptual personae is 'somewhat mysterious' (WP 61). Although personae are distinct from concepts and planes, they 'have a hazy existence halfway between concept and preconceptual plane, passing from one to the other' (WP 61). In this respect, unlike concepts which are defined in part by their relations within a plane, personae are not so confined by any particular plane but move between them, as well as chaos and concepts (WP 75). Personae, as such, are nomadic.[5]

Deleuze and Guattari describe this by considering a particular example: the idiot. As Deleuze and Guattari explain, when Descartes creates the cogito and its preconceptual plane, he does so by way of an idiot who doesn't already know what it is to think and thus must think anew: '[I]t is the Idiot who says "I" and sets up the cogito but who also has the subjective presuppositions or lays out the plane. [. . .] Here is a very strange type of persona who wants to think, and who thinks for himself, by the "natural light"' (WP 61–2). But as Deleuze and Guattari immediately ask, *where* does this idiot come from, and *how* does he appear? As it turns out, this persona had a previous life – it has a history. When located on various planes, this persona takes on a certain appearance and way of being (that is, organisation or order of becoming, the being of becoming). But conceptual personae are not confined by any one plane. Thus 'The idiot will reappear in another age, in a different context that is still Christian, but Russian now' (WP 62). From Descartes to Dostoyevsky, the idiot moves from one plane to the next. It might be thought that this movement is a becoming that cuts through or across history, but as we saw in our analysis of concepts and planes, if anything it is the opposite which is true: it is history that zigzags between planes, while becomings move at infinite speed across the surface of planes and within concepts. In aligning history with this movement, however, I am not advocating the actual over the virtual, or State striation over pure becoming. My objective is rather to go between these two – to show how the onto-logical nature of this movement is itself a between, the composite or differential of 'history/becoming' that I have now forwarded in many guises. With this in mind, it is unsurprising that when Deleuze and Guattari address the relation between the old and new idiot – that is, the question of creativity – they reiterate the double movement that was discussed above: on the one hand, the two idiots are 'most certainly not the same persona; a mutation has taken place' (WP 63). But on the other hand, as Deleuze and Guattari go on: 'And yet a slender thread links the two idiots, as if the first had to lose reason so that the second rediscovers what the other, in winning it, had lost in advance: Descartes goes mad in Russia' (WP 63). Thus once again, we find a continuity and caesura that cannot be disentangled (since it is a heterogeneous continuity). As we saw with the thread between Theseus-Ariadne-Dionysus in Chapter 1, pure becoming cannot bring about the link between Descartes and Russia alone, for it also requires an historical ontology.

These are not Deleuze and Guattari's words. In fact, according to Deleuze and Guattari, while 'philosophy constantly brings con-ceptual personae to life', the role of history is to 'go through these personae, through their changes according to planes and through their variety according to concepts' (WP 62). In other words, history is merely a reflection on the *extent* of a transformation, and plays no great part when metamorphosis is in the making. But as I have now proven in many ways, this is not the last word on history in Deleuze, for along with the image of history-as-historicism, the image that aligns history with the judging of the intellect rather than the action of intuition, we can find in Deleuze another more productive theory and use of history. We must therefore explore what role history plays not only in analysing a past persona, but more profoundly how his-torical personae themselves generate life.

A conceptual persona is not a character: 'they only nominally coincide and do not have the same role' (WP 63). Whereas a charac-ter is wedded to, on the one hand, a concept that it either promotes or denigrates, and on the other hand, a plane upon which that concept is laid out, 'conceptual personae carry out the movements that describe the author's plane of immanence, and they play a part in the very creation of the author's concepts' (WP 63). In this sense, conceptual personae come before the characters that play out a philosophy, for they indeed take part in the generation of that philosophy in the first place. Conceptual personae also have a life independent of the philosophers that both create and use them; they are not merely the instruments of a philosopher but if anything the contrary: 'The conceptual persona is not the philosopher's representative but, rather, the reverse: the philosopher is only the envelope of his principal conceptual personae who are the intercessors, the real subjects of his philosophy' (WP 64). A philosopher is thus the particular mixture of the conceptual personae that they work with and through; a philosopher is the 'idiosyncrasy of his conceptual personae' (WP 64).

If Nietzsche is Deleuze and Guattari's quintessential example of this relation, it is because the idiosyncrasy is so rich in him. As Nietzsche remarks in a famous letter to his mentor Jakob Burckhardt 'I am every name in history' (Nietzsche 1976: 685). Many Nietzschean scholars take this letter to illustrate the severity of Nietzsche's terminal madness, but Deleuze takes this proclamation quite seriously (in keeping with the relevance he finds between Nietzsche's biographical decline and his philosophy of descent). However, in discussing Nietzsche and his conceptual personae, Deleuze and Guattari make clear that these relations are above all contoured by becoming:

> [C]onceptual personae, in Nietzsche and elsewhere, are not mythical personifications or historical persons or literary or novelistic heroes. Nietzsche's Dionysus is no more the mythical Dionysus than Plato's Socrates is the historical Socrates. Becoming is not being, and Dionysus becomes philosopher at the same time that Nietzsche becomes Dionysus. (WP 65)

A philosopher's conceptual personae are thus quite distinct from historical persons (among other things). This statement must, however, be approached with caution: while it is true that conceptual personae are not historical persons and cannot be reduced to historical actuality, the studies of this book have shown how history need not be confined by its actual side either; history also has its virtual side – that side which is not enslaved by a linear chronology. Thus while it is true that 'becoming is not being', we must acknowledge that history need not be solely assigned to the side of being. If history is freed from this pigeonhole, then we will see that the historical nature of personae does not come at the expense of its becoming; personae will not be reduced to historical persons, nor will the historical nature of personae be ignored or explained away. In short, personae are historical not because they are fixed in time and place (i.e. reduced to a particular person), but because the mutating trajectory of their history (e.g. the idiot's historical trajectory from Nicholas of Cusa to Descartes to Chestov to Dostoyevsky etc.) is a part of who they are and what they do.

In order to extrapolate on how personae differ from and relate to people, as they are understood 'historically, mythologically, or commonly' (WP 64), Deleuze and Guattari make a distinction between conceptual personae and psychosocial types. Psychosocial types such as 'the father' or 'the President', 'the capitalist' or 'the proletarian', operate within and inform us about social fields. Not only do they tell us about the 'structures and functions' of a social field, but also the 'particular movements that affect the Socius' (WP 67). Thus the role of psychosocial types is 'to make perceptible, in the most insignificant or most important circumstances, the formation of territories, the vectors of deterritorialization, and the process of reterritorialization' (WP 68). While psychosocial types inform us about the relative structures and movements of a particular social field, conceptual personae cut across planes at an absolute speed that is not confined by time and place. More significantly, conceptual personae differ from psychosocial types in that they strictly have to do with *thought* – thought's territories and absolute movements: '*The role of conceptual personae is to show thought's territories, its absolute deterritorializations and reterritorializations*' (WP 69). Therefore, unlike psychosocial types, 'Conceptual personae are thinkers, solely thinkers' (WP 69); they 'are no longer empirical, psychological, and social determinations, still less abstractions, but intercessors, crystals, or seeds of thought' (WP 69).

The question then becomes, what is thought's relation to the world? For Deleuze and Guattari, thought is not reducible to a particular social field, nor is a social field reducible to an incorporeal thought. This is why 'Even if the word *absolute* turns out to be exact, we must not think that deterritorializations and reterritorializations of thought transcend psychosocial ones, any more than they are reducible to them, or to an abstraction or ideological expression of them' (WP 69–70). Absolute thoughts are conveyed in a world through types that are relative to that world. These types, on the one hand, determine the relative contour of an absolute thought. But on the other hand, types are themselves influenced by the movement that comes from without, in turn changing what they are. Thus Deleuze and Guattari describe the 'constant penetrations' (WP 67) between the two as follows:

> [Between psychosocial types and conceptual personae] is a conjunction, a system of referrals or perpetual relays. The features of conceptual personae have relationships with the epoch or historical milieu in which they appear that only psychosocial types enable us to assess. But, conversely, the physical and mental movements of psychosocial types, their pathological symptoms, their relational attitudes, their existential modes, and their legal status, become susceptible to a determination purely of thinking and of thought that wrests them from both the historical state of affairs of a society and the lived experience of individuals, in order to turn them into the features of conceptual personae, or *thought-events* on the plane laid out by thought or under the concepts it creates. Conceptual personae and psychosocial types refer to each other and combine without ever merging. (WP 70)

Conceptual personae thus form a quite complex network with psychosocial types and historical persons. To give an example, Nietzsche the historical person, in his psychosocial role as a professor, teaches the concept of the eternal return through the conceptual persona of Zarathustra and tragedy through the conceptual persona of Dionysus. Zarathustra and Dionysus, on the one hand, are necessarily 'assessed' or conveyed to the world through psychosocial types – the nobleman's as opposed to the plebeian's Zarathustra, the professor's as opposed to the poet's Dionysus – thus making conceptual personae relational to the milieu they appear in. But on the other hand, these conceptual personae change what it is to be a teacher or nobleman (Zarathustra in particular inaugurates a new pedagogy) thus turning psychosocial types into a feature of conceptual personae. These relations furthermore extend beyond any one set of person-type-persona. For instance, the historical person Deleuze constructs his plane of nomadology by in part appealing to the conceptual persona of Nietzsche the 'nomad thinker' (see DI 252–60); Deleuze could also be said to make a conceptual persona of 'the capitalist' psychosocial type – a persona that carries an absolute thought of contingency (rather than just a socio-economic system), and indeed thinks throughout all of history (the 'universal history of capitalism').

As this example shows us, conceptual personae and psychosocial types, along with historical persons, rely upon one another for their very nature and can never be considered in isolation. When added to the recognition that history, as an ontological force, cannot be confined to 'actual people' (or states of affairs) but is an integral part of conceptual personae to begin with, the notion that personae are against or without history is ameliorated.

Although Deleuze and Guattari go on in the rest of their examination of conceptual personae to further explore the relations between concepts, planes and personae, showing how they all interrelate and presuppose one another, for the sake of our current project it would be of more use to continue our analysis of the absolute movements of thought and their relations to relative social fields. This is indeed the direction that Deleuze and Guattari will take in their final chapter on the nature of philosophy – 'geophilosophy'. Let us then explore this final chapter on what is philosophy, and inquire as to what role history has to play.[6]

Historiophilosophy

At this point we are in full possession of Deleuze and Guattari's definition of philosophy:

> Philosophy presents three elements, each of which fits with the other two but must be considered for itself: *the prephilosophical plane it must lay out (immanence), the persona or personae it must invent and bring to life (insistence), and the philosophical concepts it must create (consistency).* Laying out, inventing, and creating constitute the philosophical trinity – diagrammatic, personalist, and intensive features. (WP 76–7)

This completed definition, however, only accounts for one half of Deleuze and Guattari's answer to the question 'what is philosophy?' Aside from their explication of philosophy's principle elements, it remains to be explained how these principles came about. Put otherwise, given the *internal* definition of philosophy's *de jure* principles, what are the *de facto* conditions and *external* relations between thought and the world that facilitate the birth of philosophy and contour its subsequent development? This question is of keen importance, for thought is not an entirely cerebral matter – it must always occur *somewhere*. The 'where' of philosophical thought must therefore be acknowledged as a critical factor in the determination of 'what' a thought is and 'who' it is that thinks it.

Deleuze and Guattari's short answer to the 'where' of philosophical thought is provided by the following sentence: 'thinking takes place in the relationship of territory and earth' (WP 85). According to their terminology, a territory (*territoire*) is a socially structured space that is overlaid upon the earth (*terre*), the latter of which has no intrinsic social subdivisions. All thought, as the above remark stipulates, involves a movement from one to the other. Thought is 'deterritorialised' when it is detached from a particular territory, and it is 'reterritorialised' when it conjugates with some new or other territory. Deterritorialisation thus involves movements from a territory to the earth, while the process of reterritorialisation restores territories on the earth (WP 86). Deterritorialisation is called 'relative' when 'it concerns the historical relationship of the earth with the territories that take shape and pass away on it, its geological relationship with eras and catastrophes, its astronomical relationship with the cosmos and the stellar system of which it is a part' (WP 88). Deterritorialisation is relative, in other words, when it specifically describes the movements from various territories back to *the* earth (the one and only). Deterritorialisation is absolute, on the other hand, when the earth itself 'passes into the pure plane of immanence of a Being-thought, of a Nature-thought of infinite diagrammatic movements' (WP 88). Thus while relative deterritorialisation always concerns a movement from territories to the earth of which it is a part, in absolute deterritorialisation it is the earth itself that is made relative to a plane of immanence: 'Thinking consists in stretching out a plane of immanence that absorbs the earth (or rather, "adsorbs" it)' (WP 88). By adsorbing the earth onto a plane of thought, the earth itself is made contingent to the absolute movement (speed) of thought, thus making possible 'the creation of a future new earth' through the power of thought (WP 88).

While it might appear from such a description that absolute deterritorialisation is of greater significance than relative deterritorialisation, and furthermore that absolute thought on its own is capable of creating a new reality, Deleuze and Guattari are quick to make the following disclaimer:

> Nonetheless, absolute deterritorialization can only be thought according to certain still-to-be-determined relationships with relative deterritorializations that are not only cosmic but geographical, historical, and psychosocial. There is always a way in which absolute deterritorialization takes over from a relative deterritorialization in a given field. (WP 88)

Absolute deterritorialisation, therefore, does not think alone: without the right milieu, without the appropriate relation to the relative, there will be no new earth. This could be referred to as the moment of *counter-virtualisation* in Deleuze and Guattari's work. Unlike the process of counter-actualisation, which describes the creative reinfusing and singularisation of the virtual event as it is actualised in various bodies and states of affairs, counter-virtualisation refers to the contrary process whereby the movement of virtualisation is accompanied by a counter-movement that dives back into the creative capacity of the actual. Because of this insistence on, or more accurately persistence of, actual relative milieus, even the determination of philosophy's *de jure* principles, let alone their development, must be acknowledged to have come about for particular contingent and effective reasons – it need not have happened, or need not have happened in the way that it did.[7]

So what *did* happen? Philosophy arose in Ancient Greece, Deleuze and Guattari claim, due to the confluence of three elements: immanence (the 'pure sociability' of the Greek milieu as opposed to imperial sovereignty); friendship (the 'pleasure in forming associations', including rivalry); and opinion (the 'taste for the exchange of views, for conversation') (WP 87–8). Regardless of whether one agrees with the elements listed, it is important to remember that Deleuze and Guattari's primary objective here is to show how the definition of philosophy, whatever it happens to be, is in part dependent upon the relative milieu in which it first arose. Philosophy did not just arise anywhere; it arose in Greece at a particular time. To this statement one might respond, is it not possible to speak of Chinese, Hindu, Jewish or Islamic philosophy? Deleuze and Guattari's initial answer is yes, to the extent that a philosophical structure or plane of thought can be populated by elements other than philosophical concepts (such as figures). But as they immediately qualify, it is only through the effect of the specifically Greek philosophical concept that such an apparatus indeed first became philosophical. The final answer is therefore no, there cannot be a Chinese, Hindu, Jewish or Islamic philosophy (in the beginning), insofar as these other non-Greek forms of thought deal in figures (rather than concepts) which 'unfold in wisdoms and religions according to a bifurcation that wards off philosophy in advance from the point of view of its very possibility' (WP 93). As such, philosophy did not just 'happen to occur' in Greece. Rather, philosophy, in its inception, *is and must be* Greek. This is not to say that there is an internal necessity to philosophy. On the contrary, philosophy's internal structure is dependent upon its external relations:

The birth of philosophy required an *encounter* between the Greek milieu and the plane of immanence of thought. It required the conjunction of two very different movements of deterritorialization, the relative and the absolute, the first already at work in immanence. Absolute deterritorialization of the plane of thought had to be aligned or directly connected with the relative deterritorialization of Greek society. The encounter between friend and thought was needed. In short, philosophy does have a principle, but it is a synthetic and contingent principle – an encounter, a conjunction. It is not insufficient by itself but contingent in itself. Even in the concept, the principle depends upon a connection of components that could have been different, with different neighborhoods. The principle of reason such as it appears in philosophy is a principle of contingent reason and is put like this: there is no good reason but contingent reason; there is no universal history except of contingency. (WP 93)[8]

Philosophy therefore has a principle. This principle naturally defines what philosophy is, and as such presents necessary relations *within* that principle. But as Althusser would say, this necessity was not always so – it had to *become*-necessary (see above, Chapter 4). The systematicity of philosophy is thus brought about by a contingent swerve and encounter; it is a living confirmation of contingency, not necessity. This means that philosophy, as we know it, is only so due to (in part) the Greek milieu in which it arose, but this relation is as contingent as the nature of the Greek milieu is to begin with. If this milieu had been different, so too would philosophy (if it indeed arose at all).

The primary way Deleuze and Guattari choose to demonstrate this is by considering the immense significance that Greece's geographical reality plays in its production of philosophy. As they point out, philosophy arose where it did partly due to Greece's 'fractal structure [where] each point of the peninsula is close to the sea and its sides have great length' (WP 87), as well as Greece's unique regional location which makes it 'the first to be at once near enough to and far enough away from the archaic eastern empires to be able to benefit from them without following their model' (WP 87).[9] Due to the region's variable and broken topology, as well as its bordering of an empire it is not within, the Greek world is able to develop a 'multiplicity of independent cities or distinct societies' (WP 87) – in other words, a literal heterogeneous multiplicity – that is distinct yet informed by the Orient. This constellation is also able to better accommodate, due its heterogeneous nature, those 'strangers in flight' who break with the empire (WP 87). It is for this reason that even though the first philosophers come from outside the Greek world, their thought is profoundly Greek: 'Philosophers are strangers, but philosophy is Greek' (WP 87).[10]

By illustrating the great importance of geographical features to the birth of philosophy, Deleuze and Guattari are led to conclude that: 'Philosophy is a geophilosophy in precisely the same way that history is a geohistory from Braudel's point of view' (WP 95). This invocation of Braudel, however, merits closer examination. For Braudel, history can only be appropriately understood if an appreciation is given to its geographical factors. For example, in order to understand the economic crisis in Florence between 1580 and 1585, one need first extend the scope of their research to Venice and Ferrara. From there the role of trade with the Far East will become apparent. But this influence is itself dependent upon the Moorish merchants who service the trade route through the Indian Ocean in the wake of the declining Portuguese. As is clear from this example, any history that is worth its salt will be a geohistory, spreading in this case up the Italian coast, across the eastern trade routes and throughout the Portuguese empire (Braudel 1980: 13). Nonetheless, it would, however, be false to suggest that geography alone occupies a privileged position in Braudel's history. Sociology and economics are just some of the other social sciences which Braudel's conception of history is influenced by and in relation with. How could one ever hope to fully understand the decline of the Portuguese without these other modes of inquiry? I would add philosophy to this list – the role that thinking plays in geo-socio-history. But must not history also be added to philosophy's list – the role history plays in philosophy's nature? To say that the nature of philosophy depends upon a particular milieu is therefore not just to assert the importance of geography, since every milieu, as Braudel's work shows us above all, is as much historical as it is geographical.

This can be shown if we continue to follow the movements of Deleuze and Guattari's geophilosophy. In order to further flesh out how absolute thought requires a relation to relative milieus, Deleuze and Guattari realise that a second example will be needed. Indeed, if they are to convincingly show how the nature of philosophy is in part dependent upon its relations to a milieu, Deleuze and Guattari will have to not only show how philosophy could have been other, but how it *is* other to what it *was*; they will need to compare two instances of philosophy that are different, that have different relative milieus, yet are both philosophy definitionally (as opposed to wisdoms or religions). Setting aside the birth of philosophy, Deleuze and Guattari thus turn their attention to the re-emergence of philosophy in Europe. As we saw above, various conditions of the Greek milieu combined to allow for philosophy's emergence. According to Deleuze and Guattari, analogous conditions come together once again in modern Europe. Capitalism, as it turns out, is the driving force for this conjunction: 'capitalism leads Europe into a fantastic relative deterritorialisation that is due first of all to city-towns *and that itself takes place through immanence*' (WP 97). But why does capitalism play such an important role, and where does it come from itself?

These two questions are both answered by Deleuze and Guattari through their precise definition of capitalism. As we saw in Chapter 4, capitalism arises out of an encounter between free labour and capital-money. This response to the origins of capitalism, however, is dependent upon the nature of the capitalist machine that issues it. Phrased within the language and problematic context of *What Is Philosophy?*: 'Marx accurately constructs a concept of capitalism by determining the two principal components, naked labor and pure wealth, with their zone of indiscernibility when wealth buys labor' (WP 97). But after having constructed the concept/machine of capitalism, the question still remains: 'why here now', why this encounter instead of another analogous instance? More specifically: 'Why capitalism in the West rather than in China of the third or even the eighth century?' (WP 97). The solution Deleuze and Guattari offer follows from their construction of the (well-posed) problem:

> *Only the West extends and propagates its centers of immanence.* The social field no longer refers to an external limit that restricts it from above, as in the empires, but to immanent internal limits that constantly shift by extending the system, and that reconstitute themselves through displacement. (WP 97)

Deleuze and Guattari are recounting here the shift between the despotic machine and the capitalist machine. As explained in Chapter 4, the capitalist machine differs from the despotic in that it does not striate from above or redirect flow (overcode) to a single despot. Instead, the capitalist machine decodes the entire social field and thus spreads itself across the face of the globe by becoming 'a motley painting of everything that has ever been believed' (AO 34 and 267). Capitalism as such 'has no exterior limit, but only an interior limit that is capital itself and that it does not encounter, but reproduces by always displacing it' (AO 231). European capitalism thus

173

arises from its eminent propagation of immanence, and it is for this exact reason that capitalism is so important to philosophy. What Deleuze and Guattari are looking for in their search for philosophy through history are instances of radical immanence.[11] They found it once in Ancient Greece, and they have found it again in European capitalism:

> [T]he infinite movement of thought, what Husserl calls Telos, must enter into conjunction with the great relative movement of capital that is continually deterritorialized in order to secure the power of Europe over all other peoples and their reterritorialization on Europe. Modern philosophy's link with capitalism, therefore, is of the same kind as that of ancient philosophy with Greece: *the connection of an absolute plane of immanence with a relative social milieu that also functions through immanence*. From the point of view of philosophy's development, there is no necessary continuity passing from Greece to Europe through the intermediary of Christianity; there is the contingent recommencement of a same contingent process, in different conditions. (WP 98)

As the last part of this passage perfectly illustrates, Deleuze and Guattari are not concerned with annotating how philosophy is passed from one generation to the next in causal-linear time. Their method is rather *stratigraphic*: two distant milieus or strata of existence are engendered (Greece and Europe) and connected by a bolt of lightening (absolute thought). This way of thinking, whereby non-adjacent events in time communicate with one another directly, might at first seem anti-historical. Such, however, need not be the case: on the one hand, I have shown how philosophy is not an ahistorical structure for historical ontology plays a significant part in its internal definition, while on the other hand I have shown how 'historical development' need not refer to a causal-linear progression but can instead be intensive, dynamic and stratigraphic.

To a certain extent, even some of the most widely held views about European history could be said to attest to this stratigraphy: what else is the Renaissance but a milieu that owes its nature to a leap in time from Greece to Europe, the resumption of Greece in very 'different conditions'? Historians no doubt often like to fill in the middle, but even when they do so it is not necessarily to the detriment of stratigraphy: the journey from Ancient Greece to European Renaissance, for instance, passes through the stratum of the Middle Ages, but this line is rarely conceived of as a well-measured process of progressive betterment. One may respond that to move at varying speeds, or even to have stages of historical regression, is not to move at an infinite speed or contest the causal-linear model of historical chronology. But this would be to miss my point: if the Renaissance moves at a different speed to the Middle Ages, it is because of its attempt to communicate with the Greeks *directly*, like Nietzsche's great nobles who call to one another from mountain tops across the valley. And why should this kind of relation not be considered historical? Why must the historical be confined to those accounts that respect well-measured causal-linear or teleological historicism? Credible alternative conceptions of history can certainly be forwarded, as I have illustrated. Allowing for this possibility, however, is the first necessary step.

There is another reason, more technical and specific, to resist the dismissal of history. Recalling my analysis of capitalism in Chapter 4, if capitalism is such a powerful and all-encompassing force of immanence for Deleuze and Guattari, it is not solely due to its superior power of deterritorialisation, *but also its axiomatic structure.* Deterritorialisation, as a result, is not enough on its own to secure the immanence that philosophy requires. If capitalism is to be universally immanent, an equally powerful force of reterritorialisation will be needed. In Deleuze and Guattari's present investigation, this role of capture in the process of creation is played by the modern nation-State: 'The immense relative deterritorialization of world capitalism needs to be reterritorialized on the modern nation State, which finds an outcome in democracy, the new society of "brothers", the capitalist version of the society of friends' (WP 98). Philosophy is thus 'reactivated' by capitalism, but it is reterritorialised on the democratic State.

As Deleuze and Guattari acknowledge, the democratic State might seem a poor candidate for reterritorialisation, since it is by no means a consistent territory (i.e. there are many different democratic States, with critical differences, all of which are far from 'ideal') (WP 102). The lack of a universal democratic State, however, is no obstacle to the reterritorialisation of philosophy. In fact, this is precisely Deleuze and Guattari's point: if philosophy differs today between France, England, Germany, etc., it is in part because of the ways in which these modern nation-States differ. 'Nation States [. . .] constitute the "models of realization" of this immanent axiomatic' (WP 106).[12] For every different nation-State in question we thus have a different realisation of philosophy. There are most certainly similarities between them, since all meet the requirements for the definition of philosophy.[13] But the fact that philosophy differs between nations is taken by Deleuze and Guattari as evidence for their claim that philosophy is a geophilosophy.[14]

Deleuze and Guattari's comparison of modern philosophy in different geographical locations to illustrate the importance of milieu is specifically borrowed from Nietzsche. As Deleuze and Guattari say: 'Nietzsche founded geophilosophy by seeking to determine the national characteristics of French, English, and German philosophy' (WP 102). In his discussion of 'Peoples and Fatherlands' in *Beyond Good and Evil*, Nietzsche compares philosophers and artists from France, England and Germany by referring to how they each reflect the general traits (as distilled by Nietzsche) of their respective nations. He offers such opinions as: 'They are no philosophical race, these Englishmen'; they have a 'profound normality' and 'a certain narrowness, aridity, and industrious diligence, something English in short', which places them on the side of 'knowledge' rather than 'those who can do things in the grand style, the creative' (Nietzsche 2000: 379–81). Setting aside the issue of whether Nietzsche's descriptions are accurate, the relevant question for our current investigation is: why do Deleuze and Guattari consider Nietzsche's determination of national characteristics to be specifically geographical? Is not history also an important factor in the determination of nations? One would think so, given that the majority of Nietzsche's remarks in this passage concern history and not geography. Geographical reality is certainly an important issue for Nietzsche – for example, one of the superiorities of the French character, according to Nietzsche, is that it 'contains a halfway successful synthesis of the north and the south which allows them to comprehend many things and to do things which an Englishman could never understand' (Nietzsche 2000: 384). But as evidenced by the other reasons offered for French superiority – 'their old, manifold, *moralistic* culture' and their 'capacity for artistic passions [which] has not been lacking in France for the last three centuries' – history is also clearly significant (Nietzsche 2000: 383). Thus while geographical features such as proximity (e.g. Italy's closeness to the Holy See), size (e.g. Germany as opposed to Switzerland) and terrain (e.g. is it land-locked, an island, or have a hinterland?) are critical in shaping the nature of a philosophy, it must be acknowledged that this alone cannot account for why philosophy should be a geophilosophy in Nietzsche's work, since other aspects, such as history, are equally as important to the national character of a philosophy. In this manner, it is not hard to see that Nietzsche's nationalisation of philosophy arises from and addresses much more than just geography: England may be far from Italy, but so too is Ancient Greece from Modern Greece; England may be far from Australia, but it is also closer in many ways than it is to Italy.[15]

Twice now we have therefore seen how Deleuze and Guattari preference geography when asserting the significance of relative milieus to the absolute thought of philosophy. And twice I have argued that historical reality is as significant as geographical reality in the determination of milieus and thus their impact on philosophy's nature. However, aside from this issue of comparative influence, the fact that Deleuze and Guattari endorse a programme of nationalistic caricaturisation might seem a bit strange to begin with. Such a practice, though, is not at all foreign to Deleuze, as evidenced by his nationalising of literature and style:

> American literature operates according to geographical lines: the flight towards the West, the discovery that the true East is in the West, the sense of the frontiers as something to cross, to push back, to go beyond. The becoming is geographical. There is no equivalent in France. The French are too human, too historical, too concerned with the future and the past. They spend their time in in-depth analysis. They do not know how to become, they think in terms of historical past and future. Even with the revolution, they think about a 'future of the revolution' rather than a revolutionary-becoming. (D 37)

While such a statement is guilty of indulging in generalisations (leading some commentators to even question whether Deleuze and Guattari are for or against geophilosophy (see Lampert 2006: 148–9)), it is also eminently philosophical. Deleuze and Parnet are here engaged in the abstraction of consistent virtual events from a cacophony of actual states of affairs. Given that their goal is to distil singularities of style, we must in turn admit that pointing out how historical fact is as relevant as geography to the makeup of a milieu does not really get to the heart of Deleuze and Guattari's project of geophilosophy; just as Deleuze and Guattari's nomadology is largely immune to the attacks mounted by various commentators on 'factual grounds',[16] so we must do more than point to actual facts if we are to illustrate the import of history to the nature of philosophy.

With this in mind, if the above quote from *Dialogues* is particularly instructive, it is because not only do Deleuze and Parnet differentiate between two national characters, they distinguish between geography and history itself. In other words, it is not just that America and France differ due to geography. Rather, one is geographical while the other is historical; one concerns a perpetual movement across space – a geographical intensity – while the other concerns a capturing and representation of it – an historical extensity. Such a manoeuvre is reminiscent of Deleuze's adoption of Bergsonian difference, whereby difference is not merely separated into two different natures (this nature as opposed to that), but is separated into differences in nature on the one hand and differences in degree on the other. The above distinction is also clearly related, as we saw in Chapter 3, to the sharp separation between the nomad and the State, whereby variability and geography are apportioned to the nomad and contrasted with the stasis and history of the State. Taking up this conceptual couplet again, Deleuze and Guattari suggest in their discussion of geophilosophy that while French and German philosophy are characterised by the establishment and control of foundations, English philosophy has a nomadic nature that allows for 'a movable and moving ground, a field of radical experience, an archipelagian world where they are happy to pitch their tents from island to island and over the sea' (WP 105). It is this latter geographical form that Deleuze and Guattari clearly associate their definition of philosophy with (and also the geographical features of Greece and capitalism). But insofar as this is the case, how can the nature of philosophy, for Deleuze and Guattari, be in any way historical? Paradoxically, as we will now see, it is in their discussion of philosophy's third milieu – becoming – that history arguably plays its most important role in determining the nature of philosophy, legitimising in turn an understanding of philosophy as *historiophilosophy*.

As Deleuze and Guattari conclude their examination into the relation between philosophical thought and relative milieus, the third and final milieu that they explore is not found in the past of philosophy or its present status but rather in its becoming – that which is in the process of coming about, philosophy's future. Although I have thus far critiqued Deleuze and Guattari's geophilosophy for its disregard of history, it must be acknowledged that the purpose of geophilosophy is not merely to show how philosophy is first born or how philosophies differ between different nation-States. If such were the case, then a simple contestation of their ancient history, or a recognition that philosophies differ greatly *within* a single nation, would put their entire project to rest. But arguing for a reduction of reality to either 'how it actually has been'[17] or extensive location is not Deleuze and Guattari's presiding point or objective. Indeed, much of Deleuze and Guattari's work would suggest the contrary. The Deleuzo-Guattarian nomad, for example, inhabits the same extensive space as the sedentary; they just do so in different ways (one smoothing, the other striating). Similarly, many of Deleuze's preferred novelists are said to 'speak like a foreigner in their own language' (D 4). The critical difference that is being indicated here resides not between natives who speak different languages (external difference between homogeneities) but rather in those who are foreign to themselves and thus differ from within (internal difference of heterogeneity, that which differs first and foremost from itself). In light of this, philosophy must not only have a relation to milieus in the past and present – the form of philosophy must also have a relation to its future, since by definition philosophy continually differs from itself and is thus always becoming-other: 'Becoming stranger to oneself, to one's language and nation, is not this the peculiarity of the philosopher and philosophy, their "style," or what is called a philosophical gobbledygook?' (WP 110).

For this reason, becoming, yet again, returns to the forefront of Deleuze and Guattari's understanding of philosophy. Not only is becoming central to the internal definition of philosophy (e.g. the concept's endo/exoconsistent relations of becoming), but it is also a relative milieu to which philosophy is reterritorialised on: 'The creation of concepts in itself calls for a future form, for a new earth and people that do not yet exist' (WP 108). Nevertheless, we must also again ask: does this promotion of becoming necessarily occur *at the expense* of history?

Deleuze and Guattari's concluding example in their definition of philosophy speaks to just this question ('Example 9'). It is directly foregrounded, however, in their analysis of a previous example ('Example 7'). In explaining why the principle of philosophy is contingent and not necessary, Deleuze and Guattari contrast their connection between philosophy and Greece with that of Hegel and Heidegger. In the case of Hegel, according to Deleuze and Guattari, the Greeks are the first to produce the concept, since they are the first 'to grasp the Object in a relationship with the subject' (WP 94). This relationship emerges in three successive stages: (1) contemplation of the object; (2) reflection of the subject; (3) communication of the concept with other subjects (see also WP 51). But as Deleuze and Guattari point out, at the beginning of this process 'it is not clear what distinguishes the antephilosophical stage of the Orient and the philosophical stage of Greece, since Greek thought is not conscious of the relationship to the subject that it presupposes without yet being able to reflect' (WP 94). Hegel's teleological philosophy of history, in which the Orient is prior to Greece, is therefore called into question.

Heidegger 'displaces' this problem in his history of philosophy. For Heidegger, the Orient is not prior to Greece but 'alongside' with respect to the difference between Being and beings (WP 94–5). Thus while the Orient and Greece coexist for Heidegger in a way that they did not for Hegel, their relation is equally as teleological since it is reduced to the internal structure of Being: 'What remains common to Heidegger and Hegel is having conceived of the relationship between Greece and philosophy as the origin and thus as the point of departure of a history internal to the West, such that *philosophy necessarily becomes indistinguishable from its own history*' (WP 95). In short, Deleuze and Guattari claim that Hegel and Heidegger never take philosophy's external and contingent relations seriously, for they reduce them to 'an analytic and necessary principle' (WP 94) – *Geist* or Being. Because of this, the contingent and creative relation between absolute thought and a relative milieu is replaced with a necessary and historicist relation: 'Hegel and Heidegger remain historicists inasmuch as they posit history as a form of interiority in which the concept necessarily develops or unveils its destiny' (WP 95).

What follows this critique of Hegel and Heidegger is one of the most focused and sustained discussions in Deleuze and Guattari's work on the difference between history and becoming. By the end of this passage, we are left in no doubt as to Deleuze and Guattari's placing of history on the side of necessity and capture, and becoming on the side of contingency and creation. However, if this attack on history is to be appropriately understood, two facts must be noted: (1) following as it does from their critique of Hegel and Heidegger, it is clear that by 'history' Deleuze and Guattari specifically mean *historicism* – meaning a form of history that is teleological, representational, chronological and/or mechanistically causal-linear; and (2) the alternative that Deleuze and Guattari endorse is directly credited to an *historian* – namely, Braudel. As Deleuze and Guattari specify, the correct way to ask after philosophy's contingency is to do as Braudel did: 'Why philosophy in Greece at that moment? It is the same for capitalism, according to Braudel: why capitalism in these places and at these moments?' (WP 95). To a certain extent, therefore, becoming is not opposed to history but aligned with it – an ontology of historical creativity that is other than historicism.

Deleuze and Guattari close their presentation of geophilosophy with a brief and masterful example that returns to their reading of the Event. In it, they drive home the distinction between history and becoming with respect to philosophy's reterritorialisation on the future, demonstrating how history 'is not experimentation' but at best the 'negative conditions' that make possible an experimental becoming that 'escapes history' (WP 111). But while this discussion clearly dismisses the creative capacities of history, in doing so it reaffirms my two points above: (1) the 'history' that they speak of is clearly historicism; and (2) the alternative they propose is inspired by thinkers such as Péguy, Nietzsche and Foucault who all promoted an alternative kind of *history*. Thus while Deleuze and Guattari may call on the 'aternal' and the 'untimely' in the name of becoming, it should be remembered that Péguy and Nietzsche didn't do so. For them, the terms were employed to engender an alternative historical sensibility and a *history for life* (see Chapter 1 for my demonstration of this).

Given these considerations, Deleuze and Guattari's distinction between history and becoming for the purposes of explicating their geophilosophy must be treated with extreme caution. Contrary to first appearances, the discussion of philosophy's future, its third milieu of becoming, is not necessarily at odds with history. Indeed, it is at the very moment when history appears most maligned – the moment of its execution, as it were – that an alternative form of history is called forth. In one respect, therefore, history comes to a bad end at the hands of becoming. But in another, history pulls off an extraordinary escape. To paraphrase (and pervert) Deleuze, it is as if history moves behind the back of pure becoming, 'in the moment when he blinks' (D 1). This history need not answer for the crimes of historicism, for it is what Nietzsche would call a 'history for the future' – a history, in other words, that is not opposed to becoming or to the bringing about of the future, since it is entirely commensurate with the process of creativity. If such a form of history is admitted within the purview of Deleuze and Guattari's definition of philosophy, one further transformation of its nature will be made possible: aside from the rearticulation of philosophy as a geophilosophy, philosophy will also become what could be referred to as an historiophilosophy.

*   *   *

We can now see that there are two answers to the question of what is history in Deleuze and Guattari's *What Is Philosophy?* The first goes as follows: history is opposed to becoming and associated with the actual as opposed to the virtual; history concerns states of affairs that capture the creative becomings of events; history aligns these states of affairs in a linear, chronological order which obeys a standard account of causality (unlike the becomings which cut across this history in a non-linear and simultaneous manner). But if we peer beneath the surface of Deleuze and Guattari's overt remarks on history, we will find another history which works in an entirely different way: a history which moves from the depths by zigzagging from one plane to the next; a history which intuits and endures; a history which does not follow a simple linear/chronological logic, but is non-linear, continually contingent and commensurable with what Deleuze and Guattari call 'stratigraphic time'. This history does not put an end to or capture untimely creations, but provides the means to achieve them. This history is not 'against' becoming, but is if anything its inspiration.

However, in drawing together so closely the nature of history and philosophy, a potential difficulty arises: if they share so much, then what *is* their difference? Deleuze's categorisation of Foucault is perhaps most instructive here. When describing Foucault in an interview, Deleuze notes how Foucault promotes an alternative method and ontology of history. But in doing so Deleuze insists that Foucault is not an historian:

> History's certainly part of his method. But Foucault never became a historian. Foucault's a philosopher who invents a completely different relation to history than what you find in philosophers of history. (N 94–5)

One might wonder why Foucault can be designated a philosopher who differs from all others in his particular field, yet not an historian who invents a new way of understanding and practising history. Foucault undoubtedly writes histories, as he would be the first to admit. So why would he not be an historian when he does so? The answer of course has to do with the definitions of philosophy and history that Deleuze brings to Foucault. While philosophy is a constructivism, history is an apparatus of capture. Therefore any philosophy worthy of the name is rebellious and constructive – 'to create is to resist' (WP 110) – while history, on the contrary, is institutional and instituting, a reflection and verification of the status quo. This is why is it possible for philosophers to differ radically from their tradition but not historians: differing from a tradition is philosophy definitionally, it is what true philosophers do, whereas solidifying and representing a tradition is the essence of history. These definitions place Deleuze in the curious position where if an historian constructs a concept/plane/persona in or through their historical tract, then they must be said to do so as a philosopher. Conversely, when a philosopher fails to construct their own concepts/plane/personae and instead brandishes the ready-made, they do so 'like the critic and historian of our time' (WP 83). But if one is willing to allow for a form of history that does not correspond to historicism and the State, and if philosophy is recognised to be in productive partnership with this other kind of history (in the same way that philosophy can be a geophilosophy and history a geohistory), then much of the opposition between the two, as with history and becoming, will be positively overcome. This is not to say that the two will become synonymous but rather that they will form a creative composite or differential: an historiophilosophy.

Such has therefore been the goal of this chapter: to promote an alternative nature and use of history that can be seen to have a productive role to play in Deleuze and Guattari's inquiry into 'what is philosophy'. In order to achieve this, what is required is a form of history that is truly distinct from historicism or history-as-actuality, a form of history, in other words, that is not confined to the dualism of virtual events and actual history or philosophical concepts and historical cultures, but goes beyond this simple dichotomy by effectively bringing them back together into a new monism or pluralism.[18] Although it might appear contradictory to combine history with becoming, this confusion only persists as long as we insist on a stark binary distinction that is itself devoid of transmutation. But as we have seen now in several different studies, the analytical separation of pure types is not an end in itself – it is just the beginning. And if we follow through on these various extrapolations of two, what we will find each time is a much more complex situation, where one becomes the other and both become one. Thus in reality history is not opposed to becoming but in perpetual production with it; it is never a question of one or the other, but both together as a creative composite. While it may be useful at times to distinguish radical becoming from State history, we must always be careful not to take this too far, apply it where it is inappropriate or make a micro-fascism of it.

Conclusion

In this book I have examined some of Deleuze's solo and co-authored writings to see what they might have to offer our understanding of the relation between history and becoming within a philosophy of creativity. Contrary to the belief that a Deleuzian process of creativity revolves around the promotion of becoming at the expense of history, this book has demonstrated through the course of five studies how Deleuze's work affords us with an important conception of historical creativity. By showing how history can be creative, and creativity part historical, the presumed opposition between history and becoming is overcome in favour of the composite 'history/becoming' – that differential which is irreducible to either side of the dualism and instead provides for their productive relation.

To its advantage, this reading of history and becoming within a philosophy of creativity need not ignore or explain away Deleuze's antipathy towards history. Indeed, I would be quite willing to add my voice to Deleuze's when he says: 'The thing is, I became more and more aware of the possibility of distinguishing becoming from history' (N 170). This is because I too am against the form of history that is being invoked in these statements – namely, the image of history-as-historicism or State history. In *Difference and Repetition*, this image of history is wedded to 'representation', the main antagonist of that work, and distinguished from the creativity of affirmative difference (DR 53–4). It is also variably associated by Deleuze with a mechanistic causal-linear ontology – the chronological 'order of succession' (DR 186) or 'the narrowly historical point of view of before and after' (WP 58) – and the tradition of teleology, in which history = destiny (WP 95). Although Deleuze does not go so far as to call for its elimination, since '[w]ithout history, becoming would remain indeterminate and unconditioned' (WP 96), there is no question that history is sharply separated by Deleuze from the process and act of experimentation and creation. But given this distaste for a history that is 'intended to intimidate any creation' (WP 83), is history to be abandoned to the clutches of historicism and the State apparatus of capture? Perhaps it is. Perhaps it is preferable to designate history as State history and be done with it. I am of the opinion, however, that there is something in history worth saving. For not only do I believe that history has more to offer than the image Deleuze criticises, but I would also maintain that Deleuzian philosophy itself forwards such an alternative.

What then is this alternative? I have chosen to describe it in five different ways (though there are undoubtedly others): as an intensive-depth, dynamic, nomadic, universal-contingent and as an historiophilosophy. In designating these alternatives, it must be reiterated that it has not been my intention to merely cast history in the role of pure becoming. If history is intensive, for example, it is because intensity does not solely belong to becoming, for it is *also* historical. And if history is nomadic, it is because the figure of the nomad has itself gone beyond its simple opposition to the State in search of a new composite formation. The purpose of my alternative presentations has thus been to illustrate the limitations inherent in any positioning of becoming 'against' history, whereby the former is confined by the category of virtual simultaneity and the latter by actual succession. To this end, my analyses have each strived to complexify, crack open and ultimately overcome the dualism of history and becoming, as well as several other associated dualisms, en route to the magical formula PLURALISM = MONISM (ATP 20).

In doing so, the effect has been twofold. Firstly, history has been shown to form a crucial part of Deleuze's philosophy of creativity, and not just as a negative that needs resisting. But in the process of achieving this outcome, it has also been shown how Deleuze has much to offer the philosophy of history. This twofold effect could be further pursued in a whole host of directions. To begin with, aside from those thinkers of historical creativity that I have touched on in this book – including Marx, Nietzsche, Bergson, Péguy and Braudel – there are several other figures from Deleuze's lineage, such as Spinoza, Hume and Whitehead, who would have much to offer our understanding of Deleuze's philosophy of history. Deleuze's historical ontology and methodology could also be productively compared with contemporaries of his, such as Derrida and Foucault, perhaps leading in the case of Foucault to an appreciation of nomadology and genealogy as two contrasting lines of thought issuing from Nietzsche. As for those of the 'opposed tradition', presumably Deleuze's nominated historicists – Hegel and Heidegger – would have plenty to say in response to Deleuze's rather unfavourable characterisations.

There are arguably even greater benefits to be had from pursuing connections beyond the confines of Philosophy. For instance, both Deleuzian scholarship and the discipline of historical theory (a field that has yet to show any real interest in Deleuze's work) have much to gain from one another through an increase in dialogue. Such an exchange could be particularly fruitful at present, given the general shift in historical theory away from the epistemological concerns of the late twentieth century and back towards issues of ontology (Bentley 2006: 349–50).

However, if such further investigations and conversations are to be possible, let alone productive, it will be necessary that we have recourse to a Deleuzian understanding of history and becoming that goes beyond their simple opposition. For as long as Deleuze is presumed to be 'against' history and 'for' becoming, it is hard to see how or why historical theorists should bother with Deleuze, and Deleuzians with history. But if it is acknowledged that there is another kind of history in Deleuze's work, a history that is a vital and active element in Deleuze's philosophy of creativity, then the way will be open for an engagement that can be of immense benefit to all.

Notes

Introduction

1. This modified translation is taken from Paul Patton. As he explains: 'The English text goes on to say that becoming is "the opposite" of history, thereby eliminating all the nuance of Deleuze's use of the verb "*s'opposer*".' Hence the need to accompany the suggestion of 'opposition' with the character of 'moving back and forth'. See Paul Patton 2009: 50, 53n.

2. Slavoj Žižek also distinguishes between different kinds of becoming in his *Organs without Bodies*. For Žižek, there is the sterile becoming of *The Logic of Sense* ('becoming as the impassive effect') and there is another becoming which is more productive ('becoming as the generative process' or 'the productive flux of pure becoming') (Žižek 2003: 20–1, 28, 30). Although my reading of becoming is in some ways similar to Žižek's, it also differs significantly. To begin with, Žižek's allocations are incorrect: on the one hand, the 'body without organs' that Žižek ascribes to the 'flux of becoming' is a product of and plays a significant role in *The Logic of Sense*, while on the other hand, the sterile becoming of *The Logic of Sense*, contrary to Žižek's reading, is crucial to all of Deleuze and Guattari's writings. Regardless of these discrepancies, however, the critical distinction between my project and Žižek's is that I am not at all interested in choosing sides. My primary concern is rather with how the various forms of becoming interrelate and complement one another, along with history.

3. For other examples of how DeLanda attempts to differentiate his materialist project from what he calls 'pure philosophical speculation', see DeLanda 1997: 21. DeLanda no doubt engages in such speculation himself, but this is purposely left to his conclusion, since such speculation, according to his methodology, can only be carried out *after* a sound and thorough investigation of the historical (and scientific) evidence has been completed. This also accounts for the fact that DeLanda's use of Deleuze and Guattari only really becomes fully explicit in the conclusion to his book.

4. See also Lampert 2006: 8: 'Here we see again the relation that this book will problematize. How is it that the simultaneous co-existence within an event, which makes it co-existent with any other event that

it intersects with, forms a system of distances? How is there temporal distance within simultaneity?'

5· See also Lampert 2006: 5, where he describes succession as 'merely an artifact created when we map the stages of what is primordially a set of co-existing possibilities'. DeLanda, as it happens, gives the opposite reading: instead of describing historical succession as the delaying of simultaneities, for DeLanda what is primary is the flow of succession, fixations being nothing more than the 'slowing down of this flowing reality' (DeLanda 1997: 258-9).

6. Lampert's reduction of succession to a latticework of simultaneities is arguably described well by the following passage from Bergson: 'It goes from an arrangement of things to a rearrangement, from a simultaneity to a simultaneity. Of necessity it neglects what happens in the interval; or if it does concern itself with it, it is in order to consider other arrangements in it, still more simultaneities' (Bergson 2007: 103).

7. For other commentaries on history and becoming that are content to adopt the dualism of actual history and virtual becoming *tout court*, see Gioli 2005–6: 165–6, as well as Vähämäki and Akseli Virtanen 2006.

8. As a point of difference, Peter Hallward argues that: '[Deleuze's] work, far from engaging in a description or transformation of the world, instead seeks to escape it'. Hallward even goes so far as to oppose Deleuze to Marx, claiming that Deleuze 'effectively recommends' that we contemplate the world, not change it. Hallward's position on Deleuze is thus distinct from both Holland's (politically) and DeLanda's (materially). It is also distinct from my reading, insofar as this book will seek to facilitate a détente between Deleuze and history that is at odds with Hallward's claim that 'As Deleuze presents it, the destiny of thought will not be fundamentally affected by the mediation of society, history or the world [...]'. See Hallward 2006: 7.

Chapter 1: The Depths of History

1. For Deleuze's references to this passage, see DR 189, LS 53, N 170–1 and WP 111 and 157.

2. For more on Péguy's 'mystique', see the essays in his *Temporal and Eternal*.

3. For a more detailed discussion on the connections between Riemann and Deleuze, see Plotnitsky 2006.

4. This stacking of difference produces Bergson's famous image of the cone. Although Bergson's cone is specifically a cone of memory, the image equally applies to the notion of virtual difference as understood by Deleuze. I will return to this more explicitly in Chapter 5.

5. It has been suggested by Keith Ansell Pearson that Deleuze criticises and indeed breaks with Bergson over the issue of intensity (Ansell

Pearson 1999: 74). This interpretation, based on a passage in which Deleuze appears to attack Bergson, is not entirely correct. For while this passage certainly begins with a criticism of Bergson, it is quickly retracted: 'There comes a moment, however, in this philosophy of Difference which the whole of Bergsonism represents, when Bergson raises the question of the double genesis of quality and extensity. This fundamental differenciation (quality-extensity) can find its reason only in the great synthesis of Memory which allows all the degrees of difference to coexist as degrees of relaxation and contraction, and rediscovers at the heart of duration the implicated order of that intensity which had been denounced *only provisionally* and from without' (DR 239, emphasis added). The footnote added further confirms that Deleuze's intention is not to depart from Bergson (on this issue) but if anything to show how Bergsonism can surmount this perceived problem: while duration and extensity, on the one hand, no doubt focus on the distinction between differences in kind and differences in degree, 'in another manner duration is indistinguishable from the *nature of difference* and, as such, includes all the *degrees of difference*: hence the reintroduction of intensities within duration, and the idea of a coexistence in duration of all the degrees of relaxation and contraction (the essential thesis of *Matter and Memory* and *La Pensée et le mouvant*)' (DR 331n).

6. For a thorough investigation of Deleuze's three syntheses of time for a philosophy of history, see Lampert 2006: 12–70.

7. It is significant that Deleuze invokes Althusser and Marx in this passage of *Difference and Repetition*, two thinkers who most certainly have a theory of historical production, for it indicates how there might indeed be a form of history other than historicism that is in line with Deleuze's virtual ontology. I will discuss these links with Althusser and Marx ('the historian' (ATP 428)) more closely in Chapter 4.

8. By 'science', Bergson here means that form of knowledge which concerns itself with static extensities rather than genuine durations, i.e. the intellect rather than intuition.

9. Péguy takes up many Bergsonian notions, such as duration and the cone of memory, no doubt learnt from his attendance at Bergson's lectures at the Collège de France.

10. Halévy also, to his peril, failed to adequately glorify the role that Péguy's *Cahiers* played in the Affair. See Alexander Dru's introduction to Péguy 2001: xviii.

11. In a passage that recalls both Péguy's theory of the event and writing style, Deleuze states: 'Nothing more can be said, and no more has even been said: to become worthy of what happens to us, and thus to will and release the event, to become the offspring of one's own events, and thereby to be reborn, to have one more birth, and to break with one's

carnal birth – to become the offspring of one's events and not one's actions, for the action is itself produced by the offspring of the event' (LS 149–50).

12. Keith Ansell Pearson disputes whether such connections between Bergson and Deleuze on the philosophy of history can be legitimately made, claiming that 'Questions of history and of historical memory and duration are to a large extent significantly absent from Bergson's oeuvre' (Ansell Pearson 2007). He furthermore considers the very suggestion to be 'highly provocative'. Evidence would, however, suggest otherwise. Aside from the fact that Bergson employs numerous examples throughout his writings that make use of history (both personal and social) and offer an interpretation of it, Bergson also pointedly refers to the ontology of history when elaborating on the nature of duration. Indeed, it is none other than Bergson's infamous example of sugar melting in water that suggests how a history might unfold itself gradually, 'as if it occupied a duration like our own' (Bergson 1998: 9–10; see also 35–7). I will come back to these examples in Chapter 5. For now, however, it could be simply noted that Péguy and other historical thinkers such as Arnold Toynbee were no doubt attuned to the significance of Bergson for history, though it is true that the field of Bergsonian philosophy of history is largely dormant today.

13. See NP 18: 'Dionysus carries Ariadne up to the sky; the jewels in Ariadne's crown are the stars. Is this the secret of Ariadne? The bursting constellation of a famous dicethrow? It is Dionysus who throws the dice. It is he who dances and transforms himself, who is called "Polygethes", the god of a thousand joys.'

14. For a fuller analysis of the relation between Nietzsche and Deleuze's untimely, see Lundy 2009: 188–205.

15. I am aware that this association of the eternal return with history is highly debatable, especially given Deleuze's claim that the eternal return can only concern the third time of the series, the future (DR 90). However, given Deleuze's penchant for associating Nietzsche's untimely with the eternal return, I see no reason not to do the same, though in my case with Nietzsche's original historical project in mind. Accordingly, I would argue, following Nietzsche, that even if the eternal return can only be 'properly called a belief of the future, a belief in the future' (DR 90), this belief is itself never fully without history, insofar as unhistorical forces are employed in the services of a *history for life*.

16. Other historical thinkers could be usefully added to this list. As one example, Christian Kerslake has shown how Deleuze draws from Arnold Toynbee for his concepts of nomadism and universal history. See Kerslake 2008: 17–48.

Notes

Chapter 2: The Surfaces of History

1. It could be noted that Deleuze will later explain how Chronos has his own becoming-mad. The becoming-mad of Chronos, however, is not a result of his evasion of the present but precisely the opposite: Chronos can only account for that which is not present by and in the present. Chronos, as such, becomes-mad due to the difference within him that he cannot reconcile – the difference that drives him insane: 'Saturn grumbles from deep within Zeus' (LS 164). Thus the distinction between surface and depth is maintained, despite the becoming of Chronos: 'The essential difference is no longer simply between Chronos and Aion, but between the Aion of surfaces and the whole of Chronos together with the becoming-mad of the depths' (LS 165).

2. If speed is understood loosely as a 'rate of change', then infinite speed refers to an instantaneous change.

3. It is perhaps telling that the next time Deleuze refers to a 'chessboard' it will be to describe the organising power of the State form (ATP 352–3). I will return to this point in Chapter 3.

4. As we will see in Chapter 3, this idea will form the basis for Deleuze and Guattari's motionless or 'interminably still' nomads.

5. Jay Lampert shares this rough division of *The Logic of Sense* into two halves (Lampert 2006: 97). Lampert's interest in this division, however, pertains predominantly to the quasi-cause, whereas my concern is with the complementary character of history and becoming. See Chapter 6 of his monograph for an excellent and sustained examination of the quasi-cause for a philosophy of history.

6. It has been suggested by Daniel W. Smith that the genesis of the conditions of the real, which he also refers to as 'the conditions for novelty itself', concerns 'what Deleuze calls a *static* genesis (that is, a genesis that takes place between the virtual and its actualization), and not a *dynamic* genesis (that is, an historical or developmental genesis that takes place between actual terms, moving from one actual term to another)' (Smith 2007: 7–8). Accordingly, history is downplayed in Smith's account in favour of the future. However, given my reading of the dynamic genesis as moving from depth to surface, states of affairs to incorporeal events and/or the actual to the virtual (instead of actual to actual), history – understood as historical creativity – plays a more prominent part in my interpretation of the production of the new.

7. One might note that Deleuze distinguishes in some of his later work between history and the process of development (N 49). Again, however, I would point out that by 'history' Deleuze here means historicism, not the alternative kind of history that I am attempting to describe.

8. For a comprehensive account of the linguistic and psychoanalytic

context of the stages of dynamic genesis, see Chapter 5 of Sean Bowden's outstanding *The Priority of Events: Deleuze's* Logic of Sense (2011).

9. While it is true that Deleuze will go on to show how phonemes are part of a circular system with morphemes and semantemes (LS 230), this does not alter my basic point: Deleuze is here showing how this system emerges in dynamic movements or steps, 'from the phonemic letter to the esoteric word as morpheme, and then from this to the portmanteau word as semanteme' (LS 232).

10. This description of the creative act has much resonance with Nietzsche's figure of youth. On the one hand, Nietzsche's historian of youth is able to bring forth the new due to their innocence and arrogance – their *ahistorical* and *suprahistorical* elements. But on the other hand, this creativity is also a product of the relation the youth forms with the past – their ability to hear the *voice* of the Delphic oracle.

11. In Deleuze's own example, to compare, this development occurs when the child castrates their 'imaginary phallus' and appropriates the 'symbolic phallus' of the father. By identifying with the 'law' of the father, symbolised by the phallus the father has, the child gains an organising principle that accordingly allows them to rise from their own physical surface to a metaphysical surface (LS 208).

12. See Bowden 2011. See also Williams *'Pure events are primary because of the nature of their role in the genesis of actual things when compared to the role of actual things in the genesis of pure events'* (2008: 195). For Bowden in particular, the problem of the dynamic genesis will be ancillary to the presupposed problem of pure incorporeal event, 'on which individual "things" in general ontologically depend, "all the way down"' (Bowden 2011: 13). In contrast to this, I am of the opinion that one should preference *neither* the descent from the incorporeal to the corporeal *nor* the ascent from the corporeal to the incorporeal.

13. This point will be further explored in the following chapters of this book, looking for instance at the importance of 'matter-flow' for abstract machines and the role of 'milieus' in the production of concepts.

14. Repeating his remarks on depth from DR 234–5, Deleuze will stress this association of Nietzsche with depth even further by way of a passing critique of Bachelard: 'It is strange that Bachelard, seeking to characterize the Nietzschean imagination, presents it as an "ascensional psychism". *L'Air et les songes* (Paris: Corti, 1943), ch. 5. Not only does he reduce to the minimum the role of earth and surface in Nietzsche, but he interprets Nietzschean "verticality" as being, first of all, height and ascent. But it is indeed rather depth and descent. The bird of prey does not rise, save by accident; rather, it hovers above and drops down upon it. It is even necessary to say that, for Nietzsche, depth serves the

purpose of denouncing the idea of height and the idea of ascent; height is but a mystification, a surface effect, which does not fool the eye of the depths and is undone under its gaze' (LS 347n).

15. For more on Deleuze's reading of the relation between Nietzsche's life and philosophy, see his essay 'Nietzsche' in Deleuze 2001.

16. In Chapter 3 we will see how this relation of dualism and monism is developed in Deleuze and Guattari's analysis of the nomad and the State as well as the smooth and striated. Above all, my investigation there will demonstrate how Deleuzian dualisms are themselves split and rejoined in a process of metamorphosis.

17. As Nietzsche puts it in *Beyond Good and Evil*: 'I hear with pleasure that our sun is swiftly moving toward the constellation of *Hercules* – and I hope that man on this earth will in this respect follow the sun's example'. See Nietzsche 2000: 367.

Chapter 3: Nomadic History

1. See, for example, WP 95–6, where Braudel is enlisted against history, and N 94, where Foucault is said to never have been a historian.

2. For more on the relation of Deleuze and Toynbee see Kerslake's 'Becoming against History: Deleuze, Toynbee and Vitalist Historiography' (2008). Most interestingly, Kerslake discovers how Toynbee's great project of universal history (in which this nomadism appears) is in large part inspired by his Bergsonism. This not only verifies the significance of Bergson's philosophy of history to Deleuze, but it also illustrates another way in which Deleuze uses and endorses various historical theories. I would point out, however, that Kerslake arguably overextends his analysis by implicitly suggesting that Deleuze receives his Bergson through Toynbee. As I see no reason not to allow Bergson's philosophy of history to have a direct and primary influence on Deleuze's philosophy of history, the influence of Toynbee on Deleuze's philosophy of history rather corresponds to the manner of his appearance in Deleuze's work: at first a footnote and at best a useful example of the ontology I have been explicating.

3. As we saw in Chapter 2, this was the same problem Chronos had when attempting to comprehend becoming: 'Chronos must still express the revenge taken by future and past on the present in terms of the present, because these are the only terms it comprehends and the only terms that affect it' (LS 164).

4. For the Boulez text see Boulez 1971: 87, translation modified. For more on the dissymmetrical passages between and transmutations of the smooth and the striated, see ATP 474, 480, 482, 486, 493 and 500.

5. For the relevant Nietzsche passage, see his *Genealogy of Morals*,

second essay, section 17 (Nietzsche 2000: 522–3). It could be argued that Nietzsche's 'blond beasts' are Deleuze and Guattari's nomads, but this is not claimed or shown by Deleuze and Guattari, and neither would it have any effect on the fact that the quote is used inconsistently between *Anti-Oedipus* and *A Thousand Plateaus* to describe the nature of two contrary entities – the State apparatus and the nomadic machine. As we will see in Chapter 4, this slippage between the State and the nomad is not unlike Deleuze and Guattari's slippage between the despotic and the capitalist machines when explaining the nature of universal history.

6. As Deleuze says in a similar vein: 'My favorite sentence in *Anti-Oedipus* is: "No, we've never seen a schizophrenic"' (N 12). This statement is obviously untrue, as Guattari spent many years working in an asylum treating numerous schizophrenics. But this is of course their point: true nomads and schizos are not necessarily those people that anthropologists and psychologists study and 'cure'.

7. In his work on Deleuze and history, DeLanda fails to recognise this distinction, instead claiming that the phylum and the smooth are 'nearly synonymous' (along with the BwO and the rhizome). Perhaps this is another example of DeLanda intentionally appropriating Deleuze and Guattari for the purposes of producing his own creative philosophy. But as my analysis will show, a distinction between the two is necessary if we are to distinguish between the various forms of becoming and history in Deleuze and Guattari's philosophy. See DeLanda 1997: 330n.

8. For further evidence of how the theme of flow and form discussed in the above block quotes is taken from Bergson, see ATP 374: 'This is something like intuition and intelligence in Bergson, where only intelligence has the scientific means to solve formally the problems posed by intuition, problems that intuition would be content to entrust to the qualitative activities of a humanity engaged in *following* matter.'

9. I would note here that *both* corporeal things *and* incorporeal events are ontologically defined and made up of lines. This further bolsters the intuition of this book that it is incorrect to give an ontological priority to either things or the Event. See also D 143: 'This is why the questions of schizoanalysis or pragmatics, micro-politics itself, never consists in interpreting, but merely in asking what are your lines, individual or group, and what are the dangers on each.' See also ATP 202: 'Individual or group, we are traversed by lines, meridians, geodesics, tropics, and zones marching to different beats and differing in nature.'

10. On this point Deleuze would therefore arguably lean more towards Artaud than Carroll, seeing as Carroll was never really in danger of anything – to put it one way, Carroll's nonsense was always quite sensible and inoffensive, in contrast to Artaud.

11. This increase in the number of lines from *The Logic of Sense* to *Dialogues/A Thousand Plateaus* has also been noted by Paul Patton (2009: 53n). My interpretation, however, differs slightly from Patton's. While Patton correlates the crack with the incorporeal pure event in *The Logic of Sense*, on my reading the crack in *The Logic of Sense* concerns the depths as much as the surface, since it is indeed the composite intertwining of the two. Put otherwise, the crack-up, as explained by Deleuze in *The Logic of Sense*, does not just pertain to Porcelain, but also the Volcano.

12. I have taken this phrase 'new monism' from Deleuze's reading of Bergson: 'Thus far, the Bergsonian method has shown two main aspects, the one dualist, the other monist. First, the diverging lines or the differences in kind had to be followed beyond the "turn in experience"; then, still further beyond, the point of convergence of these lines had to be rediscovered, and the rights of a new monism restored' (B 73).

13. This is also, according to Deleuze, the 'revolutionary problem': 'As we know, the revolutionary problem today is to find some unity in our various struggles without falling back on the despotic and bureaucratic organization of the party or State apparatus: we want a war-machine that would not recreate a State apparatus, a nomadic unity in relation with the Outside, that would not recreate the despotic internal unity' (DI 259). As this call to 'find some unity' demonstrates, Deleuze is by no mean anti-organisational. Rather, he is opposed to certain kinds of organisations and in favour of seeking new ones.

14. Deleuze and Guattari quote from Frank Herbert's *Dune* in order to show how a true nomad becomes one with their nomadic space: 'He moved with the random walk which made only those sounds natural to the desert. Nothing in his passage would [indicate] that human flesh moved there. It was a way of walking so deeply conditioned in him that he didn't need to think about it. The feet moved of themselves, no measurable rhythm to their pacing' (ATP 390).

15. It should be pointed out that the running together of the molecular and abstract lines *is not* what Deleuze and Parnet are referring to when they say later in *Dialogues* that the three lines could be conceived of as two. When aligning the three lines into a binary, it is explicitly the binary of the nomad and the State that they have in mind, the barbarians then being reduced to a mixture of the two. Deleuze and Parnet go on to say that we could even reduce this binary to a monism in one of two ways: either by claiming that there is only one line of pure becoming, which is then relatively or absolutely segmented (molecular or molar segmentarity), or by suggesting that one line is 'born from the explosion of the two others' (D 136–7). These reappraisals, however, pertain only to the superficiality of analysis, for the three elements remain in all of them: all

that shifts between them is the level of reducibility. Deleuze and Parnet's analysis in this passage, therefore, does not specifically speak to our current problem of deciding upon which of the three lines corresponds to the nomad.

16. See Lundy 2009: 188–205.

17. The duplicity of 'black holes' would presumably require a similar response. On the one hand, black holes are the danger of the second molecular line: 'a supple line rushes into a black hole from which it will not be able to extricate itself' (D 138). But on the other hand, black holes also reappear as the danger of the third line: 'The line of flight blasts the two segmentary series apart [molar and molecular]; but it is capable of the worst, of bouncing off the wall, falling into a black hole, taking the path of greatest regression, and in its vagaries reconstructing the most rigid of segments' (ATP 205). If we are to avoid conceptual inconsistency, this duplicity must be explained by maintaining that lines of flight are capable of sparking and turning into a molecular line that in turn plunges into a black hole.

18. These phrases are used by Deleuze in his book on Bergson to describe the movement from dualism to a new monism: '[T]he expression "beyond the decisive turn" has two meanings: First, it denotes the moment when the lines, setting out from an uncertain common point given in experience, diverge increasingly according to the differences in kind. Then, it denotes another moment when these lines converge again to give us this time the virtual image or the distinct reason of the common point. Turn and return. Dualism is therefore only a moment, which must lead to the re-formation of a monism' (B 29). See also B 73.

19. 'What a sad and sham game is played by those who speak of a supremely cunning Master, in order to present the image of themselves as rigorous, incorruptible and "pessimist" thinkers' (D 146).

20. In this passage Deleuze and Parnet are actually referring to a binary of rigid segments. The sentiment of this passage, however, can be equally applied to Deleuze's dualisms as well (nomad/State, becoming/history, etc.). If it is true that Deleuze's dualisms do not function in the same way as dualisms composed of two rigid segments, then it is precisely because they facilitate their 'between'. Deleuzian dualisms are thus no less susceptible to development via a 'third that comes from elsewhere' (e.g. the smith between or beneath the nomad and the State).

21. The 'univocity of Being' is invariably used by Deleuze in tandem with 'crowned anarchy' and 'nomadic distribution' (see DR 37). All three can be said to refer to the inauguration of 'a mobile, immanent principle of auto-unification' (LS 102), a principle which is also associated with Nietzsche's eternal return, the dice throw and the disjunctive synthesis. See LS 179–80 as well as LS 113 and 263.

22. To illustrate further, Lampert locates his two forms of history in the phrase from *A Thousand Plateaus*: 'history [in the schizo nomadic sense] is made only by those who oppose history [in the paranoiac centrist sense]' (Lampert 2006: 7, quote from ATP 295). I, however, read this statement differently. Deleuze and Guattari are certainly attempting to distinguish here between history and becoming, whereby history pertains to capture and becoming creation. But becoming is not a synonym for the second iteration of 'history' in the above sentence. Rather, those who *oppose history* are those who *become*. Another way that Deleuze and Guattari could have made the point, for instance, would be to say that territories are made by those who deterritorialise from territories and reterritorialise onto, or more precisely *into*, new ones. 'History', in this passage, therefore stands for 'historicism' pure and simple, and it is made by those who become, since historicists do not 'make' anything but merely capture what has already been created. Lampert is no doubt correct to look for a nomadic sense of history in this passage, but unfortunately one won't be found as easily as he suggests. Not only am I sceptical that Deleuze and Guattari would endorse a conception of history that was equated with pure becoming, but more importantly, I am not convinced that such an equation would be capable of producing a genuinely creative conception of history. I would thus be more inclined to note, drawing on the same passage of *A Thousand Plateaus*, that if there is a nomadic history, it will have to do with 'a bit of becoming' (ATP 296), but only a bit; it will not simply be becoming or history 'as the (good) schizo's deterritorialization of events' (Lampert 2006: 7).

Chapter 4: From Prehistory to Universal History

1. In his analysis of the same texts, Lampert answers this question of beginnings by employing a similar strategy. For Lampert, however, there are three kinds of beginnings and three answers to the question of simultaneity and succession, respective to the three kinds of social regimes/machines (see chapter 7 of Lampert's *Deleuze and Guattari's Philosophy of History* (2006), in which he will develop a distinction between 'beginning', 'origin' and 'creation'). While I agree that the three social machines each provide their own interpretation of history, each one according to its particular principle of power, and while I agree that these distinctions are critical, in particular for comprehending the nature of universal history, my analysis at this point will focus on the ontological distinction between the virtual and the actual, Aion and Chronos, rather than between the different virtual readings that social machines produce.

2. It should be noted that this example is originally forwarded by Péguy:

'There are critical points of the event just as there are critical points of temperature' (see Péguy 1931: 266–9). For Deleuze's discussions of it see LS 53, N 170–1 and WP 111 and 157.

3. I would again note that this reference is explicitly to Deleuze's understanding and use of the untimely rather than Nietzsche's. The major difference between the two is that while Deleuze uses the untimely to attack State history, Nietzsche's original intention was to show how history itself, if it was to be worthwhile, must use the unhistorical. For more on this see Lundy 2009: 188–205.

4. See *Time and Free Will*: 'Pure duration is the form which the succession of our conscious states assumes when our ego lets itself *live*, when it refrains from separating its present state from its former states. For this purpose it need not be entirely absorbed in the passing sensation or idea; for then, on the contrary, it would no longer *endure*. Nor need it forget its former states: it is enough that, in recalling these states, it does not set them alongside its actual state as one point alongside another, but forms both the past and the present states into an organic whole, as happens when we recall the notes of a tune, melting, so to speak, into one another' (Bergson 2001: 100). As this passage shows us, the critical distinction is between a present/actual state and a past/virtual state, both of which together combine to form a coexisting organic whole that allows time to endure.

5. See *Matter and Mercury* 'But the truth is that we shall never reach the past unless we frankly place ourselves within it. Essentially virtual, it cannot be known as something past unless we follow and adopt the movement by which it expands into a present image, thus emerging from obscurity into the light of day. In vain do we seek its trace in anything actual and already realized: we might as well look for darkness beneath the light' (Bergson 2004: 173). I am aware that Bergson will at times employ the term virtual to suggest a future occurrence, for instance with his discussion of a 'virtual action' that 'measures our possible action upon things, and thereby, inversely, the possible action of things upon us' (Bergson 2004: 57–60). Bergson will indeed often use 'virtual' and 'possible' interchangeably, though not always, in turn necessitating diligence on the part of the reader. However, even in those cases where they are synonymous, this does not conflict with my assessment, for the gauge upon which virtual futures are measured is in part provided by the past (e.g. our memories that are *relevant* or *appropriate* to the situation).

6. It could be further noted that the capitalist axiomatic undergoes alteration through a two-sided process: deterritorialisation and reterritorialisation. But in making this point, it must be remembered that the capitalist *machine* is not synonymous with the capitalist *axiomatic* (or the capitalist *market*) – an axiomatic (or market) is not a machine,

though it can be a part of one. Thus while it might be said that the two sides of the capitalist axiomatic are de- and reterritorialisation, it remains the case that the nature of the capitalist machine is characterised by its axiomatic structure on the one hand and its superior power of decoding/deterritorialisation on the other.

7. Interestingly, Deleuze and Guattari will also define philosophy as crisis: 'Philosophy thus lives in a permanent crisis. The plane takes effect through shocks, concepts proceed in bursts, and personae by spasms. The relationship among the three instances is problematic by nature' (WP 82). In Chapter 5 I will analyse the connections between capitalism and philosophy in greater detail, emphasising in particular their mutually immanent nature.

8. It could be argued that there is one sacred axiom of capitalism: the conjunction between free labour and capital-money. But while it is true that Deleuze and Guattari often identify this conjunction as a seminal moment in the formation of capitalism, it can also be shown, as we will see later, that Deleuze and Guattari do not always locate the birth of the capitalist machine in this conjunction, thus throwing into question whether this axiom is indeed sacred.

9. This phrase is taken by Deleuze and Guattari from Nietzsche 2005: 104. It should be noted, however, that Deleuze and Guattari alter Nietzsche's original context and intention. For Nietzsche, the phrase is directed towards the 'men of the present' who reside in the 'land of *bildung*'. More specifically, Nietzsche is criticising the contemporary man of science, who has attempted to replace belief and superstition with an adherence to unaffected reason. It is due to this presumed absolute objectivity that the contemporary man of the present appears to account for all previous 'ages and peoples'. While the capitalist may share some similarities with this description, there are also significant differences. Firstly, the capitalist is not bound by actuality like the men of the present; capitalism does not repeat the mantra 'actual are we entirely'. Secondly, although the capitalist, like the men of the present, is inscribed with an overabundance of signs that are not of his own creation, the capitalist is nevertheless productive insofar as he 'gives rise to numerous flows' that escape it (ATP 472). Which leads to a final difference: the capitalist, by not being confined to the actual and the 'unfruitful', is in fact more motley then even Nietzsche's 'actual men'; there is not even a 'skeleton' or 'lean ribs' beneath the capitalist's 'veils and wraps and colours and gestures', for even this has melted into thin air.

10. For Deleuze and Guattari's rendition of this example, see AO 223 and 225.

11. As Deleuze and Guattari succinctly put it, 'the answer lies in the State' (AO 197). Although 'so many of [capitalism's] components were already present [in China]' (WP 96), the State 'prevents them from

reaching fruition' (WP 97) by capturing and stifling the propagation of flow. The Chinese State, for example, 'closed the mines as soon as the reserves of metal were judged sufficient', and the State furthermore 'retained a monopoly or a narrow control over commerce (the merchant as functionary)' (AO 197). The West, on the contrary, 'slowly brings together and adjusts these components', and in so doing, *extends and propagates its centres of immanence*' (WP 97). Thus 'the conditions for it existed but were not effectuated or even capable of being effectuated' (ATP 452).

12. As Marx will go on to explain in this passage, this does not mean that the capitalist mode of production homogenises history. Differences between societies are indeed maintained, but these differences are themselves only determined in light of the triumph of capitalism. For example, previous economic categories such as ground rent 'cannot be understood without capital' (Marx 1975: 107). Thus the universal history of capitalism is both heterogeneous and singular. Lampert will place this aspect at the heart of Deleuze and Guattari's philosophy of history: '[T]here must be (a) one univocal sense of history, which is (b) univocalized by the last stage of history, and yet (c) distributed and differentiated throughout all stages of history' (Lampert 2006: 165). While I do not disagree, it is a goal of my analysis, as will shortly become evident, to take Deleuze and Guattari's philosophy of history beyond this aspect of retrospectivity.

13. My point here is not to say that these two aspects are unrelated, only that they are not synonymous or identical ways of describing the same thing, and thus that it is difficult to claim one of them as sacred.

14. See Read 2003a: §§5, 21–3. Although Read provides an excellent account of the retroactive nature of capitalism in his article on universal history, noting the similarities shared between the despotic and capitalist machines, he does not take this as reason to seek a form of contingency specific to capitalism, perhaps accounting for our divergent readings of contingency within Deleuze and Guattari's universal history.

15. Much could be said, and is said, on the relation between Althusser's early and late work. I will, however, limit myself to the following three observations, offered within the context of my own project. Firstly, despite Deleuze's admiration for Althusser's early work, he nevertheless notes how the Althusser of *For Marx* retains 'a principle contradiction' at its heart (DR 311). Secondly, the later work of Althusser is more clearly influenced by Deleuze, not only with respect to capitalism (see Althusser 2006: 197–8) but also Deleuze's philosophy of 'English empiricism' and 'positivity over negativity' (Althusser 2006: 189), thus modifying the dialectical contradiction of Althusser's earlier work. Thirdly, and perhaps most importantly, there is arguably

a greater concern in Althusser's later work for historical *ontology*. As Balibar puts it: 'Althusser followed a path that progressively shifted the emphasis from an epistemological problem to a political one and finally to a question regarding social and historical ontology' (Balibar 1996: 113–14).

16. As I noted in Chapter 3 Deleuze gives a quite similar description of creative emergence when remarking on the Foucauldian historian who proceeds gradually and successively: '[W]hen a new formation appears, with new rules and series, it never comes all at once, in a single phrase or act of creation, but emerges like a series of "building blocks", with gaps, traces and reactivations of former elements that survive under the new rules' (F 21–2).

17. Other examples Deleuze and Guattari provide are that point in a lovers' fight beyond which one cannot go without 'going too far' (thus bringing about separation), or that point in trade where if a primitive society goes beyond it will start to constitute a State stock (see ATP 437–40).

18. Along with these limits, Eugene Holland contends that the planet Earth is the practical limit of capitalism: 'At some point, then, the growth imperative of capitalism runs up against the carrying capacity of the planet: continuous development becomes impossible to sustain' (Holland 1999: 115). However, as terrible as the destruction of the Earth would be, I do not see why this need be the limit of capitalism's growth imperative: could not the demise of the Earth set off one of the greatest lines of flight imaginable? Could not the colonisation of other terrestrial bodies serve as a further axiom with respect to this great deterritorialisation? Deleuze and Guattari would seem to agree: '[The capitalist] world market extends to the ends of the earth before passing into the galaxy' (WP 97).

19. The references that Holland provides on this point, it could be noted, all refer to schizophrenia as the absolute limit of capitalism and/or the 'end of history', not to 'universal history'. See Holland 1999: 115, 146n.

20. It should be noted that my intention here is not to completely disassociate universal history from schizophrenia or identify universal history with capitalism only, for as my analysis has acknowledged, the schizo most certainly has a relation to universal history. My more modest intention is rather to show how capitalism is not a halfway house for universal history on the road to schizophrenia, since capitalism is already in full possession of a working universal history.

21. See Jain 2009: 7 and Holland 1999: 99–106, though in Holland's case, it should be said, he does not advocate the elimination of the axiomatic but only its subordination to the molecular and deterritorialisation.

Chapter 5: What is History in What Is Philosophy?

1. For evidence of how Deleuze and Guattari condone comparisons of the above kind, see WP 36–7.
2. See also WP 41: 'Philosophy is at once concept creation and instituting of the plane. The concept is the beginning of philosophy, but the plane is its instituting. The plane is clearly not a program, design, end, or means: it is a plane of immanence that constitutes the absolute ground of philosophy, its earth or deterritorialization, the foundations on which it creates its concepts. Both the creation of concepts and the instituting of the plane are required, like two wings or fins.'
3. In a similar way, Deleuze distinguishes between *the* virtual – the pure or absolute virtual that is chaos itself – and various virtual multiplicities, each of which are given a consistency by philosophy (compare WP 118 and 156). DeLanda makes an analogous point when distinguishing between *a* body without organs and *the* BwO: 'Because [various] BwO's, unlike pure plasma, retain forms and functions, they may be considered examples of a local BwO, that is, local limits of a process of destratification, and not *the BwO*, taken as an absolute limit' (DeLanda 1997: 261–2).
4. As shown by Christian Kerslake, Arnold Toynbee's universal history of civilisations is one such attempt to carry out a Bergsonian philosophy of history based on the notion of duration. See Kerslake 2008: 17–48.
5. It might be remarked that this description of personae favours a particular persona – Deleuze and Guattari's nomad. It is to be expected, however, that Deleuze and Guattari's definition of philosophy will itself be a creative act of philosophy, and thus partial to their own conceptual personae (the personae that speak through them).
6. It should be noted that I am only addressing Part I of *What Is Philosophy?* – that part which describes and analyses the nature of philosophy – and not Part II of the text, which supplements and fleshes out Part I by contrasting philosophy with other activities, such as science, logic and art.
7. Paul Patton makes a similar point, arguing that Deleuze and Guattari's conception of the nature and task of philosophy 'relies upon historical knowledge about the circumstances under which Philosophy emerged [and evolved]'. Patton furthermore correctly notes that philosophy, for Deleuze and Guattari, only 'achieves its utopian aims when the power of absolute deterritorialisation associated with its concepts is aligned with one or other form of relative deterritorialisation present in the *historical* milieu'. See Patton 2009: 34, emphasis added.
8. Note here how the birth and nature of philosophical reason is consistent with the nature of Deleuze and Guattari's universal history: both

are created through a contingent process while at the same time a process of contingent creativity.

9. Deleuze and Guattari give the exact same geographical reason to explain how the Aegean peoples were able to 'take advantage of the oriental agricultural stock *without having to constitute one for themselves*' (ATP 450).

10. The full quotation reads: 'As Faye says, it took a century for the name *philosopher*, no doubt invented by Heraclitus of Ephesus, to find its correlate in the word *philosophy*, no doubt invented by Plato the Athenian' (WP 87). Aside from Jean-Pierre Faye, Deleuze and Guattari also cite Clémence Ramnoux's *Histoire de la philosophie* and Nietzsche's *Naissance de la philosophy* for further confirmation of this *historical* interpretation (WP 223).

11. This search is not unlike their canvassing of the history of philosophy for moments that live up to the ultimate immanence of Spinozism – a search which turns up two names: Bergson and Christ (see WP 48–9 and 59–60).

12. This statement first appears in Deleuze and Guattari's discussion of the relation between capitalism and various States: 'The *immanent axiomatic* finds in the domains it moves through so many models, termed *models of realization*. [. . .] Thus the States, in capitalism, are not canceled [*sic*] out but change form and take on a new meaning: models of realization for a worldwide axiomatic that exceeds them' (ATP 454).

13. Of all the various similarities between different (local) States, participation in the capitalist world market would arguably be the most important, given its role in propagating immanence. See ATP 464–5.

14. According to Jay Lampert, modern philosophy would indeed reterritorialise on pure democracy if it could, but in the absence of such a pure instantiation 'modern philosophies reterritorialized on the next best thing'. 'The nation', as Lampert continues, is thus 'a false category to reterritorialize upon' – a situation that is only rescued by philosophy's third milieu (becoming and the future). The lack of 'pure democracies' and the reality of 'compromised nations', for Lampert, are thus indeed obstacles to the geophilosophy of thought. See Lampert 2006: 150. Rather than propose an 'alternative' to the reterritorialisation of thought on a nation (in order to rectify a supposed deficiency with that reterritorialisation), the purpose of my study is to show how all three milieus to which thought is reterritorialised (past, present and future) are of *equal* importance to the nature of thought, and furthermore how all three contribute to the promotion of not only a geophilosophy but also an historiophilosophy.

15. At its worse, this direct linking of geographical reality to the outcomes of philosophy would give rise to its own brand of historicism: a *geohistoricism*. Such a position is perhaps best represented today by Jared

Diamond, who argues that all of world history can be explained by longitude (see his *Guns, Germs and Steel*, 1998). While Deleuze and Guattari also wish to point out the significance of geography, producing such a geohistoricism is not their intention. For example, in giving their history of capitalism, Deleuze and Guattari demonstrate (following Braudel) the geographical significance of having a coastal capital and a network of cities that look outwards. However, the fact that China turns away from this maritime model is ultimately explained by politics, not geography (or at least not geography alone). The notion that history can be reduced to geography is thus a historicism that Deleuze and Guattari could not support: if geography is supposed to do anything for Deleuze and Guattari, it is to reaffirm the continual contingency of history, not dissolve it.

16. For a well-known critique of Deleuze and Guattari mounted on 'factual grounds', see Miller 1993: 6–35.

17. As is well known in the discipline of historical theory, this literal translation of Leopold von Ranke's infamous dictum '*wie es eigentlich gewesen*' is responsible for generating much misunderstanding of Ranke's opinions on theory. As Georg G. Iggers and Konrad Von Molke note, 'the word "*eigentlich*" which is the key to the phrase just quoted has been poorly translated into English. In the nineteenth century this word was ambiguous in a way in which it no longer is. It certainly had the modern meaning of "actually" already, but it also meant "characteristic, essential", and the latter is the form in which Ranke most frequently uses this term. This gives the phrase an entirely different meaning, and one much more in keeping with Ranke's philosophical ideas. It is not factuality, but the emphasis on the essential that makes an account historical' (Iggers and Von Molke 1973: xix–xx). This amendment, however, has little impact on my present study, since Deleuze and Guattari are not only opposed to those accounts of reality that attempt to dispense with theory, but also those accounts in which 'Every abstraction [is] detracted from the living reality of history' (Iggers and Von Molke 1973: xx).

18. To this end, the focus of this chapter can be distinguished from Jay Lampert's corresponding study. For Lampert, what is of central importance is gaining an understanding of how virtual concepts do not come from actual history but fall back into it (Lampert 2006: 152). My focus has instead been on demonstrating how history is more than mere actuality, and always already a part of philosophy's nature. The guiding objective of my project is thus not to explain 'the effectuation of virtual events in actual history' or 'the way philosophical concepts emerge in, yet remain free from, historical cultures', and neither is it to figure out how we can fall back into actual history on the presumption that *What Is Philosophy?* 'moves too far in extracting the virtual from machinic

assemblages' (Lampert 2006: 143). In my opinion, what is needed is not a theory of 'the coexistence of the stages of actual history' (Lampert 2006: 155) but rather a theory that shows how creations don't need 'falling back into history' since they never really left it to begin with. If such a theory requires a new or alternative notion of history – a notion that is distinct from historicism and closer to what Braudel, Nietzsche, et al. had in mind – then such, I would argue, is the benefit that can be had from a consideration of Deleuze and Guattari's philosophy of history.

Bibliography

Althusser, Louis (2006) *Philosophy of the Encounter: Later Writings, 1978–1987*, ed. François Matheron and Oliver Corpet, trans. G. M. Goshgarian. London and New York: Verso.

Althusser, Louis and Balibar, Étienne (1979) [1965] *Reading Capital*, trans. Ben Brewster. London: Verso edition.

Ansell Pearson, Keith (1997) *Viroid Life: Perspectives on Nietzsche and the Transhuman Condition*. London and New York: Routledge.

Ansell Pearson, Keith (1999) *Germinal Life: The Difference and Repetition of Deleuze*. London and New York: Routledge.

Ansell Pearson, Keith (2002) *Philosophy and the Adventure of the Virtual: Bergson and the Time of Life*. London and New York: Routledge.

Ansell Pearson, Keith (2007) 'Review of Jay Lampert, "Deleuze and Guattari's Philosophy of History"', *Notre Dame Philosophical Reviews*, 3 June.

Atkinson, Paul (2009) 'Henri Bergson', in Graham Jones and Jon Roffe (eds), *Deleuze's Philosophical Lineage*. Edinburgh: Edinburgh University Press, pp. 237–60.

Bachelard, Gaston (2000) 'The Instant', in Robin Durie (ed.), *Time and the Instant: Essays in the Physics and Philosophy of Time*. Manchester: Clinamen Press, pp. 64–95.

Balibar, Étienne (1996) 'Structural Causality, Overdetermination, and Antagonism', in Antonio Callari and David Ruccio (eds), *Postmodern Materialism and the Future of Marxist Theory*. Middletown: Wesleyan University Press, pp. 109–19.

Bambach, Charles R. (1990) 'History and Ontology: A Reading of Nietzsche's Second "Untimely Meditation"', *Philosophy Today*, Fall, pp. 259–72.

Bell, Jeffrey A. (2009) 'Of the Rise and Progress of Philosophical Concepts: Deleuze's Humean Historiography', in Jeffrey A. Bell and Claire Colebrook (eds), *Deleuze and History*. Edinburgh: Edinburgh University Press, pp. 54–71.

Bentley, Michael (2006) 'Past and "Presence": Revisiting Historical Ontology', *History and Theory*, 45: 349–61.

Bergson, Henri (1977) [1932] *The Two Sources of Morality and Religion*, trans. R. Ashley Audra and Cloudesley Brereton. Notre Dame: University of Notre Dame Press.

Bergson, Henri (1998) [1907] *Creative Evolution*, trans. Arthur Mitchell. Mineola, NY: Dover.

Bergson, Henri (2001) [1889] *Time and Free Will: An Essay on the Immediate Data of Consciousness*, trans. F. L. Pogson. Mineola, NY: Dover.

Bergson, Henri (2004) [1896] *Matter and Memory*, trans. Nancy Margaret Paul and W. Scott Palmer. Mineola, NY: Dover.

Bergson, Henri (2007) [1934] *The Creative Mind: An Introduction to Metaphysics*, trans. Mabelle L. Andison. Mineola, NY: Dover.

Berkowitz, Peter (1994) 'Nietzsche's Ethics of History', *Review of Politics*, 56 (1): 5–27.

Bonta, Mark and Protevi, John (2004) *Deleuze and Geophilosophy: A Guide and Glossary*. Edinburgh: Edinburgh University Press.

Boulez, Pierre (1966) *Relevés d'apprenti*. Paris: Seuil.

Boulez, Pierre (1971) *Boulez on Music Today*, trans. Susan Bradshaw and Richard Bennett. Cambridge, MA: Harvard University Press, 1971.

Bowden, Sean (2011) *The Priority of Events: Deleuze's* Logic of Sense. Edinburgh: Edinburgh University Press.

Braudel, Fernand (1980) [1969] *On History*, trans. Sarah Matthews. Chicago: University of Chicago Press.

Braudel, Fernand (2002a) [1967] *The Structures of Everyday Life: Civilization and Capitalism 15th–18th Century, Volume 1*, trans. Sian Reynolds. London: Phoenix Press.

Braudel, Fernand (2002b) [1979] *The Wheels of Commerce: Civilization and Capitalism 15th–18th Century, Volume 2*, trans. Sian Reynolds. London: Phoenix Press.

Braudel, Fernand (2002c) [1979] *The Perspective of the World: Civilization and Capitalism 15th–18th Century, Volume 3*, trans. Sian Reynolds. London: Phoenix Press.

Brobjer, Thomas H. (2004) 'Nietzsche's View of the Value of Historical Studies and Methods', *Journal of the History of Ideas*, 65 (2): 301–22.

Connolly, William E. (2011) *A World of Becoming*. Durham, NC and London: Duke University Press.

de Beistegui, Miguel (2010) *Immanence: Deleuze and Philosophy*. Edinburgh: Edinburgh University Press.

de Jong, Henk (1997) 'Review: Historical Orientation: Jorn Rusen's Answer to Nietzsche and His Followers', *History and Theory*, 36 (2): 270–88.

DeLanda, Manuel (1997) *A Thousand Years of Nonlinear History*. New York: Zone Books.

DeLanda, Manuel (2002) *Intensive Science and Virtual Philosophy*. London and New York: Continuum.

DeLanda, Manuel (2005) 'Space: Extensive and Intensive, Actual and

Virtual', in Ian Buchanan and Gregg Lambert (eds), *Deleuze and Space*. Edinburgh: Edinburgh University Press, pp. 80–8.

DeLanda, Manuel (2009) 'Molar entities and Molecular Populations in Human History', in Jeffrey A. Bell and Claire Colebrook (eds), *Deleuze and History*. Edinburgh: Edinburgh University Press, pp. 225–36.

Deleuze, Gilles (1977) [1962] 'Active and Reactive', in David Allison (ed.), *The New Nietzsche*, trans. Richard Cohen. New York: Delta, pp. 80–106.

Deleuze, Gilles (1983) [1962] *Nietzsche and Philosophy*, trans. Hugh Tomlinson. London and New York: Continuum.

Deleuze, Gilles (1990) [1969] *The Logic of Sense*, ed. Constantin V. Boundas, trans. Mark Lester with Charles Stivale. London: Continuum.

Deleuze, Gilles (1991) [1966] *Bergsonism*, trans. Hugh Tomlinson and Barbara Habberjam. New York: Zone Books.

Deleuze, Gilles (1994) [1968] *Difference and Repetition*, trans. Paul Patton. London: Athlone Press.

Deleuze, Gilles (1995) [1990] *Negotiations: 1972–1990*, trans. Martin Joughin. New York: Columbia University Press.

Deleuze, Gilles (1998) [1993] *Essays Critical and Clinical*, trans. Daniel W. Smith and Michael A. Greco. London and New York: Verso.

Deleuze, Gilles (1999a) [1956] 'Bergson's Conception of Difference', in John Mullarkey (ed.), *The New Bergson*, trans. Melissa McMahon. Manchester and New York: Manchester University Press, pp. 42–65.

Deleuze, Gilles (1999b) [1986] *Foucault*, trans. Sean Hand. London and New York: Continuum.

Deleuze, Gilles (2001a) [1973] 'Dualism, Monism and Multiplicities (Desire-Pleasure-*Jouissance*)', trans. Daniel W. Smith, *Contretemps*, 2: 92–108.

Deleuze, Gilles (2001b) *Pure Immanence: Essays on A Life*, trans. Anne Boyman. New York: Zone Books.

Deleuze, Gilles (2004) [2002] *Desert Islands and Other Texts: 1953–1974*, ed. David Lapoujade, trans. Michael Taormina. New York and Los Angeles: Semiotext(e).

Deleuze, Gilles (2006) *Two Regimes of Madness: Texts and Interviews 1975–1995*, ed. David Lapoujade, trans. Ames Hodges and Mike Taormina. New York and Los Angeles: Semiotext(e).

Deleuze, Gilles and Guattari, Félix (1984) [1972] *Anti-Oedipus: Capitalism and Schizophrenia*, trans. Robert Hurley, Mark Seem and Helen R. Lane. London and New York: Continuum.

Deleuze, Gilles and Guattari, Félix (1989) [1980] *A Thousand Plateaus: Capitalism and Schizophrenia*, trans. Brian Massumi. Minneapolis: University of Minnesota.

Deleuze, Gilles and Guattari, Félix (1994) [1991] *What Is Philosophy?*, trans. Graham Burchell and Hugh Tomlinson. New York: Columbia University Press.

Deleuze, Gilles and Parnet, Claire (2002) [1977] *Dialogues II*, trans.

Barbara Habberjam and Hugh Tomlinson. London and New York: Continuum.

Den Boer, Pim (1998) [1987] *History as a Profession: The Study of History in France, 1818–1914*, trans. Arnold J. Pomerans. Princeton: Princeton University Press.

Diamond, Jared (1998) *Guns, Germs and Steel: A Short History of Everybody for the Last 13,000 Years*. London: Vintage.

Dosse, François (1997a) [1991] *History of Structuralism: Volume I: The Rising Sign, 1945–1966*. Minneapolis: University of Minnesota Press.

Dosse, François (1997b) [1992] *History of Structuralism: Volume II: The Sign Sets, 1967–Present*. Minneapolis: University of Minnesota Press.

Dosse, François (2010) [2007] *Gilles Deleuze & Félix Guattari: Intersecting Lives*. New York: Columbia University Press.

Durie, Robin (2000) 'Splitting Time: Bergson's Philosophical Legacy', *Philosophy Today*, 44 (2): 152–68.

Durie, Robin (2002) 'Creativity and Life', *Review of Metaphysics*, 56: 357–83.

Emden, Christian J. (2006) 'Toward a Critical Historicism: History and Politics in Nietzsche's Second "Untimely Meditation"', *Modern Intellectual History*, 3 (1): 1–31.

Evans, Richard J. (1997) *In Defence of History*. London: Granta.

Fitzgerald, F. Scott (1945) [1931] *The Crack-Up*. New York: New Directions.

Foucault, Michel (1997) 'Nietzsche, Genealogy, History', in D. F. Bouchard (ed.), *Language, Counter-memory, Practice: Selected Essays and Interviews*. Ithaca, NY: Cornell University Press, pp. 139–64.

Gioli, Giovanna G. (2005–6) 'Towards a Theory of History in Gilles Deleuze', *International Journal of the Humanities*, 3 (1): 163–8.

Goodchild, Philip (1996) *Deleuze and Guattari: An Introduction to the Politics of Desire*. London: Sage.

Grosz, Elizabeth (2004) *The Nick of Time: Politics, Evolution and the Untimely*. Sydney: Allen & Unwin.

Guerlac, Suzanne (2006) *Thinking in Time: An Introduction to Henri Bergson*. Ithaca, NY: Cornell University Press.

Hacking, Ian (2004) *Historical Ontology*. Cambridge, MA: Harvard University Press.

Hallward, Peter (2006) *Out of This World: Deleuze and the Philosophy of Creation*. London and New York: Verso.

Hegel, G. W. F. (1956) [1837] *The Philosophy of History*, trans. J. Sibree. New York: Dover.

Herbert, Frank (2001) [1965] *Dune*. London: Orion.

Holland, Eugene (1999) *Deleuze and Guattari's* Anti-Oedipus: *Introduction to Schizoanalysis*. London and New York: Routledge.

Holland, Eugene (2005a) 'Capitalism + Universal History', in Adrian Parr (ed.), *The Deleuze Dictionary*. Edinburgh: Edinburgh University Press, pp. 37–9.

Holland, Eugene (2005b) 'Schizoanalysis', in Adrian Parr (ed.), *The Deleuze Dictionary*. Edinburgh: Edinburgh University Press, pp. 236–7.

Holland, Eugene (2006) 'Nonlinear Historical Materialism and Postmodern Marxism', *Culture, Theory and Critique*, 47 (2): 181–96.

Holland, Eugene (2008a) 'Schizoanalysis, Nomadology, Fascism', in Ian Buchanan and Nicholas Thoburn (eds), *Deleuze and Politics*. Edinburgh: Edinburgh University Press, pp. 74–97.

Holland, Eugene (2008b) *What Is Revolutionary about Deleuze and Guattari's Philosophy of History?* Paper delivered at the First International Deleuze Studies Conference, Cardiff, 12 August.

Holland, Eugene (2009) 'Karl Marx', in Graham Jones and Jon Roffe (eds), *Deleuze's Philosophical Lineage*. Edinburgh: Edinburgh University Press, pp. 147–66.

Iggers, Georg G. (1968) *The German Conception of History: The National Tradition of Historical Thought from Herder to the Present*. Middletown: Wesleyan University Press.

Iggers, Georg G. and Von Molke, Konrad (1973) 'Introduction' to Leopold von Ranke, *The Theory and Practice of History*. Indianapolis and New York: Bobbs-Merrill, pp. xv–lxxi.

Jain, Dhruv (2009) 'Capital, Crisis, Manifestos, and Finally Revolution', in Dhruv Jain (ed.), 'Deleuze and Marx', special issue of *Deleuze Studies*, 3: 1–7.

Kafka, Franz (1983) [1919] 'An Old Manuscript', in Franz Kafka, *The Complete Stories*, ed. Nahum N. Glazer. London: Allen Lane, pp. 415–17.

Kant, Immanuel [1781] (2008) *The Critique of Pure Reason*. Radford, VA: Wilder.

Kerslake, Christian (2008) 'Becoming against History: Deleuze, Toynbee and Vitalist Historiography', *Parrhesia*, 4: 17–48.

Keylor, William R. (1975) *Academy and Community: The Foundation of the French Historical Profession*. Cambridge, MA: Harvard University Press.

Lampert, Jay (2006) *Deleuze and Guattari's Philosophy of History*. London and New York: Continuum.

Lampert, Jay (2009) 'Theory of Delay in Balibar, Freud and Deleuze: Décalage, Nachtraglichkeit, Retard', in Jeffrey A. Bell and Claire Colebrook (eds), *Deleuze and History*. Edinburgh: Edinburgh University Press, pp. 72–91.

Lawlor, Leonard (2003) *The Challenge of Bergsonism*. London and New York: Continuum.

Lundy, Craig (2009) 'Deleuze's Untimely: Uses and Abuses in the Appropriation of Nietzsche', in Jeffrey A. Bell and Claire Colebrook (eds), *Deleuze and History*. Edinburgh: Edinburgh University Press, pp. 188–205.

Marx, Karl (1975) [1857] *Grundrisse*, trans. Martin Nicolaus. London and New York: Penguin Classics.

Marx, Karl (1977) [1867] *Capital*, Vol. I, trans. B. Fowkes. New York: Penguin.

Marx, Karl and Engels, Friedrich (1955) *Selected Correspondence*, ed. S. W. Ryanzkaya, trans. I. Lasker. Moscow: Progress.

Megill, Allan (1996) 'Review: Historicizing Nietzsche? Paradoxes and Lessons of a Hard Case', *Journal of Modern History*, 68 (1): 114–52.

Miller, Christopher L. (1993) 'The Postidentitarian Predicament in the Footnotes of *A Thousand Plateaus*: Nomadology, Anthropology, and Authority', *Diacritics*, 23 (3): 6–35.

Miller, Henry (1960) [1941] *Wisdom of the Heart*. New York: New Directions.

Mullarkey, John (1999) *Bergson and Philosophy*. Edinburgh: Edinburgh University Press.

Nietzsche, Friedrich (1976) *The Portable Nietzsche*, ed. and trans. Walter Kaufmann. New York: Penguin Books, pp. 661–83.

Nietzsche, Friedrich (1983) [1874] *Untimely Meditations*, trans. R. J. Hollingdale. Cambridge: Cambridge University Press.

Nietzsche, Friedrich (1995) [1874] *Unfashionable Observations*, trans. Richard T. Gray. Stanford: Stanford University Press.

Nietzsche, Friedrich (2000) *Basic Writings of Nietzsche*, trans. Walter Kaufmann. New York: Modern Library.

Nietzsche, Friedrich (2005) [1883–5] *Thus Spoke Zarathustra*, trans. Graham Parkes. Oxford and New York: Oxford University Press.

Patton, Paul (1984) 'Conceptual Politics and the War Machine in "Mille Plateaux"', *SubStance*, 13 (3/4), Issue 44–45: 61–80.

Patton, Paul (2000) *Deleuze and the Political*. London and New York: Routledge.

Patton, Paul (2006) 'The Event of Colonisation', in Ian Buchanan and Adrian Parr (eds), *Deleuze and the Contemporary World*. Edinburgh: Edinburgh University Press, pp. 108–24.

Patton, Paul (2008) 'Becoming-Democratic', in Ian Buchanan and Nicholas Thoburn (eds), *Deleuze and Politics*. Edinburgh: Edinburgh University Press, pp. 178–95.

Patton, Paul (2009) 'Events, Becoming and History', in Jeffrey A. Bell and Claire Colebrook (eds), *Deleuze and History*. Edinburgh: Edinburgh University Press, pp. 33–53.

Patton, Paul (2010) *Deleuzian Concepts: Philosophy, Colonization, Politics*. Stanford: Stanford University Press.

Péguy, Charles (1931) [1909–12] *Clio*. Paris: Gallimard.

Péguy, Charles (2001) *Temporal and Eternal*, trans. Alexander Dru. Indianapolis: Liberty Fund.

Plato (1961) 'Philebus', in *Plato: The Collected Dialogues*, ed. E. Hamilton and H. Cairns, trans. R. Hackforth. Princeton: Princeton University Press.

Pletsch, Carl (1977) 'History and Friedrich Nietzsche's Philosophy of Time', *History and Theory*, 16 (1): 30–9.

Plotnitsky, Arkady (2006) 'Manifolds: on the Concept of Space in Riemann and Deleuze', in Simon Duffy (ed.), *Virtual Mathematics: The Logic of Difference*. Bolton: Clinamen Press, pp. 187–208.

Protevi, John (2009) 'Geohistory and Hydro-Bio-Politics', in Jeffrey A. Bell and Claire Colebrook (eds), *Deleuze and History*. Edinburgh: Edinburgh University Press, pp. 92–102.

Ramadanovic, P. (2001) 'From Haunting to Trauma: Nietzsche's Active Forgetting and Blanchot's Writing of the Disaster', *Postmodern Culture*, 11 (2).

Read, Jason (2003a) 'A Universal History of Contingency: Deleuze and Guattari on the History of Capitalism', *Borderlands*, 2 (3).

Read, Jason (2003b) *The Micro-Politics of Capital: Marx and the Prehistory of the Present*. Albany, NY: State University of New York Press.

Reill, Peter Hanns (1980) 'Barthold Georg Niebuhr and the Enlightenment Tradition', *German Studies Review*, 3 (1): 9–26.

Runia, Eelco (2006) 'Presence', *History and Theory*, 45: 1–29.

Smith, Daniel W. (2007) 'The Conditions of the New', *Deleuze Studies*, 1: 1–21.

Sowerwine, Charles (2001) *France since 1870: Culture, Politics and Society*. New York: Palgrave.

Spengler, Oswald (1924) 'On the German National Character', first published in *Deutsches Adelsblatt*, XLII (1924). For this version visit the Oswald Spengler Collection at: http://home.alphalink.com.au/~radnat/spengler/gercharacter.htm.

Spengler, Oswald (1937) 'Nietzsche and His Century', first published in *Reden und Aufsätze* (1937) Munich. For this version visit the Oswald Spengler Collection at: http://home.alphalink.com.au/~radnat/spengler/nietzschecentury.htm.

Surin, Kenneth (2006) '1,000 Political Subjects ...', in Ian Buchanan and Adrian Parr (eds), *Deleuze and the Contemporary World*. Edinburgh: Edinburgh University Press, pp. 57–78.

Widder, Nathan (2002) *Genealogies of Difference*. University of Illinois Press.

Widder, Nathan (2008) *Reflections on Time and Politics*. University Park, PA: Pennsylvania State University Press.

Vähämäki, Jussi and Virtanen, Axseli (2006) 'Deleuze, Change, History', in Martin Fuglsang and Bent Meier Sørensen (eds), *Deleuze and the Social*. Edinburgh: Edinburgh University Press, pp. 207–28.

Williams, James (2003) *Gilles Deleuze's* Difference and Repetition: *A Critical Introduction and Guide*. Edinburgh: Edinburgh University Press.

Williams, James (2008) *Gilles Deleuze's* Logic of Sense: *A Critical Introduction and Guide*. Edinburgh: Edinburgh University Press.

Williams, James (2009) 'Ageing, Perpetual Perishing and the Event as Pure Novelty: Péguy, Whitehead and Deleuze on Time and History', in Jeffrey A. Bell and Claire Colebrook (eds), *Deleuze and History*. Edinburgh: Edinburgh University Press, pp. 142–60.

Žižek, Slavoj (2003) *Organs without Bodies: Deleuze and Consequences*. New York: Routledge.

Index